Springer
Berlin
Heidelberg
New York
Barcelona
Budapest
Hong Kong
London
Milan
Paris
Santa Clara
Singapore
Tokyo

Nicholas R. Jennings
Michael J. Wooldridge (Eds.)

Agent Technology

Foundations, Applications, and Markets

Springer

Editors:

Nicholas R. Jennings
Michael J. Wooldridge
Queen Mary and Westfield College, University of London
Department of Electronic Engineering
London E1 4NS, UK
E-mail: (n.r.jennings/m.j.wooldridge)@qmw.ac.uk

Cataloging-in-Publication data applied for

Die Deutsche Bibliothek – CIP-Einheitsaufnahme

Agent technology : foundations, applications, and markets / Nicholas R. Jennings ; Michael J. Wooldridge (ed.). – Berlin ; Heidelberg ; New York ; Barcelona ; Budapest ; Hong Kong ; London ; Milan ; Paris ; Santa Clara ; Singapore ; Tokyo : Springer, 1998

ISBN 978-3-642-08344-0

Springer-Verlag Berlin Heidelberg New York
a member of BertelsmannSpringer Science+Business Media GmbH

© UNICOM Seminars Ltd/Springer-Verlag Berlin Heidelberg 2010
Printed in Germany

Preface

Agent technology is one of the most vibrant and fastest growing areas of information technology – new agent-based products, applications, and services are being announced on an almost daily basis. The reason for this intense interest is that the metaphor of autonomous problem solving entities cooperating and coordinating to achieve their desired objectives is an intuitive and natural way of conceptualising many problems. Moreover, the conceptual apparatus of agent technology provides a powerful and useful set of structures and processes for designing and building complex software applications.

Agent Technology: Foundations, Applications, and Markets identifies and distills the key conceptual foundations of agent-based computing and presents them in the context of a variety of commercial and industrial application domains. This makes it the first book to be targeted specifically at a broad audience of software managers, designers, and developers who are considering whether and where agent technology will be useful for their organization. For those who are familiar with the foundations of agent technology, the book provides an indication of the likely future direction of the field and a number of case studies offering insights into the problems and benefits of developing and deploying agent-based applications.

As agent technology matures and moves into the mainstream of software development, we expect to see the everyday pragmatic issues of agent-based software development increasingly debated. We believe this volume represents the first major contribution to this debate. We hope and expect that it will stimulate interest not just from those already working in the field, but from practitioners in all information technology disciplines.

December 1997   Nick Jennings and Mike Wooldridge

Contents

Part 1: Introductory Papers

1   Applications of Intelligent Agents   3
     N. R. Jennings and M. Wooldridge

2   A Brief Introduction to Software Agent Technology   29
     H. S. Nwana and D. T. Ndumu

3   Agent Software for Near-Term Success in Distributed Applications   49
     S. C. Laufmann

Part 2: Vision Papers

4   Practical Design of Intelligent Agent Systems   73
     P. C. Janca and D. Gilbert

5   Vendors of Intelligent Agent Technologies: A Market Overview   91
     C. Guilfoyle

6   Brokering the Info-Underworld   105
     J. D. Foss

7   Personal Agents: A Walk on the Client Side   125
     P. Kearney

Part 3: Systems and Their Applications

8   Rational Software Agents: From Theory to Practice   139
     M. Georgeff and A. Rao

9   Agent-Oriented Techniques for Traffic and Manufacturing Applications: 161
     Progress Report
     B. Burmeister, S. Bussmann, A. Haddadi and K. Sundermeyer

10   Co-operating Agents: Concepts and Applications   175
     H. Haugeneder and D. Steiner

11   Intelligent Agents in Telecommunications   203
     R. Weihmayer and H. Velthuijsen

12   Managing Heterogeneous Transaction Workflows with   219
     Co-operating Agents
     M. N. Huhns and M. P. Singh

13 Software Technologies for Building Agent Based Systems   241
    in Telecommunication Networks
    M. Plu

14 Intelligent Agents in Portfolio Management   267
    K. P. Sycara, K. Decker and D. Zeng

15 The FinCEN AI System: Finding Financial Crimes in a Large Database 283
    of Cash Transactions
    H. G. Goldberg and T. E. Senator

16 Adding Value with Intelligent Agents in Financial Services   303
    D. Wenger and A. R. Probst

part **1**

Introduction

1 Applications of Intelligent Agents

N. R. Jennings and M. Wooldridge
Queen Mary & Westfield College
University of London

1.1 Introduction

Intelligent agents are a new paradigm for developing software applications. More than this, agent-based computing has been hailed as 'the next significant breakthrough in software development' (Sargent, 1992), and 'the new revolution in software' (Ovum, 1994). Currently, agents are the focus of intense interest on the part of many sub-fields of computer science and artificial intelligence. Agents are being used in an increasingly wide variety of applications, ranging from comparatively small systems such as email filters to large, open, complex, mission critical systems such as air traffic control. At first sight, it may appear that such extremely different types of system can have little in common. And yet this is not the case: in both, the key abstraction used is that of an *agent*. Our aim in this article is to help the reader to understand why agent technology is seen as a fundamentally important new tool for building such a wide array of systems. More precisely, our aims are five-fold:

- to introduce the reader to the concept of an agent and agent-based systems,
- to help the reader to recognize the domain characteristics that indicate the appropriateness of an agent-based solution,
- to introduce the main application areas in which agent technology has been successfully deployed to date,
- to identify the main obstacles that lie in the way of the agent system developer, and finally
- to provide a guide to the remainder of this book.

We begin, in this section, by introducing some basic concepts (such as, perhaps most importantly, the notion of an agent). In Section 1.2, we give some general guidelines on the types of domain for which agent technology is appropriate. In Section 1.3, we survey the key application domains for intelligent agents. In Section 1.4, we discuss some issues in agent system development, and finally, in Section 1.5, we outline the structure of this book.

Before we can discuss the development of agent-based systems in detail, we have to describe what we mean by such terms as 'agent' and 'agent-based system'. Unfortunately, we immediately run into difficulties, as some key concepts in agent-based computing lack universally accepted definitions. In particular, there is no real agreement even on the core question of exactly what an agent is (see

Franklin and Graesser (1996) for a discussion). However, we believe that most researchers would find themselves in broad agreement with the following definitions (Wooldridge and Jennings, 1995).

First, an agent is a computer system situated in some environment, and that is capable of *autonomous action* in this environment in order to meet its design objectives. Autonomy is a difficult concept to pin down precisely, but we mean it simply in the sense that the system should be able to act without the direct intervention of humans (or other agents), and should have control over its own actions and internal state. It may be helpful to draw an analogy between the notion of autonomy with respect to agents and encapsulation with respect to object-oriented systems. An object encapsulates some state, and has some control over this state in that it can only be accessed or modified via the methods that the object provides. Agents encapsulate state in just the same way. However, we also think of agents as encapsulating *behavior*, in addition to state. An object does not encapsulate behavior: it has no control over the execution of methods – if an object x invokes a method m on an object y, then y has no control over whether m is executed or not – it just *is*. In this sense, object y is not autonomous, as it has no control over its own actions. In contrast, we think of an agent as having *exactly* this kind of control over what actions it performs. Because of this distinction, we do not think of agents as invoking methods (actions) on agents – rather, we tend to think of them *requesting* actions to be performed. The decision about whether to act upon the request lies with the recipient.

Of course, autonomous computer systems are not a new development. There are many examples of such systems in existence. Examples include:

- any process control system, which must monitor a real-world environment and perform actions to modify it as conditions change (typically in real time) – such systems range from the very simple (for example, thermostats) to the extremely complex (for example, nuclear reactor control systems),
- software daemons, which monitor a software environment and perform actions to modify the environment as conditions change – a simple example is the UNIX xbiff program, which monitors a user's incoming email and obtains their attention by displaying an icon when new, incoming email is detected.

It may seem strange that we choose to call such systems agents. But these are not *intelligent* agents. An intelligent agent is a computer system that is capable of *flexible* autonomous action in order to meet its design objectives. By *flexible*, we mean that the system must be:

- *responsive*: agents should perceive their environment (which may be the physical world, a user, a collection of agents, the Internet, etc.) and respond in a timely fashion to changes that occur in it,
- *proactive*: agents should not simply act in response to their environment, they should be able to exhibit opportunistic, goal-directed behavior and take the initiative where appropriate, and

- *social*: agents should be able to interact, when they deem appropriate, with other artificial agents and humans in order to complete their own problem solving and to help others with their activities.

Hereafter, when we use the term 'agent', it should be understood that we are using it as an abbreviation for 'intelligent agent'. Other researchers emphasize different aspects of agency (including, for example, mobility or adaptability). Naturally, some agents may have additional characteristics, and for certain types of applications, some attributes will be more important than others. However, we believe that it is the presence of all four attributes in a single software entity that provides the power of the agent paradigm and which distinguishes agent systems from related software paradigms – such as object-oriented systems, distributed systems, and expert systems (see Wooldridge (1997) for a more detailed discussion).

By an *agent-based* system, we mean one in which the key abstraction used is that of an agent. In principle, an agent-based system might be conceptualized in terms of agents, but implemented without any software structures corresponding to agents at all. We can again draw a parallel with object-oriented software, where it is entirely possible to design a system in terms of objects, but to implement it without the use of an object-oriented software environment. But this would at best be unusual, and at worst, counterproductive. A similar situation exists with agent technology; we therefore expect an agent-based system to be both designed and implemented in terms of agents. A number of software tools exist that allow a user to implement software systems as agents, and as societies of cooperating agents.

Note that an agent-based system may contain any non-zero number of agents. The *multi*-agent case – where a system is designed and implemented as several interacting agents, is both more general and significantly more complex than the *single*-agent case. However, there are a number of situations where the single-agent case is appropriate. A good example, as we shall see later in this chapter, is the class of systems known as *expert assistants*, wherein an agent acts as an expert assistant to a user attempting to use a computer to carry out some task.

1.2 Agent Application Domain Characteristics

Now that we have a better understanding of what the terms 'agent' and 'agent-based system' mean, the obvious question to ask is: *what do agents have to offer?* For any new technology to be considered as useful in the computer marketplace, it must offer one of two things:

- the ability to solve problems that have hitherto been beyond the scope of automation – either because no existing technology could be used to solve the problem, or because it was considered too expensive (difficult, time-consuming, risky) to develop solutions using existing technology; or

- the ability to solve problems that can already be solved in a significantly better (cheaper, more natural, easier, more efficient, or faster) way.

1.2.1 Solving New Types of Problem

Certain types of software system are inherently more difficult to correctly design and implement than others. The *simplest* general class of software systems are *functional*. Such systems work by taking some input, computing a function of it, and giving this result as output. Compilers are obvious examples of functional systems. In contrast, *reactive* systems, which maintain an ongoing interaction with some environment, are inherently much more difficult to design and correctly implement. Process control systems, computer operating systems, and computer network management systems are all well-known examples of reactive systems. In all of these examples, a computer system is required that can operate independently, typically over long periods of time. It has long been recognized that reactive systems are among the most complex types of system to design and implement (Pnueli, 1986), and a good deal of effort has been devoted to developing software tools, programming languages, and methodologies for managing this complexity – with some limited success. However, for certain types of reactive system, even specialized software engineering techniques and tools fail – new techniques are required. We can broadly subdivide these systems into three classes:

- open systems,
- complex systems, and
- ubiquitous computing systems.

1.2.1.1 Open Systems

An open system is one in which the structure of the system itself is capable of dynamically changing. The characteristics of such a system are that its components are not known in advance, can change over time, and may be highly heterogeneous (in that they are implemented by different people, at different times, using different software tools and techniques). Computing applications are increasingly demanded by users to operate in such domains. Perhaps the best-known example of a highly open software environment is the Internet – a loosely coupled computer network of ever expanding size and complexity. The design and construction of software tools to exploit the enormous potential of the Internet and its related technology is one of the most important challenges facing computer scientists in the 1990s, and for this reason, it is worth using it as a case study. The Internet can be viewed as a large, distributed information resource, with nodes on the network designed and implemented by different organizations and individuals with widely varying agendas. Any computer system that must operate on the Internet must be capable of dealing with these different organizations and agendas, without constant guidance from users (but within well-defined bounds). Such functionality is almost certain to require techniques based on negotiation or cooperation, which lie very firmly in the domain of multi-agent systems (Bond and Gasser, 1988).

1.2.1.2 Complex Systems

The most powerful tools for handling complexity in software development are *modularity* and *abstraction*. Agents represent a powerful tool for making systems modular. If a problem domain is particularly complex, large, or unpredictable, then it may be that the only way it can reasonably be addressed is to develop a number of (nearly) modular components that are specialized (in terms of their representation and problem solving paradigm) at solving a particular aspect of it. In such cases, when interdependent problems arise, the agents in the systems must cooperate with one another to ensure that interdependencies are properly managed. In such domains, an agent-based approach means that the overall problem can be partitioned into a number of smaller and simpler components, which are easier to develop and maintain, and which are specialized at solving the constituent sub-problems. This decomposition allows each agent to employ the most appropriate paradigm for solving its particular problem, rather than being forced to adopt a common uniform approach that represents a compromise for the entire system, but which is not optimal for any of its subparts. The notion of an autonomous agent also provides a useful *abstraction* in just the same way that procedures, abstract data types, and, most recently, objects provide abstractions. They allow a software developer to conceptualize a complex software system as a society of cooperating autonomous problem solvers. For many applications, this high-level view is simply more appropriate than the alternatives.

1.2.1.3 Ubiquity

Despite the many innovations in human-computer interface design over the past two decades, and the wide availability of powerful window-based user interfaces, computer-naïve users still find most software difficult to use. One reason for this is that the user of a software product typically has to describe each and every step that needs to be performed to solve a problem, down to the smallest level of detail. If the power of current software applications is ever to be fully utilized by such users, then a fundamental rethink is needed about the nature of the interaction between computer and user. It must become an equal partnership – the machine should not just act as a dumb receptor of task descriptions, but should *cooperate* with the user to achieve their goal. As Negroponte wrote, 'the future of computing will be 100% driven by delegating to, rather than manipulating computers' (Negroponte, 1995). To deliver such functionality, software applications must be:

- *autonomous*: given a vague and imprecise specification, it must determine how the problem is best solved and then solve it, without constant guidance from the user,

- *proactive*: it should not wait to be told what to do next, rather it should make suggestions to the user,
- *responsive*: it should take account of changing user needs and changes in the task environment, and
- *adaptive*: it should come to know user's preferences and tailor interactions to reflect these.

In other words, it needs to behave as an intelligent agent. These considerations give rise to the idea of an agent acting as an 'expert assistant' with respect to some application, knowledgeable about both the application itself and the user, and capable of acting *with* the user in order to achieve the user's goals. We discuss some prototypical expert assistants in Section 1.3.

1.2.2 Improving the Efficiency of Software Development

Agent technology gives us the tools with which to build applications that we were previously unable to build. But it can also provide a better means of concept-ualizing and/or implementing a given application. Here, three important domain characteristics are often cited as a rationale for adopting agent technology (cf. Bond and Gasser, 1988):

- data, control, expertise, or resources are inherently distributed,
- the system is naturally regarded as a society of autonomous cooperating com-ponents, or
- the system contains legacy components, which must be made to interact with other, possibly new software components.

1.2.2.1 Distribution of Data, Control, Expertise, or Resources

When the domain involves a number of distinct problem solving entities (or data sources) that are physically or logically distributed (in terms of their data, control, expertise, or resources), and which need to interact with one another in order to solve problems, then agents can often provide an effective solution. For example, in a distributed health care setting, general practitioners, hospital specialists, nurses, and home care organizations have to work together to provide the appropriate care to a sick patient (Huang et al., 1995). In this domain, there is:

- *distribution of data*: the general practitioner has data about the patient, which is very different from that of the hospital nurse – even though it concerns the same person,
- *distribution of control*: each individual is responsible for performing a different set of tasks,
- *distribution of expertise*: the specialist's knowledge is very different from that of either the general practitioner or the nurse, and

- *distribution of resources*: a specialist is responsible for the beds required by their patients, a general practitioner for paying hospital bills, etc.

In cases like this, agents provide a natural way of modeling the problem: real-world entities and their interactions can be directly mapped into autonomous problem solving agents with their own resources and expertise, and which are able to interact with others in order to get tasks done. Also, in the case of distributed data sources, (as in sensor networks (Lesser and Corkill, 1983) and seismic monitoring (Mason, 1995)), the use of agents means that significant amounts of processing can be carried out at the data source, with only high-level information exchanged. This alleviates the need to send large amounts of raw data to a distant central processor, thus making more efficient use of communications bandwidth.

1.2.2.2 Natural Metaphor

The notion of an autonomous agent is often the most appropriate metaphor for presenting a given software functionality. For example:

- a program that filters email can be presented to its user via the metaphor of a *personal digital assistant* (Maes, 1994), and
- meeting scheduling software can naturally be presented as an empowered, autonomous, social agent that can interact with other similar agents on the user's behalf.

In such applications, the fact that these functions are implemented through a series of local agents also means that they can be *personalized* to reflect the preferences of their user. Finally, in computer games (Wavish and Graham, 1995) and virtual reality systems (Bates, 1994), characters can naturally be represented as agents.

1.2.2.3 Legacy Systems

Large organizations have many software applications (especially information systems) that perform critical organizational functions. To keep pace with changing business needs, these systems must be periodically updated. However, modifying such *legacy systems* is in general very difficult: the system's structure and internal operation will become corrupted with the passage of time, designs and documentation are lost, and individuals with an understanding of the software move on. Completely rewriting such software tends to be prohibitively expensive, and is often simply impossible. Therefore, in the long term, the only way to keep such legacy systems useful is to incorporate them into a wider cooperating community, in which they can be exploited by other pieces of software. This can be done, for example, by building an 'agent wrapper' around the software to enable it to inter-operate with other systems (Genesereth and Ketchpel, 1994; Jennings et al., 1993).

The process of transforming a software application such as a database into an agent is sometimes referred to as *agentification* (Shoham, 1993).

1.2.3 The Limitations of Agent Solutions

Although agent technology has an important role to play in the development of leading-edge computing applications, it should not be oversold. Most applications that currently use agents could be built using non-agent techniques. Thus the mere fact that a particular problem domain has distributed data sources or involves legacy systems does not *necessarily* imply that an agent-based solution is the most appropriate one – or even that it is feasible. As with all system designs, the ultimate choice is dictated by many factors. This section has identified the types of situation in which an agent-based solution *should be considered*, as opposed to those in which it *should be deployed*. Moreover, it should be noted that the very nature of the agent paradigm leads to a number of problems, common to all agent-based applications:

- *No overall system controller.* An agent-based solution may not be appropriate for domains in which global constraints have to be maintained, in domains where a real-time response must be guaranteed, or in domains in which dead-locks or livelocks must be avoided.
- *No global perspective.* An agent's actions are, by definition, determined by that agent's local state. However, since in almost any realistic agent system, complete global knowledge is not a possibility, this may mean that agents make globally sub-optimal decisions. The issue of reconciling decision making based on local knowledge with the desire to achieve globally optimal performance is a basic issue in multi-agent systems research (Bond and Gasser, 1988).
- *Trust and delegation.* For individuals to be comfortable with the idea of delegating tasks to agents, they must first *trust* them. Both individuals and organizations will thus need to become more accustomed and confident with the notion of autonomous software components, if they are to become widely used. Users have to gain confidence in the agents that work on their behalf, and this process can take time. During this period, the agent must strike a balance between continually seeking guidance (and needlessly distracting the user) and never seeking guidance (and exceeding its authority). Put crudely, an agent must know its limitations.

1.3   Agent Application Domains

> *Agents are the next major computing paradigm and will be pervasive in every market by the year 2000.* (Janca, 1995)

There are several orthogonal dimensions along which agent applications could be classified. They can be classified by the type of the agent, by the technology used to implement the agent, or by the application domain itself. We choose to use the domain type, since this view fits best with the objectives and structure of the rest of this chapter (see Nwana (1996) for an alternative typology). Our aim in producing this classification scheme is simply to give a feel for the breadth and variety of agent applications. More comprehensive descriptions of specific agent systems can be found in (AA97; Chaib-draa, 1995; Nwana, 1996; PAAM 1996; van Parunak, 1996).

1.3.1 Industrial Applications

Industrial applications of agent technology were among the first to be developed: as early as 1987, Parunak reports experience with applying the contract net task allocation protocol in a manufacturing environment (see below). Today, agents are being applied in a wide range of industrial applications.

1.3.1.1 Process Control

Process control is a natural application for intelligent agents and multi-agent systems, since process controllers are themselves autonomous reactive systems. It is not surprising, therefore, that a number of agent-based process control applications should have been developed. The best known of these is ARCHON, a software platform for building multi-agent systems, and an associated methodology for building applications with this platform (Jennings, 1995). ARCHON has been applied in several process control applications, including electricity transportation management (the application is in use in northern Spain), and particle accelerator control. ARCHON also has the distinction of being one of the earliest field-tested multi-agent systems in the world. Agents in ARCHON are fairly heavyweight computational systems, with four main components: a *high-level communication module* (HLCM), which manages inter-agent communication; a *planning and coordination module* (PCM), which is essentially responsible for deciding what the agent will do; *an agent information management module* (AIM), which is responsible for maintaining the agent's model of the world, and finally, an *underlying intelligent system* (IS), which represents the agent's domain expertise. The HLCM, PCM, and AIM together constitute a kind of 'agent wrapper', which can be used to encapsulate an existing intelligent system (or indeed any pre-existing software application) and turn it into an agent.

1.3.1.2 Manufacturing

Parunak (1987) describes the YAMS (Yet Another Manufacturing System), which applies the well-known Contract Net protocol (Smith, 1980) to manufacturing control. The basic problem can be described as follows. A manufacturing enterprise is modeled as a hierarchy of *workcells*. There will, for example, be workcells for milling, lathing, grinding, painting, and so on. These workcells will be further grouped into flexible manufacturing systems (FMS), each of which will provide a functionality such as assembly, paint spraying, buffering of products, and so on. A collection of such FMSs is grouped into a factory. A single company or organization may have many different factories, though these factories may duplicate functionality and capabilities. The goal of YAMS is to efficiently manage the production process at these plants. This process is defined by some constantly changing parameters, such as the products to be manufactured, available resources, time constraints, and so on. In order to achieve this enormously complex task, YAMS adopts a multi-agent approach, where each factory and factory component is represented as an agent. Each agent has a collection of plans, representing its capabilities. The contract net protocol allows tasks (i.e., production orders) to be delegated to individual factories, and from individual factories down to FMSs, and then to individual workcells. The contract net is based on the idea of negotiation, and hence YAMS views the problem of deciding how best to process a company's product manufacturing requirements as a negotiation problem. A some-what similar approach was developed in (Wooldridge et al., 1996), where the problem of determining an optimal production sequence for a factory was analyzed using the tools of game and negotiation theory.

1.3.1.3   Air Traffic Control

Kinny et al. (1996) describe a sophisticated agent-realized air traffic control system known as OASIS. In this system, which is undergoing field trials at Sydney airport in Australia, agents are used to represent both aircraft and the various air traffic control systems in operation. The agent metaphor thus provides a useful and natural way of modeling real-world autonomous components. As an aircraft enters Sydney airspace, an agent is allocated for it, and the agent is instantiated with the information and goals corresponding to the real-world aircraft. For example, an aircraft might have a goal to land on a certain runway at a certain time. Air traffic control agents are responsible for managing the system. OASIS is implemented using the AAII's own dMARS system. This system allows an agent to be implemented using the belief-desire-intention model of agency – one of the most popular approaches to reasoning about agents in theoretical multi-agent systems.

1.3.2   Commercial Applications

1.3.2.1   Information Management

As the richness and diversity of information available to us in our everyday lives has grown, so the need to manage this information has grown. The lack of effective information management tools has given rise to what is colloquially known as the information overload problem. Put simply, the sheer volume of information available to us via the Internet and World Wide Web (WWW) represents a very real problem. The potential of this resource is immediately apparent to anyone with more than the most superficial experience of using the WWW. But the reality is often disappointing. There are many reasons for this. Both human factors (such as users getting bored or distracted) and organizational factors (such as poorly organized pages with no semantic markup) conspire against users attempting to use the resource in a systematic way. We can characterize the information overload problem in two ways:

- *Information filtering*. Every day, we are presented with enormous amounts of information (via email and newsnet news, for example), only a tiny proportion of which is relevant or important. We need to be able to sort the wheat from the chaff, and focus on information we *need*.
- *Information gathering*. The volume of information available prevents us from actually *finding* information to answer specific queries. We need to be able to obtain information that meets our requirements, even if this information can only be collected from a number of different sites.

One important contributing factor to information overload is almost certainly that an end user is required to constantly *direct* the management process. But there is in principle no reason why such searches should not be carried out by agents, acting autonomously to search the Web on behalf of some user. The idea is so compelling that many projects are directed at doing exactly this. Three such projects are described below:

- Maxims: (Maes, 1994) describes an electronic mail filtering agent called Maxims. The program 'learns to prioritize, delete, forward, sort, and archive mail messages on behalf of a user' (p. 35). It works by 'looking over the shoulder' of a user as he or she works with their email reading program, and uses every action the user performs as a lesson. Maxims constantly makes internal predictions about what a user will do with a message. If these predictions turn out to be inaccurate, then Maxims keeps them to itself. But when it finds it is having a useful degree of success in its predictions, it starts to make suggestions to the user about what to do.
- Newt: (Maes, 1994) also describes an example of an Internet news filtering program called Newt. This program, implemented in C++ on a UNIX platform, takes as input a stream of usenet news articles, and as output gives a subset of these articles that it is recommended the user reads. The Newt agent is 'programmed' by means of training examples: the user gives Newt examples of articles that would and would not be read, and this feedback is used to modify an internal 'model' (we use the term very loosely) of the user's interests. The user can, if desired, explicitly program Newt by giving it precise rules (e.g., "give me all articles containing the word 'agent'"). Newt retrieves words of interest from an article by performing a full-text analysis using the vector space model for documents.

- The Zuno Digital Library: A digital library is an organized, managed collection of data, together with services to assist the user in making use of this data. The Zuno Digital Library (ZDL) system is a multi-agent system that enables a user to obtain a single, coherent view of incoherent, disorganized data sources such as the World Wide Web, a user's own data, collections of articles on publishing house sites, and so on (Zuno, 1997). Agents in ZDL play one of three roles:

    - *consumer* – representing end users of the system, who can be thought of as consuming information;
    - *producer* – representing 'content providers', who own the information that customers consume; and
    - *facilitator* – mapping between consumers and producers.

Consumer agents in the system are responsible for representing the user's interests. They maintain models of users, and use these models to assist them, by proactively providing information they require, and shielding them from information that is not of interest. ZDL thus acts both as an information *filter* and an information *gatherer*.

1.3.2.2   Electronic Commerce

Currently, commerce is almost entirely driven by human interactions; humans decide when to buy goods, how much they are willing to pay, and so on. But in principle, there is no reason why *some* commerce cannot be *automated*. By this, we mean that some commercial decision making can be placed in the hands of agents. Lest the reader suppose that this is fanciful, and that no sensible commercial organization would make their decision making (and hence money spending) the responsibility of a computer program, it should be remembered that this is precisely what happens today in the electronic trading of stocks and shares. Widespread electronic commerce is, however, likely to lie some distance in the future. In the near term, electronic trading applications are likely to be much more mundane and small scale. As an example, Chavez and Maes (1996) describe a simple 'electronic marketplace' called Kasbah. This system realizes the market-place by creating 'buying' and 'selling' agents for each good to be purchased or sold respectively. Commercial transactions take place by the interactions of these agents.

1.3.2.3   Business Process Management

Company managers make informed decisions based on a combination of judge-ment and information from many departments. Ideally, all relevant information should be brought together before judgement is exercised. However obtaining pertinent, consistent and up-to-date information across a large company is a complex and time consuming process. For this reason, organizations have sought to develop a number of IT systems to assist with various aspects of the management of their business processes. Project ADEPT (Jennings et al., 1996) tackles this problem by viewing a business process as a community of negotiating, service-providing agents. Each agent represents a distinct role or department in the enterprise and is capable of providing one or more services. For example, a design department may provide the service of designing a telecom network, a legal department may offer the service of checking that the design is legal, and the marketing department may provide the service of costing the design. Agents who require a service from another agent enter into a negotiation for that service to obtain a mutually acceptable price, time, and degree of quality. Successful negotiations result in binding agreements between agents. This agent-based approach offers a number of advantages over more typical workflow solutions to this problem. The proactive nature of the agents means services can be scheduled in a just-in-time fashion (rather than pre-specified from the beginning), and the responsive nature of the agents means that service exceptions can be detected and handled in a flexible manner. The current version of the system has been tested on a British Telecom (BT) business process involving some 200 activities and nine departments and there are plans to move toward full scale field trials.

1.3.3 Medical Applications

Medical informatics is a major growth area in computer science: new applications are being found for computers every day in the health industry. It is not surprising, therefore, that agents should be applied in this domain. Two of the earliest applications are in the areas of health care and patient monitoring.

1.3.3.1 Patient Monitoring

The Guardian system described in (Hayes-Roth et al., 1989) is intended to help manage patient care in the Surgical Intensive Care Unit (SICU). The system was motivated by two concerns: first, that the patient care model in a SICU is essentially that of a team, where a collection of experts with distinct areas of expertise cooperate to organize patient health care; and second, that one of the most important factors in good SICU patient health care is the adequate sharing of information between members of the critical care team. In particular, specialists tend to have very little opportunity to monitor the minute-by-minute status of a patient; this task tends to fall to nurses, who, in contrast, often do not have the expertise to interpret the information they obtain in the way that an appropriate expert would. The Guardian system distributes the SICU patient monitoring function among a number of agents, of three different types:

- *perception/action agents* – responsible for the interface between Guardian and the world, mapping raw sensor input into a usable symbolic form, and translating action requests from Guardian into raw effector control commands,

- *reasoning agents* – responsible for organizing the system's decision making process, and
- *control agents* – of which there will only ever be one, with overall, top-level control of the system.

These agents are organized into hierarchies, and the system as a whole is closely based on the blackboard model of control, wherein different agents ('knowledge sources') cooperate via sharing knowledge in a common data structure known as a blackboard.

1.3.3.2 Health Care

Huang et al. (1996) describe a prototypical agent-based distributed medical care system. This system is designed to integrate the patient management process, which typically involves many individuals. For example, a general practitioner may suspect that a patient has breast cancer, but this suspicion cannot be confirmed or rejected without the assistance of a hospital specialist. If the specialist confirms the hypothesis, then a care programme must be devised for treating the patient, involving the resources of other individuals. The prototype system allows a natural representation of this process, with agents mapped onto the individuals and, potentially, organizations involved in the patient care process. Agents in the prototype contain a knowledge-based (intelligent) system, containing the domain expertise of the agent, a human-computer interface, allowing the user to add, remove, or view system goals, and a communications manager, which realizes the message-passing functionality of agents. The intelligent system component is based on the KADS model of expertise, and the whole agent architecture is implemented in PROLOG. Message passing is realized via extensions to standard email.

1.3.4 Entertainment

The leisure industry is often not taken seriously by the computer science community. Leisure applications are frequently seen as somehow peripheral to the 'serious' applications of computers. And yet leisure applications such as computer games can be extremely lucrative – consider the number of copies of id Software's 'Quake' sold since its release in 1996. Agents have an obvious role in computer games, interactive theater, and related virtual reality applications: such systems tend to be full of semi-autonomous animated characters, which can naturally be implemented as agents.

1.3.4.1 Games

Wavish et al. (1996) describe several applications of agent technology to computer games. For example, they have developed a version of the popular Tetris computer game, where a user must try to make a wall out of irregularly shaped falling blocks. The agent in the game takes the part of the user, who must control where the blocks fall. Trying to program this agent using traditional symbolic AI techniques would require going through a knowledge elicitation stage, representing knowledge about the game and the role of the user in terms of symbolic data structures such as rules, and so on. This approach would be entirely unrealistic for a game like Tetris, which has hard real-time constraints. Wavish and colleagues thus use an alternative *reactive* agent model called RTA (Real Time Able). In this approach, agents are programmed in terms of *behaviors*. These behaviors are simple structures, which loosely resemble rules but do not require complex symbolic reasoning.

1.3.4.2 Interactive Theater and Cinema

By interactive theater and cinema, we mean a system that allows a user to play out a role analogous to the roles played by real, human actors in plays or films, interacting with artificial, computer characters that have the behavioral characteristics of real people. Agents that play the part of humans in theater-style applications are often known as *believable* agents, a term coined by Joe Bates. His vision is of

> *[Agents that] provide the illusion of life, thus permitting ... [an] audience's suspension of disbelief.* (Bates, 1994)

A number of projects have been set up to investigate the development of such agents. For example, (Hayes-Roth et al., 1995) describe a *directed improvization* system, in which human players act out roles in a dynamic narrative, creating a new, user directed 'work'.

1.3.5 Comments

At a certain level of abstraction, many of the above applications share common features. Individual agents are designed and built to enact particular roles. These agents are autonomous, goal directed entities, which are responsive to their environment. They must typically interact with other agents in order to carry out their role. Such interactions are a natural consequence of the inevitable interdependencies which exist between the agents, their environment, and their design objectives. As the agents are autonomous, the interactions are usually fairly sophisticated – involving cooperation, coordination and negotiation. Following on from this view, two important observations can be made about developing agent-based applications:

- The detailed problem solving actions of the agent can only be determined at run time. Individual behavior is regulated by a complex interplay between the agent's internal state and its external influences (its environment and the other agents). Thus the precise 'trajectory' that an agent will follow can only be discovered by running the agent in its environment.
- Because the behavior of individual agents is not uniquely determined at design time, the behavior of the system as a whole can also only emerge at run time.

These points have some obvious (and perhaps alarming) implications for the use of an agent-based approach in safety-critical application domains such as air traffic control, where it is essential that the system satisfies its specification. We comment on this issue in Section 1.4.

The above applications also illustrate that there are several different dimensions along which we can analyze agent-based systems:

- *Sophistication of the Agents.* Agents can be seen as performing three broad types of behavior. At the simplest level, there is the 'gopher' agent, which carries out comparatively simple tasks, based on well-defined, pre-specified rules and assumptions. The next level of sophistication involves 'service performing' agents, which carry out a high-level, but still well-defined task at the request of a user (e.g., arrange a meeting or find an appropriate flight). Finally, there are the predictive/proactive agents, capable of flexible auto-nomous behavior in the way we discussed above. Simple examples are agents that volunteer information or services to a user, without being asked, whenever it is deemed to be appropriate.
- *Role of the Agents.* Agents play many types of role. For example, in several of the industrial and commercial applications discussed above, the role of the agent system is to provide a decision support functionality. The agents act autonomously and proactively to gather information and to make recommen-dations, but a human operator makes the ultimate decisions. In contrast, in the entertainment domain (for example), the agent completely automates a problem solving role – it is thus delegated a particular activity and is entirely respon-sible for carrying it out.
- *Granularity of View.* In some of the applications discussed above, the signi-ficant unit of analysis and design is the *individual* agent, whereas in other applications it is the *society* of agents that is key. The decision about whether to adopt a single-agent or multi-agent approach is generally determined by the domain, and is similar in nature to decisions about whether monolithic, centralized solutions or distributed, decentralized solutions are appropriate. Single-agent systems are in a sense much simpler than multi-agent systems, since they do not require the designer to deal with issues such as cooperation, negotiation, and so on.

1.4 The Agent Development Bottleneck

At the time of writing, expertise in designing and building agent applications is scarce. There is little in the way of production-quality software support for building agent applications, and still less general understanding of the issues that need to be addressed when building such systems. Worse, most of today's agent systems are built from scratch, using bespoke tools and techniques, which cannot easily be applied to other types of system. This is particularly worrying because a lot of infrastructure is required before the main components of an agent system can be built. At the moment, most developers rebuild this infrastructure from scratch in every new case; this process is clearly not sustainable.

However, there is an increasing awareness that this situation must change if agents are to make it into the mainstream of software development (Kinny, 1996; Wooldridge, 1997). Support is required throughout the agent system development process. In what follows, we use a traditional software engineering model as a basis for structuring our discussion of this issue. We begin our discussion with requirements specification, since the stage that precedes it – requirements analysis – does not differ in any significant way from that for other types of software system. The requirements analysis stage typically concludes with a *user require-ments document* – a statement of the properties that the analyst or developer believes the user (client) wants of the new system. This document is usually written in non-technical language, so that it can be understood by both client and developer.

1.4.1 Requirements Specification

Once an understanding is reached of the client's needs with respect to the newly commissioned system, a precise statement is required of what the developers intend to build. This document tends to be written as formally as possible – it aims to be a precise statement of the properties of the system that the developers will build. A number of approaches have been developed to agent system requirements specification, and in particular to formal (mathematical) approaches (Wooldridge, 1997). The details of these formalisms tend to be rather complex, but broadly speaking, they characterize agents as *rational decision makers*. By this, we mean systems whose internal state can be expressed in terms of 'mentalistic' constructs such as belief, desire, and intention. An agent's decision making can then be characterized in terms of these constructs. It may be difficult to see how one might specify a computer system in this way, but the idea is really quite straightforward. One builds a specification out of a set of 'rules' (strictly speaking, logical formulas), somewhat like this:

> if   *agent 1 believes that agent 2 believes runway 1 is clear*
> then   *agent 1 should believe that agent 2 has erroneous information,*
> and *agent 1 should intend that agent 2 is informed of its error.*

One might wonder why terms such as 'believe' and 'intend' are used. Beliefs are generally used to refer to the information that agents have about their environment. This information can be incorrect – in just the same way that information we have about the environment (our beliefs) could be wrong. The term intention is used to refer to a goal that the agent will pursue until it either succeeds or fails completely – it admits the possibility of failure, a realistic possibility in many complex systems, one which traditional formalisms tend to ignore. The chapter by Georgeff and Rao is the clearest expression of this view in this volume. The reader is also referred to (Wooldridge, 1997) for a detailed discussion on these approaches.

1.4.2 System Design

The design of robust, efficient systems is one of the most important issues addressed by software engineers, and a great deal of effort has been devoted to making system design a methodical, rigorous process. At the time of writing, comparatively few workers in the agent research community have considered how design methodologies might be applied to agent systems. This situation must clearly change if agent systems are to become widely used, and in particular, the following key questions need to be addressed:

- *Adopting an agent-based approach.* In much of the work that goes under the agent banner, the rationale behind the choice of an agent-based approach (over other, arguably simpler alternatives) is unclear. The analysis of appropriate domain properties (Sections 1.2 and 1.3) represents a step toward this end.
- *Macro-system Structure.* Once given an abstract, high-level system speci-fication, we need to transform this specification into agents, and relate these agents to one another in a system structure. This process is known as *refine-ment*. In just the same way that object-oriented design methodologies exist, which give guidelines relating to the identification of objects and object inter-dependencies, so we might expect soon to see *agent-oriented design method-ologies*, which offer clear guidelines about how to decompose a problem into agents and what effects a given decomposition is likely to have on the system performance. The design problem is exacerbated by the fact that legacy systems often need to be incorporated in agent systems. Thus design needs to be done both from a top-down perspective (how should the problem be decomposed ideally?) and from a bottom-up perspective (what software groupings already exist and cannot be changed?). Both perspectives must be accommodated.

1.4.3 System Implementation

An agent system design will both describe the various different roles that exist within the system and characterize the relationships that exist between these roles. However, the design will not generally prescribe an implementation of these agents. So, having identified the various agent roles in a system, the next step is to determine how each of these roles can be best realized. An agent architecture needs to be devised or adopted for each role, which will deliver the required functional and non-functional characteristics of the role.

Many agent architectures have been developed by the intelligent agents community, with many different properties (Wooldridge and Jennings, 1995). At one extreme, there are 'strong AI' systems, which allow users to build agents as knowledge-based systems, or even as logic theorem provers. In order to build agents using such systems, one goes through the standard knowledge-based system process of knowledge elicitation and representation, coding an agent's behavior in terms of rules, frames, or semantic nets. At the other extreme, there are many agent frameworks that simply offer enhanced versions of (for example) the Java programming language – they include no AI techniques at all. Neither of these extremes is strictly right or wrong: they both have merits and drawbacks. In general, of course, the simplest solution that will effectively solve a problem is often the best. There is little point in using complex reasoning systems where simple Java-like agents will do. Obviously, more detailed guidelines to assist with this decision making process are desirable.

1.4.4 System Testing, Debugging, and Verification

As long ago as 1987, Les Gasser wrote:

> *Concurrency, problem-domain uncertainty, and non-determinism in execution together conspire to make it very difficult to comprehend the activity in a distributed intelligent system [...] we urgently need graphic displays of system activity linked to intelligent model-based tools which help a developer reason about expected and observed behavior.* (Gasser, 1987)

Gasser's comments remain as true of agent system development in the late 1990s as they did of the mid-1980s. Sadly, testing and debugging are still much neglected areas of the agent development process. Developers need assistance with *visualizing* what is happening, and need *debugging* facilities to step through the execution and amend behavior where appropriate. Visualization is particularly important – determining what is happening in asynchronous, concurrent systems is an exceedingly difficult task. This is true both within an agent and even more so between agents. Traditional debugging features which allow execution to be stopped, internal states to be examined, states to be changed, message arrivals to be simulated, and so on are also essential. In most systems these features and tools are developed from scratch – clearly an undesirable state of affairs.

1.5   The Structure of This Book

The chapters in this book cover a wide spectrum of issues related to the applications of intelligent agents and multi-agent systems. There are introductory chapters that explain the basic concepts and summarize the state of the art, there are vision chapters which look to the future of agent applications (from both a technical and a marketing perspective), and, finally, there are experience chapters, which deal with specific agent systems and applications.

In more detail:

- Technological issues that are addressed include: architectures for individual agents and multi-agent systems; frameworks for implementing agent applications; methodologies for designing agents and multi-agent systems; techniques for attaining efficient and coherent communication, cooperation and coordination; and techniques for personalizing agents to reflect the needs of individual users.
- Predictions are made about the following issues: the types of markets where agents are likely to have the highest impact; the economic value of various agent markets; the time scales by which agent technology will enter various aspects of mainstream software solutions; and the (technical and non-technical) obstacles that need to be overcome if agents are to achieve their potential.
- Application domains for which agent systems are described include: telecommunications systems, personal digital assistants, information management, information economies, business applications, air traffic control, computer simulation, transportation management, and financial management.

The range of author affiliations (British Telecom, US West, IBM, GPT, Sharp, Daimler-Benz, Siemens, GTE Labs, France Telecom, US Treasury, and Swiss Bank Corporation) covers a significant proportion of the large commercial organizations that are currently investing in agent technology, and illustrates forcefully the pervasive nature of this exciting new technology.

1.5.1   Introductory Chapters

These two chapters introduce the basic terms and concepts of agent systems. They provide the underpinning for the remainder of this book and offer a good point of entry to those who are new to the field.

Nwana and Ndumu provide a broadly based and up-to-date introduction to the basic concepts and terminology of agent systems. They define a typology that specifies the range of agents which currently exist, offer an assessment of the key problems and promises of the different agent types, and describe a number of exemplar systems.

Laufmann takes a complementary approach to that of Nwana and Ndumu. He identifies and specifies an ideal intelligent agent, and shows how the current agent landscape can be divided by considering extant systems as highlighting particular attributes of this ideal model. He espouses three different, but related, views of agents – agents as automated personal assistants, agents as cooperating problem solvers, and agents as communicating software entities. He then concentrates on the third view and outlines a strategy for software development that should lead to substantially improved agent applications in the near term.

1.5.2 Vision Chapters

These four chapters assess where agents are today and where they are likely to be in five to ten years time. When taken together, the chapters convey the excitement and potential of this field and highlight the key open problems.

Janca presents an analysis of the current state of agent-enabled applications and describes how this is likely to change in the coming years. He identifies two broad classes of agents – user interface agents which act on behalf of the user (capturing their goals and translating these into actions) and process agents which are responsible for enacting these goals. Based on an analysis of the current market for agent technology (see also the contribution by Guilfoyle) he notes that the current generation of applications exist in self-contained niches, that the agents use proprietary formats, and that there are no standards for interconnection (see contributions by Huhns and Singh and Kearney). To circumvent these short-comings, he presents an agent design model which acts as a unifying framework for agent applications and which can have standard re-useable parts. In this view, building different applications becomes more of a 'plug-and-play' than a 'start from scratch' endeavor. Finally, he presents a series of commercial challenges that need to be overcome before agents can reach their full potential.

Guilfoyle presents an analysis of the market for agent technology (also see Janca's contribution). She identifies the main areas in which agent technology is likely to have an impact and the main vendors that are currently active in this field. She assesses the current trends of agent applications and offers various predictions about how the size and direction of the market will expand over time.

Foss concentrates on the concept of information brokerage (one of the key agent application domains identified by Janca and Guilfoyle). He outlines the role of intelligent agents as an intermediary service between consumers and infor-mation sources, and presents a vision of a future commercial information trading environment which is rich enough for true electronic commerce to take place. This view includes dealing adequately with the currently neglected issues of taxation, rights, royalties, and revenues. A case is then made for the pivotal role of agent technology in this vision (see Plu's contribution for an indication of how such a vision can begin to be realized using current generation technology).

Kearney concentrates solely on one class of agents – personal digital assistants (PDAs). Again, this is an important current and future market for agent technology as identified by Janca and Guilfoyle. For this application class, he posits a role for agent software which involves mediating between the individual user and a range of online services (see also the contributions of Foss and Janca). He suggests a path from the current state of the art through successive generations of PDAs to a state in which agents are ubiquitous providers of personalized services. For this vision to be attained, he identifies agent interoperability as the key problem to be solved (see also the contribution by Huhns and Singh).

1.5.3 Systems and Their Applications

The chapters in this section represent the current state of the art in applied agent systems. They outline the types of agent frameworks and architectures that are currently being used to develop and implement agent systems and discuss, in detail, a wide range of agent applications built using this technology.

Georgeff and Rao present results related to the design and implementation of rational software agents. In this work, they address one of the fundamental problems of agent research – the gap between theory and practice. This gap is currently large and both sides of the field plough along in isolation. However, in their work, the authors use a formal framework to specify and implement their agents. The particular class of agents they address are Belief-Desire-Intention (BDI) agents (also see the contribution by Burmeister et al.). Thus, they sketch the theoretical foundation of their agents and how they are realized in a practical agent implementation. They then discuss how this implementation was used to build large-scale, real-world agent applications in the domains of air traffic management, business process management, and air combat modeling.

Burmeister et al. discuss how agent based techniques can be applied in the domains of traffic management and manufacturing. They present their core technology for realizing their agent applications: COSY, a modular agent architecture based on the concepts of behaviors, resources, and intentions (see also the contribution by Georgeff and Rao); and DASEDIS, a development environment for building such agents (cf. the development environment of Haugeneder and Steiner). The application of this architecture to two traffic applications (traffic management and freight logistics) and two manufacturing applications (flexible manufacturing and plant control) is then discussed.

Haugeneder and Steiner present a conceptual design and specification of an agent architecture and a multi-agent language (called MAIL) for implementing single agents and cooperative interaction among them. This design is then refined into a multi-agent environment for constructing cooperative applications based on this model (cf. the DASEDIS framework of Burmeister et al.). Finally, the architecture and the environment are demonstrated on two sample applications in the areas of group scheduling and road traffic management (see also the contribution of Burmeister et al.).

Weihmayer and Velthuijsen provide an overview of the role of agent systems in the domain of telecommunications. They identify the types of telecommunications applications for which agent solutions have been constructed. These include process support (see also contributions by Huhns and Singh and Janca), network control, service management (see also Plu's contribution), network management, transmission switching, and network design. They then discuss the justification for the intense interest on the part of telecommunications organizations in agent technology, present a number of detailed system case studies, and, finally, offer a balanced analysis of the future of agents in telecommunications.

Huhns and Singh describe how a set of autonomous agents can cooperate to provide coherent management of transaction workflows. In particular, they concentrate on the problem of how agents with diverse and heterogeneous information models can interoperate with one another (cf. the approach advocated by Kearney). Their approach to such interoperation is predicated on the fact that the agents maintain models of their information and resources. These models are then mapped into a common ontology to ensure coherent semantics among the cooperating group. Their approach is exemplified by considering a multi-agent system for telecommunication service provisioning.

Plu presents an agent-based view of how organizations can design and build computer infrastructures that provide sophisticated information and electronic commerce services to many customers. Using the ISO standard architecture for open distributed processing, he shows, with the aid of scenarios, the central role that agent technology can play at many of the model's distinct levels. He also discusses issues related to mobile agents – identifying when they are appropriate and the types of advantages they confer over their static counterparts.

Sycara et al. present the design and implementation of a series of agents for the tasks of filtering, evaluating, and integrating information on the Internet. Their agents team up, on demand, depending on the user, the task, and the situation, to retrieve and filter information. The agents and their organizational structure also adapt to the prevailing task and user. Their system is demonstrated in the domain of financial portfolio management (see also Wenger and Probst's contribution).

Goldberg and Senator detail the FAIS system, which links and evaluates reports of large cash transactions to identify potential money laundering activities.

The system, which has been operational since 1993, is designed and implemented as a cooperative endeavor involving humans and software agents (see Haugeneder and Steiner's contribution for further thoughts on such human-computer cooperation). The main focus of the presently implemented system is knowledge discovery and information analysis in large data spaces. However, as the system's range of applicability has increased, so the need for greater agent-to-agent cooperation has emerged. To this end, the authors describe the next generation of FAIS and discuss how adopting an agent-based perspective eases the system migration task.

Wenger and Probst analyse the potential role and impact of the agent paradigm in the general area of providing financial services. They highlight the characteristics of typical agent-based applications and provide illustrative scenarios for the domains of mortgage sales, corporate financial management, and portfolio management (see also the contribution by Sycara et al.). They then discuss the various ways in which intelligent agents can add value to financial operations, present a detailed scenario based on an investment sales transaction service, and assess the future role of agent technology in this market segment.

References

AA97 (1997) *Proceedings of the First International Conference on Autonomous Agents '97*, Marina del Rey, CA. ACM Press.

Bates, J. (1994) The role of emotion in believable agents. *Communications of the ACM*, 37(7), 122–125.

Bond, A. H., Gasser, L. (Eds.) (1988) *Readings in Distributed Artificial Intelligence*. Morgan Kaufmann.

Chaib-draa, B., (1995) Industrial applications of distributed AI. *Communications of the ACM*, 38(11), 47–53.

Chavez, A., Maes, P. (1996) Kasbah: An agent marketplace for buying and selling goods. *Proceedings of First International Conference on the Practical Application of Intelligent Agents and Multi-Agent Systems*, London, UK.

Crabtree, B., Jennings, N. R. (Eds.) (1996) *Proceedings of First International Conference on the Practical Application of Intelligent Agents and Multi-agent Systems*, London, UK.

Franklin, S., Graesser, A. (1996) Is it an agent, or just a program? *Proceedings Third International Workshop on Agent Theories, Architectures and Languages*, Budapest, Hungary, 193–206.

Gasser, L., Braganza, C., Herman, N. (1987) MACE: A flexible testbed for distributed AI research. In: M. N. Huhns (Ed.) *Distributed AI*. Morgan Kaufmann.

Genesereth, M. R., Ketchpel, S. P. (1994) Software agents. *Communications of the ACM*, 37(7), 48–53.

Hayes-Roth, B., Hewett, M., Waashington, R., Hewett, R., Seiver, A. (1995) Distributing intelligence within an individual. In: L. Gasser, M. N. Huhns (Eds.) *Distributed AI*, Volume II, 385–412. Morgan Kaufmann.

Huang, J., Jennings, N. R., Fox, J. (1995) An agent-based approach to health care management. *Int. Journal of Applied Artificial Intelligence*, 9(4), 401–420.

Janca, P. C. (1995) Pragmatic application of information agents. BIS Strategic Report.

Jennings, N. R., Varga, L. Z., Aarnts, R. P., Fuchs, J., Skarek, P. (1993) Transforming stand-alone expert systems into a community of cooperating agents. *Int. Journal of Engineering Applications of Artificial Intelligence*, 6(4), 317–331.

Jennings, N. R., Corera, J. M., Laresgoiti, I. (1995) Developing industrial multi-agent systems. In: *Proceedings of the First International Conference on Multi-agent Systems*, (ICMAS-95), 423-430.

Jennings, N. R., Faratin, P., Johnson, M. J., Norman, T. J., O'Brien, P., Wiegand, M. E. (1996) Agent-based business process management. *Int. Journal of Cooperative Information Systems*, 5(2, 3), 105–130.

Lesser, V. R., Corkill, D. D. (1983) The distributed vehicle monitoring testbed: a tool for investigating distributed problem solving network. *AI Magazine*, Fall, 15–33.

Maes, P. (1994) Agents that reduce work and information overload. *Communications of the ACM*, 37(7), 31–40.

Mason, C. L. (1995) Cooperative interpretation of seismic data for nuclear test ban treaty verification: a DAI approach. *Int. Journal of Applied Artificial Intelligence*, 9(4), 371–400.

Negroponte, N. (1995) *Being Digital*. Hodder and Stoughton.

Ovum Report (1994) Intelligent agents: the new revolution in software.

PAAM'97 (1997) *Proceedings of the First International Conference on the Practical Application of Intelligent Agents and Multi-agent Systems*, London.

Parunak, H. V. D. (1987) Manufacturing experience with the contract net. In: M. N. Huhns (Ed.) *Distributed AI*. Morgan Kaufmann.

Parunak, H. V. D. (1996) Applications of distributed artificial intelligence in industry. In: G. M. P. O'Hare, N. R. Jennings (Eds.) *Foundations of Distributed Artificial Intelligence*, 139–164. Wiley.

Pnueli, A. (1986) Specification and development of reactive systems. In: *Information Processing 86*, Elsevier/North-Holland.

Sargent, P. (1992) Back to school for a brand new ABC. In: *The Guardian*, 12 March, p. 28.

Shoham, Y. (1993) Agent-oriented programming. *Artificial Intelligence*, 60(1), 51-92.

Smith, R. (1980) The contract net protocol. *IEEE Trans. on Computers*, C-29(12), 1104–1113.

Wavish, P., Graham, M. (1996) A situated action approach to implementing characters in computer games. *Int. Journal of Applied Artificial Intelligence*, 10(1), 53–74.

Wooldridge, M., Jennings, N. R. (1995) Intelligent agents: theory and practice. *The Knowledge Engineering Review*, 10(2), 115–152.

Wooldridge, M. (1997) Agent based software engineering. *IEE Proceedings on Software Engineering*, 144(1), 26–37.

Wooldridge, M., Bussmann, S., Klosterberg, M. (1996) Production sequencing as negotiation. In: *Proceedings of the First International Conference on the Practical Application of Intelligent Agents and Multi-agent Systems*, London.

Zuno Ltd (1997) See http://www.dlib.com/.

2 A Brief Introduction to Software Agent Technology[1]

H. S. Nwana
D. T. Ndumu
BT Research Labs

2.1 Introduction

Software agent technology is a rapidly developing area of research. Application domains in which agent solutions are being applied or researched into include workflow management, telecommunications network management, air traffic control, business process re-engineering, data mining, information retrieval/management, electronic commerce, education, personal digital assistants (PDAs), e-mail filtering, digital libraries, command and control, smart databases, and scheduling/diary management. Indeed, as Guilfoyle (1995) notes:

> *in 10 years time most new IT development will be affected, and many consumer products will contain embedded agent-based systems.*

In this chapter, we overview the evolving area of software agents. The over-use of the word 'agent' has tended to mask the fact that, in reality, there is a truly heterogeneous body of research being carried out under this banner. This chapter overviews the rationales, hypotheses, goals, and state-of-the-art demonstrators of the various agent types currently under investigation by researchers.

2.2 What Is an Agent?

We have as much chance of agreeing on a consensus definition for the word 'agent' as artificial intelligence (AI) researchers have of arriving at one for 'artificial intelligence.' Arguably, software agents date back to the early days of AI work, to Carl Hewitt's (1977) concurrent actor model. In this model, Hewitt proposed the concept of a self-contained, interactive, and concurrently executing object which he termed an 'actor.' This object had some encapsulated internal state and could respond to messages from other similar objects.

---

[1] This chapter is an abridged version of (Nwana, 1996).

When we really have to, we define an agent as referring to a component of software and/or hardware that is capable of acting exactingly in order to acomplish tasks on behalf of its user. Given a choice, we would rather say it is an umbrella term that covers a range of other more specific agent types, and then go on to list and define these other agent types.

2.2.1 A Typology of Agents

There are several dimensions to classify *existing* software agents. Firstly, agents may be classified by their mobility, i.e., by their ability to move around some network. This yields the classes of *static* or *mobile* agents.

Secondly, they may be classed as either *deliberative* or *reactive*. Deliberative agents derive from the deliberative thinking paradigm which holds that agents possess an internal symbolic reasoning model, and they engage in planning and negotiation with other agents in order to achieve their goals. Work on reactive agents originate from research carried out by Brooks (1986) and Agre and Chapman (1987). These agents do not have any internal, symbolic models of their environment, and they act using a stimulus/response type of behavior by responding to the present state of the environment in which they are embedded (Ferber, 1994).

Thirdly, agents may be classified along several attributes which ideally they *should* exhibit. At BT Laboratories, we have identified a minimal list of three: autonomy, learning, and cooperation. *Autonomy* refers to the principle that agents can operate on their own without the need for human guidance, even though this would sometimes be invaluable. A key element of autonomy is proactiveness, i.e., the ability to 'take the initiative' (Wooldridge and Jennings, 1995). *Cooperation* with other agents is paramount: it is the *raison d'être* for having multiple agents. Further, the communication required to ensure cooperation generally involves high-level messages. Lastly, for agents to be truly 'intelligent', they would have to *learn* as they react and/or interact with their external environment; such that with time, their performance increases. We use these three characteristics in Figure 2.1 to derive three types of agents: *collaborative agents, interface agents*, and truly *smart agents*.

We must emphasize that these distinctions are *not* definitive. For example, with collaborative agents, there is more emphasis on cooperation and autonomy than on learning; but we do not imply that collaborative agents never learn. We do *not* consider anything else lying outside the 'circles' to be agents. For example, most expert systems are largely autonomous; but, typically, they do not cooperate or learn. Ideally, agents should do all three equally well, but this is the *aspiration* rather than the reality. Truly smart agents do not yet exist!

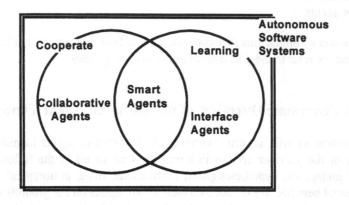

Figure 2.1. A part view of an agent typology

Fourthly, agents may sometimes be classified by their roles (particularly, if the roles are major ones), e.g., world wide web (WWW) information gathering agents. Essentially, such agents help manage the vast amount of information in wide area networks like the Internet. We refer to this class of agents as *information* or *Internet agents*. Again, information agents may be static or mobile and deliberative or reactive.

Fifthly, we have also included the category of *hybrid* agents that combine two or more agent philosophies in a single agent.

There are other attributes of agents that we consider secondary to those already mentioned. For example, is an agent versatile (i.e., does it have many goals or does it engage in a variety of tasks)? Is an agent benevolent or unhelpful, antagonistic or altruistic? Does an agent lie knowingly or is it always truthful? Is it temporally continuous? Some researchers also attribute emotional attitudes to agents – do they get 'fed up' when asked to do the same thing time and time again (Bates, 1994)? Some agents are also imbued with *mentalistic* attitudes such as beliefs, desires, and intentions (Rao and Georgeff, 1995; Jennings, 1993). Such attributes as these provide for a stronger definition of agenthood.

In essence, *agents exist in a truly multi-dimensional space*. However, for the sake of clarity of understanding, we have 'collapsed' this space into a single list. Hence, we identify seven types of agents:

- Collaborative agents
- Interface agents
- Mobile agents
- Information/Internet agents

- Reactive agents
- Hybrid agents
- Smart agents

There are some applications that combine agents from two or more of these categories, and we refer to these as *heterogeneous agent systems*.

2.3   A Panoramic Overview of the Different Agent Types

In this section we will, in turn, overview all the types of agents identified in our typology of the previous section in terms of some or all of the following: their essential metaphors, hypotheses/goals, motivations, roles, prototypical examples, and potential benefits. We do not overview smart agents on the grounds that this is the *aspiration* of agent researchers rather than the *reality*.

2.3.1   Collaborative Agents

As shown in Figure 2.1, collaborative agents emphasize autonomy and co-operation with other agents in order to perform tasks for their owners in open and time-constrained multi-agent environments. They may learn, but this aspect is not typically a major emphasis of their operation, though some perform limited parametric or rote learning. To coordinate their activities, they may have to negotiate in order to reach mutually acceptable agreements. Collaborative agents tend to be static, large, coarse-grained agents. They may be benevolent, rational, truthful, some combination of these, or none of them. As noted earlier, some researchers give stronger definitions of such agents, hence, the class of collaborative agents may itself be perceived as a broad grouping.

2.3.1.1   Motivation and Benefits

The rationale for having collaborative agent systems is a specification of the goal of distributed AI (DAI), which may be summarized as '*creating a system that interconnects separately developed collaborative agents, thus enabling the ensemble to function beyond the capabilities of any of its members*' (Huhns and Singh, 1994). Thus, DAI research, and hence collaborative agents research, aims to:

- solve problems that are too large for a centralized single agent to do due to resource limitations or the sheer risk of having one centralized system;
- allow for the interconnection and interoperation of existing legacy systems, e.g., expert systems, decision support systems, and conventional programs; and

- provide solutions to inherently distributed problems. For instance, solutions that draw from distributed information sources, e.g., distributed online information sources or distributed sensor networks (see DVMT, Durfee et al., 1987); and solutions where the expertise is distributed, e.g., in health care provision or air traffic control (see OASIS, Rao and Georgeff, 1995).

The potential benefits of collaborative agents research, inherited from DAI, include modularity (which reduces complexity), speed (due to parallelism), reliability (due to redundancy), and flexibility (i.e., new tasks are composed more easily from the more modular organization). Collaborative agents also inherit benefits from AI such as operation at the knowledge level, easier maintenance, reusability, and platform independence.

2.3.1.2 A Prototypical Example: The Pleiades System

The Pleiades project (see URL1) applies collaborative agents in the domain of organizational decision making over the 'InfoSphere' (which refers essentially to a collection of Internet-based heterogeneous resources).

Pleiades is a distributed collaborative agent-based architecture which has two layers of abstraction: the first layer contains *task-specific* collaborative agents and the second *information-specific* collaborative agents (Figure 2.2). This architecture has been used to develop a visitor hosting system in which agents cooperate in order to create and manage a visitor's schedule for Carnegie Mellon University. In the architecture, task-specific agents perform a particular task for their users, e.g., arranging appointments and meetings with other task agents. These agents coordinate and schedule plans based on the context. They collaborate with one

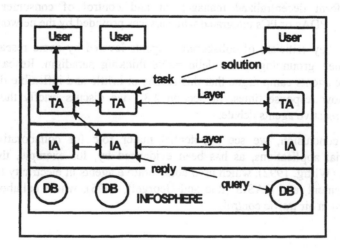

Figure 2.2. The Pleiades distributed system architecture (adapted from Sycara, 1995)

another (within Layer 1) to resolve conflicts or integrate information. In order to garner the information required at this level, they request information from information-specific agents. Information agents, in turn, may collaborate with one another (within Layer 2) to provide the information requested back to the Layer 1 requesting agent. The sources of the information are the many databases in the infosphere. Ultimately, the task agents propose a solution to their users.

Task agents encode a model of the task domain and knowledge of how to perform tasks, as well as an acquaintance model detailing the capabilities of other task or information agents. They also possess some learning mechanisms. Information agents possess knowledge of the various information sources and how to access them, and an acquaintance model specifying the abilities of other information agents (Sycara, 1995).

Individually, an agent consists of a planning module linked to its local beliefs and facts database. It also has a local scheduler, a coordination module, and an execution monitor. Thus, agents can instantiate task plans, coordinate these plans with other agents and schedule/monitor the execution of their local actions. Interestingly, the architecture has no central planner and hence agents must all engage in coordination by communicating to others their constraints, expectations, and other relevant information.

2.3.1.3   A Brief Critical Review of Collaborative Agent Systems Work

There are many other useful pieces of work on collaborative agents. At BT Laboratories, two prototype collaborative agent-based systems, ADEPT and MII, have been developed recently. ADEPT (O'Brien and Wiegand, 1996) employs collaborative agents in the application area of business process re-engineering while MII (Winter et al., 1996) demonstrates that collaborative agents can be used to perform decentralized management and control of consumer electronics, typically PDAs or PCs integrated with services provided by the network operator.

The key criticism of collaborative agents leveled by some researchers stems from their grounding in the deliberative thinking paradigm. Researchers in the reactive agents camp argue that this results in brittle and inflexible demonstrators with slow response times. In Section 2.3.5 we discuss briefly the deliberative versus reactive agents debate.

In conclusion, we see a potential major role for collaborative agents in industrial applications, as has been evidenced by, for example, the ARCHON project (Wittig, 1992), which used collaborative agents in electricity transportation management, and OASIS (Rao and Georgeff, 1995), where collaborative agents are used in air traffic control.

2.3.2   Interface Agents

Interface agents (see Figure 2.1) emphasize autonomy and learning in order to perform tasks for their owners. Maes (1994) points out that the key metaphor underlying interface agents is that of a *personal assistant* who is *collaborating with the user* in the same work environment. Note the subtle emphasis and distinction between collaborating with *the user* and collaborating with *other agents* as is the case with collaborative agents.

Essentially, interface agents support and provide proactive assistance, typically to a user learning to use a particular application such as a spreadsheet or an operating system. The user's agent observes and monitors the actions taken by the user in the interface (it 'watches over the shoulder of its user'), learns new short-cuts, and suggests better ways of doing the task. As for learning, typically, interface agents learn to assist their users in the following four ways: (i) by observing and imitating the user, (ii) through receiving positive and negative feedback from the user, (iii) by receiving explicit instructions from the user, and (iv) by asking other agents for advice. Generally, the learning modes are by rote memory-based learning or parametric, though other techniques such as evolutionary learning are also being introduced. Their cooperation with other agents, if any, is limited typically to asking for advice.

Maes (1995) specifies two preconditions to be fulfilled by suitable application programs for interface agents: firstly, that there is substantial repetitive behavior in using the application program (otherwise, the agent will not be able to learn anything) and, secondly, that this repetitive behavior is potentially different for different users (otherwise, use a knowledge-based approach).

2.3.2.1   Benefits/Roles

The general benefits of interface agents are threefold. First, they make less work for the end user and application developer. Secondly, the agent can adapt, over time, to its user's preferences and habits. Finally, know-how among the different users in a community may be shared (e.g., when agents learn from their peers). Perhaps these will be better understood by discussing a few of the roles for which interface agents have been built.

Kozierok and Maes (1993) describe an interface agent, Calendar Agent, that assists its user in scheduling meetings. Over time, it can learn the preferences and commitments of its user, e.g., she does not like to attend meetings on Friday afternoons, she prefers meetings in the morning, etc. The learning techniques employed are memory-based learning and reinforcement learning.

Liebermann (1995) describes Letizia, a keyword and heuristic-based search agent, which assists in web browsing. Since most browsers encourage depth-first browsing, Letizia conducts a breadth-first search concurrently for other useful locations that the user may be interested in. It does this by 'guessing' the user's intention from her browsing behavior, e.g., she keeps returning to some particular page, and proceeding to search using the search engine. This enables it to recommend some other useful, serendipitous locations.

Maes (1994) describes a news filtering agent, NewT, that helps users filter and select articles from a continuous stream of Usenet Netnews. NewT agents are trained by presenting to them positive and negative examples of what should or should not be retrieved. They are message-content and keyword-based but also exploit other information such as the author and source.

There is no denying the fact that interface agents can be deployed in real applications in the short term because they are simple, operate in limited domains, and require no cooperation.

2.3.3 Mobile Agents

2.3.3.1 Hypothesis, Motivation and Benefits

Mobile agents are software processes capable of roaming wide area networks (WANs) such as the WWW, interacting with foreign hosts, performing tasks on behalf of their owners and returning 'home' having performed the duties set them. These duties may range from making a flight reservation to managing a tele-communications network. Mobile agents are agents because they are autonomous and they cooperate, albeit differently to collaborative agents. For example, they may cooperate by one agent making the location of some of its internal objects and methods known to other agents.

The key hypothesis underlying mobile agents is the idea that in certain applications, they provide a number of *practical*, though *non-functional*, advantages that escape their static counterparts. For example, imagine having to download many images just to pick out one. Is it not more natural to get your agent to 'go' to that location, do a local search, and only transfer the chosen compressed image back across the network?[2]

2.3.3.2 How Mobile Agents Work: A Brief TeleScript View

TeleScript is an interpreted object-oriented and remote programming language which allows for the development of distributed applications (URL2). Figure 2.3 summarizes a part view of the TeleScript architecture. The TeleScript Development Environment (TDE) comprises, among other things, the engine (interpreter and runtime development environment), browser, debugger, and associated libraries.

---

[2] This example was provided by our colleague Barry Crabtree.

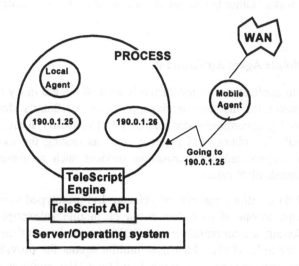

Figure 2.3. A part view of TeleScript architecture (adapted from Wayner, 1995)

TeleScript applications consist of TeleScript agents operating within a 'world' or cyberspace of places and engines, both of which are objects. The top class in TeleScript's object hierarchy is the *process*. A TeleScript engine is itself a preemptive multitasking interpreter that can run multiple processes. Hence, the engine can host multiple agents that share data/information between themselves. Furthermore, a *place* is a process that can contain an arbitrary number and depth of other places. *Agents*, unlike *places*, are objects that cannot contain other processes, but they can 'go' from place to place. An agent requiring a service defined at some given place must go to that place and call the operations there (see Figure 2.3). Thus, 'go' is the primitive that allows for inter-process communication. Two or more agent processes can *meet* in a place and make use of each other's services.

A 'go' requires a destination *place* and the host engine packages up the agent along with its data, stack, and instruction pointer and ships it off to this destination place which may be across a vast WAN. At its destination, the other TeleScript-enabled engine unpacks it, checks its authentication, and it is then free to resume execution at this new place. When it finishes, it returns to its original host having performed the task required by its owner.

It is also important to point out that mobile agent systems need not only be constructed using a remote programming language like TeleScript. Indeed, Appleby & Steward (1994) at BT Laboratories prototyped an award-winning C/C++ programmed mobile agent-based system for controlling telecommunications networks. Other languages to consider include Java, Xlisp, Agent-Tcl, and Safe-Tcl.

2.3.3.3   Mobile Agent Applications

Mobile agent applications do not currently abound but are likely to increase in the future. However, the first commercial application was Sony's Magic Link PDA or personal intelligent communicator (see URL3). Essentially, it assists in managing a user's e-mail, fax, phone, and pager as well as linking the user to TeleScript-enabled messaging and communication services such as America Online and AT&T PersonaLink Services.

Plu (1995) mentions that France Telecom has prototyped some services based on TeleScript. In one of their demonstrators, mobile TeleScript agents integrate railway ticketing and car rental services. IBM plans to launch their Communication System (Reinhardt, 1994) which uses mobile agents for providing a communications super-service capable of routing and translating communications from one service and medium to another, e.g., mobile to desktop, PDA to fax, and speech to text.

2.3.4   Information/Internet Agents

2.3.4.1   Hypothesis, Motivation and Benefits

Information agents perform the role of managing, manipulating, or collating information from many distributed sources. The motivation for developing information agents is at least twofold. Firstly, there is simply a need for tools to manage the information explosion of the WWW. Everyone on the WWW would benefit from them in the same way as they are benefiting from search facilitators such as Spiders, Lycos, or Webcrawlers. Secondly, there are vast financial benefits to be gained. Recall that Netscape Corporation grew from relative obscurity to a billion-dollar company almost overnight – and a Netscape or Mosaic client simply offers general browsing capabilities, albeit with a few add-ons. Whoever builds the first usable Netscape equivalent of a proactive, dynamic, adaptive, and cooperative WWW information manager is certain to reap enormous financial rewards.

Before we proceed, we should clarify that there is a rather fine distinction, if any, between information agents and some agents we earlier classed as interface or collaborative agents (e.g., NewT and Letizia). In this text, information agents are defined by what *they do*, in contrast to collaborative or interface agents, which we defined by what *they are*.

2.3.4.2 How Information Agents Work

Internet agents could be mobile; however, this is not the norm as yet. Typical static ones are embedded within an Internet browser and use a host of Internet management tools such as spiders and search engines in order to gather the information. Etzioni and Weld (1994) describe a state-of-the-art Internet agent called the Internet softbot (software robot). It allows a user to make a high-level menu-based request such as 'Send the budget memos to Mitchell at CMU' and 'Get all of Ginsberg's technical reports that are not stored locally,' and the softbot is able to use search and inference knowledge to determine *how* to satisfy the request in the Internet. In doing so, it is able to tolerate ambiguity, omissions, and the inevitable errors in the user's request. Etzioni & Weld use a strong analogy to a real robot in order to describe their softbot's interface to the Internet. For example, they describe the softbot's *effectors* to include ftp, telnet, mail, and numerous file manipulation commands such as mv or compress. The *sensors* provide the softbot with information about the external world and they include Internet facilities such as archie, gopher, and netfind.

2.3.4.3 A Brief Critical Review of Information Agents Work

We expect information agents to be a major growth area in the next couple of years. At BT Laboratories, Davies and Weeks (1995) designed and implemented the Jasper agent. Jasper agents work on behalf of a user or a community of users, and are able to store, retrieve, summarize, and inform other agents of information useful to them found on the WWW. As a user works with her Jasper agent, a profile of her interests is built dynamically based on keywords. A Jasper agent is able to suggest interesting WWW pages to a user by matching her profile with those of other users in the community. A successful match results in the user being told of other WWW pages that her peers find 'interesting.'

The key problem with static information agents is in keeping their indexes up-to-date in an environment which is prone to complete chaos. Thus, it is probable that the majority of future information agents will be of the mobile variety: they would be able to navigate the WWW and store its topology in a database, say, at their home site. The local database may then be locally queried by the user.

2.3.5 Reactive Software Agents: An Overview

Also often referred to as autonomous agents, reactive agents represent a special category of agents that do *not* possess internal, symbolic models of their environments; instead they respond in a stimulus-response manner to the present state of the environment in which they are embedded. Work on reactive agents dates back to such research as that of Brooks (1986) and Agre and Chapman (1987), but many theories, architectures, and languages for these sorts of agents have been developed since.

Maes (1991a) highlights the three key ideas underpinning reactive agents. Firstly, *emergent functionality*: reactive agents are relatively simple and they interact with other agents in basic ways. Nevertheless, complex patterns of behavior *emerge* from these interactions when the ensemble of agents is viewed globally. Hence, there is no *a priori* specification (or plan) of the behavior of the set-up of reactive agents. Secondly, *task decomposition*: a reactive agent is viewed as a collection of modules that operate autonomously and are responsible for specific tasks (e.g., sensing, motor control, computations). Communication between the modules is minimized and of quite a low-level nature. No global model exists within any of the agents and, hence, the global behavior has to emerge. Thirdly, reactive agents *tend* to operate on representations that are close to raw sensor data, in contrast to the high-level symbolic representations that abound in the other types of agents discussed so far.

2.3.5.1 Hypothesis, Motivation, and Benefits

The essential hypothesis of reactive agent-based systems is a specification of the *physical grounding hypothesis*. The *physical symbol system hypothesis*, which underpins classical AI, holds that for a physical system to demonstrate intelligent action it should be a symbol processing system. The physical grounding hypothesis challenges this long-held view, arguing that it is fundamentally flawed and that it imposes severe limitations on symbolic AI-based systems. This new hypothesis states that in order to build a system that is intelligent, it is necessary to have representations grounded in the physical world (Brooks, 1991a). Brooks argues that this hypothesis obviates the need for symbolic representations or models because the world becomes its own best model. Furthermore, this model is always kept up-to-date since the system is connected to the world via sensors and/or actuators. Hence, the reactive agents hypothesis may be stated as follows: intelligent agent systems can be developed from simple agents that do not have internal symbolic models, and whose 'intelligence' derives from the emergent behavior of the interactions of the various agents.

The key benefit that has motivated reactive agents work is the hope that they would be more robust and fault-tolerant than other agent-based systems, e.g., a single agent in an ensemble may be lost without any catastrophic effects. Other benefits include flexibility and adaptability in contrast to the inflexibility, slow response times, and brittleness of classical AI systems.

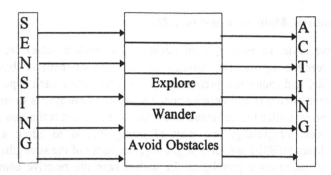

Figure 2.4. Brooks' subsumption architecture

2.3.5.2 Reactive Agent Applications

There are relatively few reactive software agent-based applications. Partly for this reason, there is no standard mode to their operation; rather, they tend to depend on the reactive agent architecture chosen.

Perhaps the most celebrated reactive agent architecture is Brooks' (1991b) *subsumption architecture*. It consists of a set of modules, each of which is described in a subsumption language based on augmented finite state machines (AFSM). An AFSM is triggered into action if its input signal exceeds some threshold, though this is also dependent on the values of suppression and inhibition signals into the AFSM. Note that AFSMs represent the only processing units in the architecture, i.e., there are no symbols as in classical AI work. The modules are grouped and placed in layers (which work asynchronously) such that modules in a higher level can inhibit those in lower layers (see Figure 2.4). Each layer has a hard-wired purpose or *behavior*, e.g., to avoid obstacles or to enable/control wandering. This architecture has been used to construct at least ten mobile robots.

Arguably, the most basic reactive architecture is that based on situated-action rules. A situated action agent acts essentially in ways that are 'appropriate' to its situation, where 'situation' refers to a potentially complex combination of internal and external events and states (Connah, 1994). Situated-action 'agents' have been used in PENGI, a video game (Agre and Chapman, 1987), and by Ferber (1994) to simulate ant societies where each ant is modeled as an agent, and a limited ecosystem composed of biotopes, shoals of fish, and fishermen.

2.3.6 Hybrid Agents

2.3.6.1 Hypothesis, Motivation and Benefits

So far, we have reviewed five types of agents: collaborative, interface, mobile, Internet, and reactive agents. The debates as to which of them is 'better' are academic, sterile, and rather too premature to get into. Since each type has (or promises) its own strengths and deficiencies, the trick, as always, is to maximize the strengths and minimize the deficiencies of the most relevant technique for your particular purpose. Frequently, one way of doing this is to adopt a *hybrid* approach, like Maes (1991b), which brought together some of the strengths of both the deliberative and reactive paradigms. In such a case the reactive component, which would take precedence over the deliberative one, brings about the following benefits: robustness, faster response times, and adaptability. The deliberative part of the agent would handle the longer-term goal-oriented issues. Hence, hybrid agents refer to those whose constitution is a combination of two or more agent *philo-sophies* within a singular agent.

2.3.6.2 Hybrid Agent Architectures

As is the case with reactive agents, there are few hybrid agent architectures. Typically, however, they have a layered architecture, as exemplified by Muller et al.'s (1995) InteRRaP architecture.

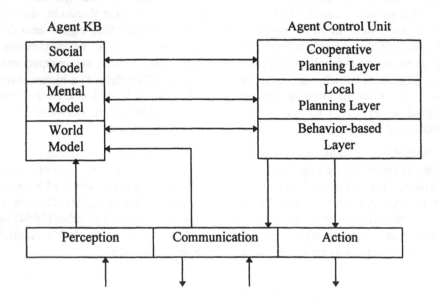

Figure 2.5. The InteRRaP hybrid architecture (adapted from Fisher et al., 1996)

Muller et al.'s InteRRaP architecture (Figure 2.5) comprises three control layers: the behavior-based layer (BBL), the local planning layer (LPL) and the cooperative planning layer (CPL). The reactive part of the framework is implemented by the BBL which contains a set of situation-action rules. These describe the agent's reactive skills for implementing fast situation recognition in order to react to time-critical situations. The intermediate LPL implements local goal-directed behavior while the topmost CPL enables the agent to plan/cooperate with other agents in order to achieve multi-agent plans, as well as resolve conflicts. LPL and CPL allow for more deliberation. These layers all work asynchronously with different models in the agent's knowledge base: BBL, LPL, and CPL operate with the world, mental models, and social models respectively. The InteRRaP architecture has been evaluated by constructing a FORKS application that simulates forklift robots working in an automated loading dock environment.

2.3.7 Heterogeneous Agent Systems

2.3.7.1 Hypothesis, Motivation and Benefits

Heterogeneous agent systems refer to an integrated set-up of at least two or more agents that belong to two or more different agent classes. A heterogeneous agent system may also contain hybrid agents. Genesereth and Ketchpel (1994) articulate clearly the motivation for heterogeneous agent systems. The essential argument is that the world abounds with a rich diversity of software products. Though these programs work in isolation, there is an increasing demand to have them *inter-operate* – hopefully, in such a manner that they provide more added value as an ensemble than they do individually. Indeed, a new domain called *agent-based software engineering* has been invented in order to facilitate the interoperation of miscellaneous software agents. A key requirement for interoperation among heterogeneous agents is having an agent communication language (ACL), with an agent-independent semantics, through which the different software agents can communicate with each other.

2.3.7.2 How Heterogeneous Agent Systems Work

To commence, we provide the rather *specific* definition of the word 'agent' proffered in agent-based software engineering. It defines a software agent as such '*if and only if it communicates correctly in an agent communication language*' (Genesereth and Ketchpel, 1994). If new agents are constructed such that they abide by this dictum, then putting them together in a heterogeneous set-up is possible, though not trivial. However, with legacy software, they need to be converted into software agents first. The latter authors note that there are three ways of doing this conversion. Firstly, the legacy software may be totally rewritten – a most costly approach. Secondly, a *transducer* approach may be used. The transducer is a *separate* piece of software which acts as an interpreter between the agent communication language and the legacy software's native communication protocol. This is the favored approach in many situations where the legacy code may be too delicate to tamper with or is unavailable. Lastly, in the *wrapper* technique, some code is 'injected' into the legacy program in order to allow it to communicate in ACL. The wrapper can directly access and modify the program's data structures. This is clearly a more interventionist approach, but offers greater efficiency than the transduction approach.

Once the agents are available, there are two possible architectures to choose from: one in which all the agents handle their own coordination and another in which groups of agents can rely on special system programs to achieve coordination. The disadvantage of the former is that the communication overhead does not ensure scalability. As a consequence, the latter, federated approach is typically preferred. Here, agents do not communicate directly with one another but do so through intermediaries called *facilitators*. Essentially, the agents surrender some of their autonomy to the facilitators who are able to locate other agents on the network capable of providing various services. The facilitators also establish connections across environments and ensure correct 'conversation' among agents; ARCHON (Wittig, 1992) and PACT (Cutkosky et al., 1993) used such an architecture.

This concludes our panoramic overview of the different classes of agents identified in Section 2.2.

2.4 Conclusion

> *Smart agents are here to stay. Once unleashed, technologies do not disappear (Norman, 1994)*

This chapter has pilfered from a diverse literature in order to overview the rapidly evolving area of software agents. We have overviewed the area from the viewpoint of the clear diversity of agents being researched into in universities and research laboratories worldwide. We hope this chapter provides a useful contribution to understanding this exciting field of software agents. Nwana (1996) presents an extended, more comprehensive version of this chapter.

Acknowledgements

We would like to thank the members of the Intelligent Systems Unit, BT Laboratories, who provided feedback that improved the quality of this chapter. The authors bear all responsibility for any misunderstandings and/or errors therein. This work was funded by BT Laboratories.

References

Agre, P. E., Chapman, D. (1987) Pengi: an implementation of a theory of activity. In: *Proceedings of the Sixth National Conference on Artificial Intelligence*, San Mateo, CA, 268–272. Morgan Kaufmann.

Appleby, S., Steward, S. (1994) Mobile software agents for control in telecommunications networks. *BT Technol Journal*, 12(2), 104–113.

Bates, J. (1994) The role of emotion in believable characters. *Communications of the ACM*, 37(7), 122–125.

Brooks, R. A. (1986) A robust layered control system for a mobile robot. *IEEE J. Robotics and Automation*, 2(1), 14–23.

Brooks, R. A. (1991) Elephants don't play chess. In: P. Maes (Ed.) *Designing Autonomous Agents: Theory and Practice from Biology to Engineering and Back*, 3–15. MIT Press, London.

Brooks, R. A. (1991) Intelligence without representation. *Artificial Intelligence*, 47, 139–159.

Chaib-draa, B., Moulin, B., Mandiau, R., Millot, P. (1992) Trends in distributed artificial intelligence. *Artificial Intelligence Review*, 6, 35–66.

Connah, D. (1994) The design of interacting agents for use in interfaces. In: M. D. Brouwer-Janse, T. L. Harringdon (Eds.) *Human-Machine Communication for Educational Systems Design*, NATO ASI Series F, Vol. 129. Springer-Verlag, Berlin.

Cutkosky, M. R., Engelmore, R. S., Fikes, R. E., Genesereth, M. R., Gruber, T. R., Tenenbaum, J. M., Weber, J. C. (1993) PACT: an experiment in integrating concurrent engineering systems. *IEEE Computer*, 1, January, 28–37.

Davies, N. J., Weeks, R. (1995) Jasper: communicating information agents. In: *Proceedings of the fourth International Conference on the World Wide Web*, Boston, MA, December.

Durfee, E. H., Lesser, V. R., Corkill, D. (1987) Coherent cooperation among communicating problem solvers. *IEEE Transactions on Computers*, C-36(11), 1275–1291.

Etzioni, O., Weld, D. (1994) A softbot-based interface to the Internet. *Communications of the ACM*, 37 (7), 72–76.

Ferber, J. (1994) Simulating with reactive agents. In: E. Hillebrand, J. Stender (Eds.) *Many Agent Simulation and Artificial Life*, 8–28. IOS Press, Amsterdam.

Fischer, K., Muller, J. P., Pischel, M. (1996) Unifying control in a layered agent architecture. *Technical Report TM-94-05*, German Research Center for AI - (DFKI GmbH).

Genesereth, M. R., Ketchpel, S. P. (1994) Software agents. *Communications of the ACM*, 37(7), 48–53.

Guilfoyle, C. (1995) Vendors of agent technology. *UNICOM Seminar on Intelligent Agents and their Business Applications*, 8-9 November, London, 135–142.

Hewitt, C. (1977) Viewing control structures as patterns of passing messages. *Artificial Intelligence*, 8(3), 323–364.

Huhns, M. N., Singh, M. P. (1994) Distributed artificial intelligence for information systems, CKBS-94 Tutorial, June 15, University of Keele, UK.

Jennings, N. R. (1993) Specification and implementation of a belief desire joint-intention architecture for collaborative problem solving. *J. Intelligent and Cooperative Information Systems*, 2(3), 289–318.

Kozierok, R., Maes, P. (1993) A learning interface agent for scheduling meetings. In: *Proceedings ACM-SIGCHI International Workshop on Intelligent User Interfaces*, Florida, 81–93.

Lieberman, H. (1995) Letizia: an agent that assists web browsing. In: *Proceedings IJCAI 95*, AAAI Press.

Maes, P. (Ed.) (1991) *Designing Autonomous Agents: Theory and Practice from Biology to Engineering and Back*. MIT Press, London.

Maes, P. (1991) Situated agents can have goals. In: P. Maes (Ed.) *Designing Autonomous Agents: Theory and Practice from Biology to Engineering and Back*, 49–70. MIT Press, London.

Maes, P. (1994) Agents that reduce work and information overload. *Communications of the ACM*, 37 (7), 31–40.

Maes, P. (1995) Intelligent software. *Scientific American*, 273 (3), September.

Muller, J. P., Pishel, M., Thiel, M. (1995) Modeling reactive behavior in vertically layered agent architectures. In: M. Wooldridge, N. Jennings (Eds.) *Intelligent Agents*. Lecture Notes in Artificial Intelligence, Vol. 890, 261–276. Springer-Verlag,.Berlin.

Norman, D. (1994) How might people interact with agents. *Communications of the ACM*, 37(7), 68–76.

Nwana, H. S. (1996) Software agents: an overview. To appear in *Knowledge Engineering Review*.

O'Brien, P., Wiegand, M. (1996) Agents of change in business process management. *BT Technol J.*, October, To appear.

Plu, M. (1995) Software agents in telecommunications network environments. *UNICOM Seminar on Intelligent Agents and their Business Applications*, 8-9 November, London, 225–243.

Rao, A. S., Georgeff, M. P. (1995) BDI agents: from theory to practice. In: *Proceedings First International Conference on Multi-Agent Systems (ICMAS-95)*, San Francisco, CA, June, 312–319.

Reinhardt, A. (1994) The network with smarts. *Byte*, October, 51–64.

Sycara. K. (1995) Intelligent agents and the information revolution. *UNICOM Seminar on Intelligent Agents and their Business Applications*, 8-9 November, London, 143–159.

URL1: http://www.cs.cmu.edu/afs/cs.cmu.edu/project/theo-5/www/pleiades.html.

URL2: http://www.genmagic.com.

URL3: http://www.sel.sony.com.

Wayner, P. (1995) *Agents Unleashed: A Public Domain Look at Agent Technology*. AP Professional, Boston, MA.

Winter, C. S., Titmuss, R., Crabtree, B. (1996) Intelligent agents, mobility and multimedia information. *Proceedings First International Conference on the Practical Application of Intelligent Agents and Multi-Agent Technology (PAAM '96)*, London, 22-24 April.

Wittig, T. (Ed.) (1992) *ARCHON: An Architecture for Multi-Agent Systems*. Ellis Horwood, London.

Wooldridge, M., Jennings, N. (1995) Intelligent agents: theory and practice. *The Knowledge Engineering Review*, 10 (2), 115–152.

3 Agent Software for Near-Term Success in Distributed Applications

S. C. Laufmann
U S West Advanced Technologies

3.1 Introduction

The world is moving rapidly toward the deployment of geographically and organizationally diverse computing systems. Accordingly, the technical difficulties associated with distributed, heterogeneous computing applications are becoming increasingly apparent. Applications such as distributed information systems and electronic commerce are placing new demands on software infrastructures.

The notion of *agents* is becoming increasingly popular in addressing these difficulties. However, there is no widely accepted definition for, or approach to, agents. Agent terminology is used to refer to a wide range of solutions being proposed by different organizations for different purposes. These solutions may address very different applications or domains, contain implicit though important limiting assumptions, or use different vocabularies. The term *agent* is itself quite evocative of human problem-solving skills and is often used without a precise definition, or with no definition at all.

As a result, there is substantial confusion regarding the technologies that surround this term and its uses. Section 3.2 addresses this confusion by describing and comparing three related, but fundamentally different views of agents – agents as automated personal assistants, agents as cooperating problem solvers, and agents as communicating software entities. Section 3.3 looks at the characteristics of two classes of applications that are commonly used to motivate agent research and application – distributed information systems and information-based commerce. Section 3.4 identifies a unique opportunity for near-term success in these application areas – one that offers a practical path for extension as new technological solutions emerge in the future. Section 3.5 examines the approach, and Section 3.6 summarizes and draws conclusions.

3.2 Perspectives on Agent Technologies

In an early effort to develop artificial intelligence for distributed information access, the tasks and skills of a human data analyst were studied, eventually

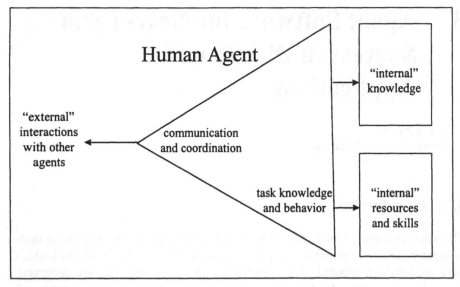

Figure 3.1. A simple conceptual model of a human problem solving agent

leading to the simple conceptual model shown in Figure 3.1 (Laufmann, 1992; Laufmann et al., 1991a; 1991b). In this model, the human problem solver's skills are grouped into three categories: *communication and interaction* – the ability to interact with other human agents using shared protocols and languages to achieve coordinated activity, implying some level of shared context and understanding; *task knowledge and behavior* – the ability or resources to perform one or more task-specific activities (this can be viewed as a set of *skills*); and *general knowledge and behavior* – the ability to perform general task-independent behaviors such as cooperative planning, prioritizing tasks, reasoning about internal capabilities, predicting performance on future tasks, recovering from unexpected difficulties, negotiating for services, and the like. This component captures the behaviors most closely resembling *general intellect*. Individual capabilities may vary widely in each of these components.

Though this model is simple, it is useful both for understanding the nature of human problem solvers and in creating artificial agents for various applications. In addition, it provides a useful tool for differentiating and categorizing agent technologies.[1]

---

[1]While this is a useful model, there are some areas of agent research that do not fit well into it, especially those addressing reactive agents or emergent behaviors (for an example, see (Minsky, 1986)). Such work is by definition at a lower level of granularity than that captured by this model.

The following sections present three different perspectives, or views, of artificial agents. Each emphasizes a different component of this model. In each, the set of necessary and sufficient conditions for determining membership in the class of entities known as 'agents' tends to be based on characteristics within just one of the three components of this model.[2] Most of the agent-related work in research and industry can be categorized using this model, though a thorough assessment of such work is beyond the scope of this article. (Wooldridge and Jennings (1995) and Nwana (1996) offer recent categorizations and assessments of agent-related work.) Rather, this model is simply one mechanism to bring clarity to the agent discussion and (hopefully) dispel some confusion about agent technology and systems by helping to identify the different philosophical tendencies that underlie the work. Furthermore, the model offers clues for new areas of work that may show promise, as discussed in Section 3.4.

Areas of emphasis are typically associated closely with the motivation underlying a body of work. In general, work motivated by a specific application will tend to focus primarily on what the agent does rather than on how it is done (Section 3.2.1). Similarly, work motivated by a thorny technical problem will tend to focus more on how it is done than on a specific application (Section 3.2.2). And work motivated by interoperability problems in distributed and heterogeneous computing environments, as in (Laufmann, 1996), will tend to focus on the communication and coordination aspects of the problem (Section 3.2.3).

3.2.1 Agents as Automated Personal Assistants

The notion of *agents* is often associated with that of automated personal assistants. As such, the agents perform some kind of task(s) for a person. This view emphasizes the *type of application* to which the agent is targeted (i.e., that of assisting a human), and is based on certain task knowledge and behaviors, or *task-specific skills* (see Figure 3.2). Thus, the necessary and sufficient conditions for inclusion within the set of agents are based primarily on *what* the agent does, without substantial regard for *how* it is done.

This view of agents does not preclude capabilities within individual agents that fall into the other categories in the model. In fact, many agents will require capabilities in the other areas as well. However, the definitional line that separates agents from non-agents, in this perspective, is based on certain behaviors that fall within the category of *task knowledge and behavior*. Similarly, each of the other perspectives stresses one component of the model in defining agents, though without precluding capabilities in the other areas.

---

[2] While the definition of agents within a given approach is often based in a single component in the model, it is common, in practice, for the associated prototype or operational systems to include capabilities in the other model components as well.

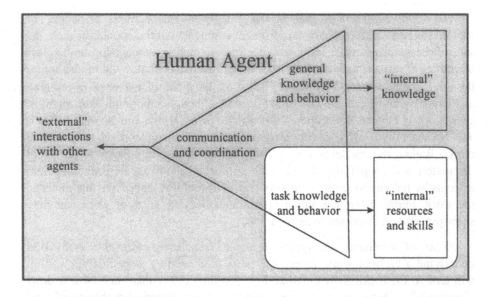

Figure 3.2. Agents with emphasis on task knowledge and behavior

This view is probably the most common in current use, and is especially noticeable in the popular press. One frequently cited application based on this view is information filtering or gleaning agents, for a particular use or for a particular user. There are many individual applications of this kind, including many research prototypes and commercial products. This approach to agents is exemplified in the work of Maes (1994). Other examples include interface agents (Dent et al., 1992; Mitchell et al., 1994) and network agents (Etzioni and Weld, 1994).

3.2.2 Agents as Cooperating Problem Solvers

In the second view, agents utilize advanced reasoning capabilities to perform cooperative work effectively, presumably to effect some result that none would be capable of achieving alone. In this sense, an agent is capable of behaviors that lead to cooperative problem solving. This definition stresses the general knowledge and behavior, or *general intellect*, component of the agent (see Figure 3.3). In this view, the intellect component incorporates methods and behaviors that might lead to cooperative or collaborative work. Thus, this perspective emphasizes *how* things are done, rather than *what* type of task is done. This approach generally assumes an environment which is composed of multiple entities (i.e., other agents) that are fundamentally capable of working together in similar ways.

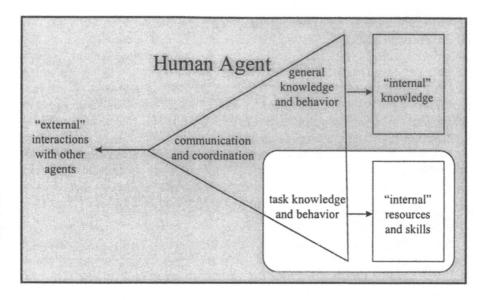

Figure 3.3. Agents with emphasis on the general knowledge and behavior

This view is probably the oldest in current use, but its use has been primarily within the research community addressing the field of Distributed Artificial Intelligence (DAI). In common use, these agents are entities that call upon substantial internal capabilities to negotiate for services or resources, or that cooperate to solve complex or distributed problems. They often incorporate mechanisms for storing and maintaining 'mental models' of other agents. There are many examples of this approach – including various agent modeling techniques (Cohen and Levesque, 1990; Rao and Georgeff, 1991; Singh, 1994), agent-oriented programming (Shoham, 1990), Softbots (Etzioni et al., 1994; Weld and Etzioni, 1994), and cyc-based agents (Mayfield et al., 1995).

3.2.3 Agents as Communicating Software Modules

A third view toward defining agents is based largely on specific mechanisms for communication and interaction. Each agent is capable of interacting in ways that all agents share. In this approach the notion of agent is most closely associated with the *communication and interaction* between agents, rather than on what they do as individuals, or by what means they accomplish their individual task(s). In order to communicate effectively, agents must share communication protocols and languages, and the knowledge necessary to properly interpret and understand messages. These mechanisms and knowledge, along with the ability to act upon them, become the basis for the necessary and sufficient definition of an agent.

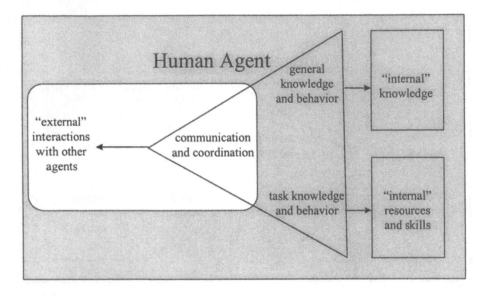

Figure 3.4. Agents with emphasis on the communication and interaction

This is a pragmatic view in that the focus is not on *what* is done or *how* it is done. Rather, the key idea is that the agents are all capable of communicating and thereby coordinating their activities with one another. This is referred to by Wooldridge and Jennings as the *social*, or *macro*, level (Wooldridge and Jennings, 1995). The emphasis of systems based on this view is the ways in which the agents communicate and interact in achieving related or joint activities (see Figure 3.4). The underlying model becomes the glue that holds the agent community together and allows it to operate as a whole.

In practice, these agents are software module 'instances' that are built on general purpose software that encodes and standardizes the means and methods of communication and interaction. They are coordination shells that make the key communication and interaction functions relatively transparent. This approach appears to be the least common in current use. Examples include the 'information agents' described by Papazoglou et al. (1992), applications motivating the development of the Knowledge Query Manipulation Language (KQML) (Finin et al., 1994; Genesereth and Ketchel, 1994), the Carnot Project (Huhns et al., 1992), coarse-grained agents (Lahfmann, 1992; Laufmann et al., 1991), and the Contract Net system (Smith, 1980; Smith and Davis, 1980).

3.3   Application Requirements

It is becoming readily apparent that the effectiveness of the interactions among computing systems is essential to the success of large-scale, distributed applications. Thus, it is critical for systems to work together to achieve better results faster and at reduced cost. Nearly all modern computing systems must operate in a distributed, heterogeneous environment, with multiple users performing different tasks, often tasks other than those for which the component systems were originally designed.

Thus, programs must often interact with other component systems in order to accomplish their goals. These interactions are essentially social in nature, and are therefore beyond the traditional realm of computation. Gelernter and Carriero (1992) distinguish between models of *computation*, upon which the bulk of computer science has traditionally focused, and models of *coordination*, which address the interactions among various entities and their resources.

Each of the following sections briefly presents and evaluates the main requirements of a major distributed, heterogeneous application class.

3.3.1 Distributed Information Systems

Distributed information systems are rapidly becoming the norm. These systems cross geographical, and often organizational, boundaries and are typically broadly heterogeneous, not only in hardware and software, but also in utility and semantics. Systems designed for one use are routinely adapted to other uses for which they were not originally designed. The spectrum of uses and users grows as the systems become 'legacy' systems. The life cycle of information systems is thus characterized by enhancement and sometimes radical adaptation as the surrounding environment changes. These changes are unpredictable and unavoidable, and may result from a variety of factors, including changes in corporate structure or strategy, regulatory or legal changes, aging and emerging technologies, or changes in markets and products.

Individual systems must interoperate in various ways with other systems during their lifespan, creating interoperation difficulties which must be resolved along the way. These problems can include semantic mismatches, different communication and coordination policies and languages (e.g., terminal-oriented systems that must inter-operate with distributed object systems), and differing mechanisms and ontologies for sharing information and constraints. In addition, distributed information systems exhibit the properties of *open systems* (Bond and Gasser, 1988; Hewitt, 1985; 1986), including asynchronous, concurrent processing in multiple nodes, inconsistent states and information between component systems, and completely decentralized control – properties that must be addressed in creating an overall system within which individual systems interoperate. These issues are discussed in more detail in (Laufmann, 1994).

The effort expended in developing and maintaining distributed information systems is focusing increasingly on the code that integrates each system with the others with which it must interact. As an example, Figure 3.5 shows the legacy service order processing system that has evolved over three decades in a major telephone company in the United States. A substantial majority of the code and the costs associated with maintaining the overall system are expended on the coordination of the individual systems with the other components involved in the process. While this example may seem extreme, it is not uncommon for environments such as this to exist in larger, long-established enterprises, especially those that have been involved in various corporate reorganizations or mergers.

3.3.2 Information Commerce Applications

Another emerging application area is *information-based commerce*, wherein commercial enterprises buy and sell information, or in which information is the medium of exchange in the buying or selling of other goods or services. This application shares most of the basic problems of the distributed information systems discussed above.[3] In addition to the problems described above, participants in the information marketplace also face a series of pragmatic issues related to authentication, security, privacy, financial transaction methods and policies, tracking and accounting, billing, payment assurances, version compatibility and consistency, and related operation systems support issues, which must all be supported in a distributed environment. Of critical importance to the participants in the information marketplace is retention of local functional autonomy and independence, so that their individual operations and activities are neither controlled nor threatened by other forces or entities in the network. Further discussion of these issues is given in (Laufmann, 1994).

In practice, it is expected that information commerce will one day grow to include nearly all suppliers and consumers of goods and services, covering the entire value chain from wholesalers of raw materials and basic services to complex, consumer-level goods and services. It will also eventually include all mass market consumers. The infrastructure and tools to facilitate information commerce must support very large numbers of interactions as this application matures.

As above, many of these issues are related to communication and interaction in order to effectively coordinate multiple resources in a distributed, heterogeneous environment.

---

[3] This is not surprising, since electronic commerce must inevitably be based at some point on a foundation of distributed information systems.

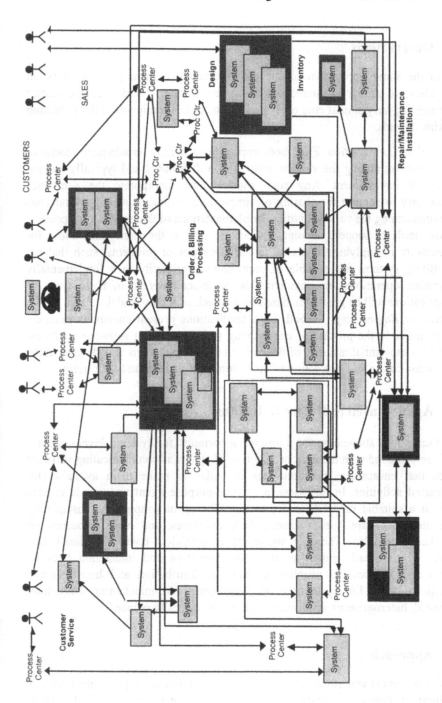

Figure 3.5. The legacy service order processing system for a major telephone company in the United States

3.3.3 Observations

Both of the above applications occur with increasing frequency and on a broad scale. They are similar in nature, exhibiting very similar technical characteristics and presenting very similar core problems. Each application involves the following two critical needs:

- *Model of Coordination*. First, both applications require an adequate model of coordination among the various entities in a distributed and typically hetero-geneous environment. Any such model must incorporate the semantics necessary to support the sharing of simple information, knowledge, and con-straints among the various entities. Implementations of this model must provide basic tools to support ongoing operations, and at the same time allow for flexibility in applying the model to various types of problems, such that the resulting systems are capable of continuous availability in a fundamentally dynamic operational environment. The wide-scale spread of these types of applications will be greatly hindered by the lack of such a model.
- *Software Engineering*. Second, both applications present enormous practical difficulties in the process of engineering and maintaining software solutions. Often a substantial majority of the code in such applications is dedicated to the communication and interaction of the component systems and their users.

3.4   Agent-Based Software Solutions

The observations above describe a unique opportunity for systems development – one closely aligned with the third perspective of agents as communicating software entities that encapsulate functionalities in order to make them available for coordinated activities. In this view, a general-purpose agent wrapper is created based on a suitable model of coordination. The agent wrapper is subsequently instantiated to encapsulate programs, data, interfaces, and other resources for networked availability. These agents, in effect, provide a layer of *virtual homo-geneity*, which greatly simplifies the communication and interaction between systems and reduces the negative impacts of distribution and heterogeneity. Consequently, the life cycle costs of developing and maintaining large-scale distributed, heterogeneous applications can be substantially reduced.

3.4.1 Approach

In order to implement software agents, we must adopt an appropriate *model of coordination*, based on a practical *software engineering* strategy. The following describes one approach, based on experimental work performed in the develop-ment of coarse-grained agents (CGAs) for various distributed information systems and information commerce applications. These agents and examples are further discussed below.

3.4.1.1 Strategy

The overall strategy begins with the best currently available technology, then is extended or adapted as better technologies become available. The long-term goal is to develop and deploy a suitable model of coordination, implemented as an integral part of the distributed computing infrastructure, and based on the following characteristics:

- The model of coordination must be *explicit.*
- This model must be *reusable* without substantial modification for a wide variety of applications.
- The model must be of *minimal size and complexity* including only those components that are absolutely necessary, as increased complexity will make widespread adoption and future changes more difficult.
- Insofar as is practicable, the model should be implemented as a *wholly separable* software component, so it can be incrementally upgraded and enhanced, independent of the encapsulated functionalities. Separability allows improvement in the distributed system as a whole with little or no change to the individual component systems, applications, data, or interfaces. This notion is more fully discussed in (Laufmann, 1994).
- This model must be *deployable now*, in a way that exploits the capabilities of current technology.
- This model must be *readily extensible,* and thus positioned to take advantage of new, emerging techniques and tools as they become available. Improvements and enhancements can occur in the underlying implementations of individual components (speed, efficiency, platform dependencies), the robustness of the system as a whole (general purpose robustness and recovery mechanisms), and various internal reasoning capabilities. The capability to dynamically define and distribute extensions would be a significant future addition.

3.4.1.2 Model

In this approach, each agent is an autonomous individual within a possibly large society of other individuals.[4] Each agent is capable of interacting with others in some way to solve problems. Each adheres to societal 'norms' of communication and basic behavior. Each possesses its owns skills and abilities, which it makes available to the society. Each is essentially supportive in its dealings with other

---

[4]For our purposes, we view these agents as computer artifacts – programs that run in one or more processes on a host computer. However, the ideas here are also essentially true of human agents, and can be extended to include them as well.

agents in the environment. Agents provide a middleware layer of *virtual homogeneity* within which concepts like negotiation and collaboration can one day be built, and above which a new and broad range of functional heterogeneity can be constructed and deployed. This approach is a form of *agent-based software engineering* (Genesereth and Ketchpel, 1994).

For our purposes, then, the notion of *agent* is based on a set of well-defined behaviors in a social environment rather than on adherence to some particular implementation. Thus, agents are defined by a set of necessary and sufficient properties, which are in turn based on a set of protocols, languages, and relevant behaviors.[5] The necessary and sufficient properties that define an agent are different from the functionalities that the agent makes available to 'the world.' Those protocols, languages, commands, and functions included in the definition are required of *every* agent, while other definitions, commands, and functions are optional, and may be shared only by those agents for which they are relevant. For example, a specific agent may not need to handle a language for sharing knowledge if that agent has no explicit internal knowledge base. Similarly, an agent that cannot perform high-speed matrix multiplication need not understand or handle a matrix multiplication language.

We call these agents *coarse-grained agents* (CGAs), to differentiate them from the various forms of finer grained agents discussed in the DAI research literature (e.g., Agha, 1986; Dent et al., 1992; Rao and Georgeff, 1991). As a form of agent-based software engineering, CGAs provide a foundational mechanism upon which many kinds of distributed applications may be constructed. CGAs are based on the following architectural properties.

- *Heterogeneity*. CGAs cannot be assumed to be homogeneous beyond the level of the communication protocols. Each may be a specialized problem-solver, with an internal structure and composition 'optimized' for its own skills and resources. CGAs can be implemented in different languages on different hardware. This approach offers practical advantages in computing efficiency and in system development and deployment.
- *Persistence*. CGAs must generally be persistent, minimally existing for several seconds and possibly for many years. They are expected to survive machine downtimes, though possibly with some loss of state. The relative permanence of CGAs makes certain architectural complexities more cost effective than they would be for shorter-lived agents.

---

[5] Because agent implementations need adhere only to the minimal set of protocols, languages, and behaviors that define an agent, and not to any particular internal model, it is possible that some implementations will be based on a model different in some ways than that described in this report.

- *Supportive.* CGAs are essentially helpful. Each attempts to handle every request made of it. This is an attitude that is both useful and natural, characterizing the behavior of many natural social systems.
- *Autonomy.* Each CGA has its own (possibly implicit) set of goals and priorities, and its own processes within which it performs its internal functions.
- *Independence.* No two CGAs can be assumed to share the same information, knowledge, or beliefs, beyond those required to support the necessary and sufficient behaviors included in the definition of agents.
- *Multilingual.* CGAs may be multilingual, allowing communication at various functional levels for varying purposes. Inter-agent communication should not rely on homogeneity beyond the communication protocols, and should therefore be independent of any CGA's internal construction or resources.

CGAs are based on a simple conceptual model, as shown in Figure 3.6. This model is derived from the human agent model in Figure 3.1, but presents a more systems-oriented view of the same properties. As in the human agent model, each CGA has three main components – communication, task-specific knowledge and behavior (i.e., skills), and general knowledge and behavior. As with humans, individual CGAs may also vary widely in these capabilities. For example, some rather useful agents may require no general knowledge capabilities.

This model incorporates two additional notions:

- *Functional plugs.* Since each of these components is designed to be extended as new technologies and tools emerge, each of the three components of an agent may be viewed as a series of empty 'plugs' into which various tools may be placed to extend the functionality of the agent.
- *Agent core.* The core consists of internal functions that act as 'glue' to hold the three components and their modules together, providing support functions for general operations like asynchronous message sending and receiving (to communicate with other agents), multitasking, and shared memory between the agent's multiple tasks.

This model may be implemented in different ways. However, the intent is to create fully reusable shells for different physical platforms with appropriate hooks, or stubs, for the models and components we do not yet know how to construct (e.g., most general knowledge and behaviors), within which we can embed a wide variety of useful functionalities (i.e., the agent's individual, task-specific skills), and with a minimal shared coordination backbone (i.e., the communication and interaction component).

With this foundation we can gain experience with the known components by deploying systems for which substantial, dynamic social knowledge and other intellectual capabilities are not normally required. We can use the same shell to experiment with various proposed model extensions for cooperation and collaboration. It may be possible to conduct experiments using agents that have been

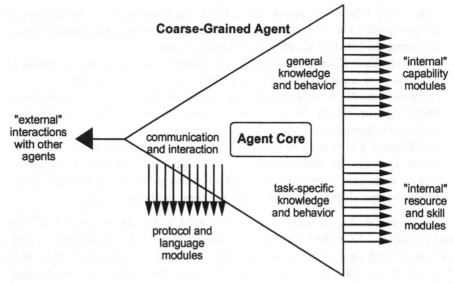

Figure 3.6. Coarse-grained agent functional model

deployed for one or more applications, providing the opportunity to examine various proposed models in real-life applications.

Toward this end, the agent shell should be designed to support the following uses:

- To quickly wrap (in an agent 'skin') a set of functionalities, to enable very rapid prototyping and/or deployment of application components in a distributed environment. This has proven quite successful in a laboratory setting (see Section 3.4.2).
- To wrap and make available over a network pre-existing functionalities such as legacy systems. Agents thus provide a means for integrating pre-existing systems and code into a new, coordinated environment, though with some limitations in the capabilities of those agents.
- To provide a platform for rapid experimentation and deployment of future technological advances, without significantly inhibiting use of the platform for current generation systems.

3.4.2 Applications

This approach has been explored in our laboratory for six years. During this time it has been extensively applied to each of the application domains discussed in Section 3.3.

The initial application, known as 'oMIE,' explored ways to provide direct user access to a remote and complex legacy system, using several specialized service agents to support various parts of the overall task, including locating the legacy system, encoding and decoding alphanumeric data codes, assisting users to formulate unambiguous information requests, translating user terms into vocabulary meaningful to the specific legacy database, and formulating correct query syntax. Using CGAs as our foundation, we were able to implement these very different functionalities with little regard for the locations and host platforms of the other components, which were written in different languages (Macintosh Common Lisp and Symbolics Lisp) and located on four separate machines running two different operating systems (Macintosh and Symbolics). Each agent was dramatically different in terms of internal capabilities and tools, yet the layer of virtual homogeneity effectively hid these differences (Laufmann, 1992; Laufmann, 1996).

The second series of applications were related to the information marketplace. Here, agents 'wrap' individual service provider businesses, such as Fred's Catalog Store, as well as various facilitation functions, such as service registration and indexing. Although this domain is quite different from the oMIE application, the same foundation of coarse-grained agents was used, though a third version of the CGA implementation was added, written in C/C++ and running on a Unix workstation. The reuse of the agent software dramatically reduced the time required to implement individual services and make them available over a network. Based on the realized simplicity of this process, a series of automated service creation tools was designed to automatically instantiate new agents on available machines as new services were created. More information about these can be found in (Laufmann, 1994; Laufmann, 1996).

In addition, we are 're-hosting' a legacy system from a mainframe to multiple, distributed platforms and constructing servers for consumer-level kiosks to deploy sales tools in remote locations, both based on the CGA approach. A recent article describes these applications in greater detail (Laufmann, 1997).

These and other related experiences have realized implementational efficiencies in two important ways. First, the time required to distribute an implemented functionality was substantially reduced. Second, the intuitive co-ordination model and the well-defined interfaces imposed by the model reduced the cognitive load on the developers of the component systems, reducing both the cognitive complexity of the problem and the number of errors produced during implementation.These findings are consistent with the findings of object-oriented programming research, which is based on a similar though less extreme approach to modularity (Micallef, 1988; Stefik and Bobrow, 1986).

3.4.3 Related Work

The body of related work is very large, and will be only briefly summarized here.

Many of the ideas related to communication, coordination, and cooperation have their roots in the classical DAI work on Contract Net (Davis and Smith, 1983; Smith, 1980; 1981; Smith and Davis, 1980). Though that work was undertaken for rather different purposes, the work remains relevant to both the distributed information systems and information commerce applications.

This approach is probably most similar, at least in goals and design, to agent-based software engineering, as described in (Genesereth and Ketchpel, 1995). CGAs share much of the software engineering motivation of that work. However, the approach we have taken differs slightly, both in focus and extent, with less emphasis on knowledge-intensive applications.

Others have taken similar technological approaches. For example, the information agents of Papazoglou et al. (1992) work to overcome the inherent problems of inter-operability in a large distributed and heterogeneous network. Also, the Knowledgeable Agent-oriented System (KAoS) takes a very similar approach, and was motivated by very similar problems (Bradshaw et al.,1995). Other examples may be found in (Burmeister et al., 1995; Haugeneder and Steiner, 1995; Jennings, 1994).

There are a variety of similar applications being explored, though using different technical approaches. Among these are Carnot, which facilitates information system interoperability through a global knowledge base (Collet et al., 1991; Huhns et al., 1992), and work on information agents for the Loom Interface Module, where agents use knowledge bases to translate information requests (McKay et al., 1996).

In many respects, the ideas and work described here have followed the path described by Asimov (Asimov, 1987). We initially set out to study and replicate to the greatest extent possible the problem solving activities of human agents, and along the way created something that is in some ways better than the original and in some ways worse. By carefully exploiting the successful parts, the result is made useful for particular types of applications, without replacing the original target system.

3.5 Discussion

The approach described above offers several advantages that can contribute to near-term success in commercial applications in distributed and heterogeneous environments. These advantages are derived from the goals presented in Section 3.4.1.1.

First, a coherent model of coordination can be designed, implemented, deployed, and maintained explicitly, as opposed to the implicit models used in much current software engineering practice. This model becomes the conceptual glue that holds distributed, heterogeneous applications together. It offers practical advantages by reducing the complexity of the communication and interaction solutions for a large variety of applications, especially those that must be deployed within distributed networks.

Second, this model is application-independent, and therefore fully reusable for a variety of applications. It enables the development of large-scale, multi-application networks of skill-based individual agents.

Third, by implementing the 'agentness' of agents as separable software, possibly as shared libraries of functions, agents gain a fully separable path for upgrades and enhancements as new technical approaches emerge. This yields substantial benefits in the design, development, and maintenance of large-scale systems.

Fourth, this model, based on what may be practically deployed now, is quite useful in a variety of applications, and can produce immediate savings by reducing the costs of the software life cycle for distributed, heterogeneous applications.

Fifth, this model (and presumably its implementations as well) may be readily and easily extended to incorporate new functionality, such as that defined by researchers in DAI or by developers and practitioners of personal assistant applications, or as new network protocols or communication systems become available.

Much work remains to be done in order to achieve the full potential of the current opportunity. Included in this are 'standardized' definitions of the necessary and sufficient properties of agents and the development of agent libraries, based on these definitions, for a variety of hardware and software platforms. Future extensions will emerge through the research community and may include plug-in modules for more complex forms of interaction, in support of cooperative and collaborative activities, such as agent negotiation, agent modeling, and performance histories and predictions. Other possible improvements and extensions may be based on the use of *speech act theory* (Flores et al., 1988; Searle, 1979) as a foundation for the roles and rules of coordinated behavior in various types of discourses (Laufmann et al., 1991; Smith and Cohen, 1995), or in extending the Knowledge Query Manipulation Language (KQML) (Finin et al., 1994; Finin et al., 1993) with new performatives.

3.6 Conclusions

The three agent perspectives discussed herein are distinct, though they involve some overlap. Of these three, the third suggests an intriguing opportunity for near-term success in developing solutions for large-scale distributed, heterogeneous applications. By applying our agent approach to the common technological issues surrounding the development and deployment of distributed, heterogeneous systems, we can move forward with realizable benefits in the short term, and potential growth into the longer term.

Laboratory experimentation indicates the potential of this approach for a variety of distributed applications, both in decreased time to implement distributed solutions, and in decreased cognitive load on the developers of distributed applications. These observations indicate that the time is right to begin deploying agent-based software engineering solutions to distributed problems, but with a view toward upgrading in the future to take advantage of emerging technologies.

Acknowledgments

The ideas and work described here are the result of hundreds of hours of interactions with key colleagues, including Ed Freeman, Rick Blumenthal, Bill McIver, Dave Wroblewski, Tim McCandless, Mitch Nathan, Simo El-Khadiri, Srdjan Kovacevic, Robert Joseph, Nina Berry, and Mike Novak.

Special thanks go to colleagues who have critically addressed various components of this work in the past, including Mike Huhns, Mike Papazoglou, Roger King, Nick Jennings, Hector Garcia-Molina, Terry Winograd, Doug Lenat, Dexter Pratt, Karen Lochbaum, and Mark Derthick.

References

Agha, G. A. (1986) *ACTORS: A Model of Concurrent Computation in Distributed Systems*. The MIT Press, Cambridge, MA.

Asimov, I. (1987) If AI = the human brain, cars should have legs. *Information-WEEK*, March, 56.

Bond, A. H., Gasser, L. (1988) An analysis of problems and research in DAI. In: A. H. Bond, L. Gasser (Eds.) *Readings in Artificial Intelligence*, 3–35. Morgan Kaufmann Publishers, Los Altos, CA.

Bradshaw, J. M., Dutfield, S., Carpenter, B., Jeffers, R., Robinson, T. (1995) KAoS: a generic agent architecture for aerospace applications. In: *Proceedings of the CIKM'95 Intelligent Information Agents Workshop*, Baltimore, MD.

Burmeister, B., Bussmann, S., Haddadi, A., Sundermeyer, K. (1995) Agent-oriented techniques for traffic and manufacturing applications: progress report. In: *Proceedings of the Agent Software Seminar*, 122–131, London, England. Unicom Seminars.

Cohen, P. R., Levesque, H. J. (1990) Intention is choice with commitment. *Artificial Intelligence*, 42(2-3), 213–261.

Collet, C., Huhns, M. N., Shen, W.-M. (1991) Resource integration using a large knowledge base in Carnot. *IEEE Computer*, December, 55–62.

Davis, R., Smith, R. G. (1983) Negotiation as a metaphor for distributed problem solving. *Artificial Intelligence*, 20(1), 63–109.

Dent, L., Boticario, J., McDermott, J., Mitchell, T., Zabowski, D. A. (1992) A personal learning apprentice. In: *Proceedings of the Tenth National Conference on Artificial Intelligence*, 96–103, San Jose, CA. AAAI Press.

Etzioni, O., Levy, H. M., Segal, R. B., Thekkath, C. A. (1994) OS agents: using AI techniques in the operating system environment. Technical report #93-04-04, Department of Computer Science and Engineering, University of Washington.

Etzioni, O., Weld, D. (1994) A softbot-based interface to the Internet. *Communications of the ACM*, 37(7), 72–76.

Finin, T., Fritzson, R., McKay, D., McEntire, R. (1994) KQML as an agent communication language. In: *Proceedings of the Third International Conference on Information and Knowledge Management*, 456–463. Gaithersburg, MD. ACM Press.

Finin, T., Weber, J., Wiederhold, G., Genesereth, M., Fritzson, R., McKay, D., McGuire, J., Pelavin, R., Shapirof, S., Beck, C. (1993) DRAFT specification of the KQML agent-communication language. DARPA Knowledge Sharing Initiative External Interfaces Working Group.

Flores, F., M. Graves, Hartfield, B., Winograd, T. (1988) Computer systems and the design of organizational interaction. *ACM Transactions on Office Information Systems*, 6(2), 153–172.

Gelernter, D., Carriero, N. (1992) Coordination languages and their significance. *Communications of the ACM*, 35(2), 97–107.

Genesereth, M. R., Ketchpel, S. P. (1994) Software agents. *Communications of the ACM*, 37(7), 48–53, 147.

Haugeneder, H., Steiner, D. (1995) Cooperating agents: concepts and applications. In: *Proceedings of the Agent Software Seminar*, 80–106, London, England. Unicom Seminars.

Hewitt, C. E. (1985) The challenge of open systems. *BYTE*, April, 223-242.

Hewitt, C. E. (1986) Offices are open systems. *ACM Transactions on Office Information Systems*, 4(3), 271–287.

Huhns, M. N., Jacobs, N., Ksiezyk, T., Shen, W. M., Singh, M. P., Cannata, P. E. (1992) Integrating enterprise information models in Carnot. In: *Proceedings of the International Conference on Intelligent and Cooperative Information Systems*, 32–42, Rotterdam, Netherlands.

Jennings, N. (1994) Cooperation in industrial multi-agent systems. *World Scientific*, London.

Laufmann, S. C. (1992) Coarse-grained distributed agents for transparent access to remote information. In: M. P. Papazoglou, J. Zeleznikow (Eds.) *The Next Generation of Information Systems – from Data to Knowledge*, Lecture Notes in Artificial Intelligence Vol. 611, 223–237. Springer-Verlag, Berlin.

Laufmann, S. C. (1994) The information marketplace: the challenge of information commerce. In: *Proceedings of the Second International Conference on Cooperative Information Systems,* 147–157, Toronto, Canada.

Laufmann, S. C. (1996) The information marketplace: achieving success in commercial applications. In: N. Adam, Y. Yesha (Eds.) *Electronic Commerce: Current Research Issues and Applications,* Lecture Notes in Computer Science Vol. 1028, 115–147. Springer-Verlag, Berlin.

Laufmann, S. C. (1996) Toward agent-based software engineering for information-dependent enterprise applications. *Journal of Software Engineering,* in press.

Laufmann, S. C., Blumenthal, R. L., Thompson, L. M., Bowen, B. (1991) Direct end-user access to remote information. In: *Proceedings of the Conference on Organizational Computing Systems,* 16–28, Atlanta. ACM Press.

Laufmann, S. C., Nathan, M. J., Blumenthal, R. L. (1991) An architecture to support cooperation among coarse-grained distributed problem solvers. In: *Proceedings of the AAAI-91 Workshop on Cooperation Among Heterogeneous Intelligent Agents,* Anaheim, CA.

Maes, P. (1994) Agents that reduce work and information load. *Communications of the ACM,* 37(7), 31–40, 146.

Mayfield, J., Finin, T., Narayanaswamy, R., Shah, C., MacCartney, W., Goolsbey, K. (1995) The Cycic friends network: getting Cyc agents to reason together. In: *Proceedings of the CIKM'95 Intelligent Information Agents Workshop,* Baltimore, MD.

McKay, D. P., Pastor, J., McEntire, R., Finin, T. (1996) An architecture for information agents. In: *Proceedings of the Third International Conference on Artificial Intelligence Planning Systems* (ARPI Supplement). AAAI Press.

Micallef, J. (1988) Encapsulation, reusability and extensibility in object-oriented programming languages. *Journal of Object Oriented Programming,* 1(1), 12–36.

Minsky, M. (1986) *The Society of Mind.* Simon and Schuster, New York.

Mitchell, T., Caruana, R., Freitag, D., McDermott, J., Zabowski, D. (1994) Experience with a learning personal assistant. *Communications of the ACM,* 37(7), 81–91.

Nwana, H. S. (1996) Software agents: an overview. *The Knowledge Engineering Review,* 11(3), 1–40.

Papazoglou, M. P., Laufmann, S. C., Sellis, T. K. (1992) An organizational framework for cooperating intelligent information systems. *International Journal on Intelligent and Cooperative Information Systems,* 1(1), 169–202.

Rao, A. S., Georgeff, M. P. (1991) Modeling rational agents within a BDI-architecture. In: *Proceedings of the Second International Conference on Knowledge Representation and Reasoning,* 473–484. Morgan Kaufmann.

Searle, J. R. (1979) *Expression and Meaning: Studies in the Theory of Speech Acts.* Cambridge University Press, Cambridge, MA.

Shoham, Y. (1990) Agent-oriented programming. Technical report #STAN-CS-90-1335, Stanford University.

Singh, M. P. (1994) *Multi-agent Systems: A Theoretical Framework for Intentions, Know-How, and Communications,* Lecture Notes in Artificial Intelligence Vol. 799. Springer-Verlag, Berlin.

Smith, I. A., Cohen, P. R. (1995) Toward a semantics for a speech act based agent communications language. In: *Proceedings of the CIKM'95 Intelligent Information Agents Workshop*, Baltimore, MD.

Smith, R. G. (1980) The contract net protocol: high-level communication and control in a distributed problem solver. In: A. H. Bond, L. Gasser (Eds.) *Readings in Distributed Artificial Intelligence*, 357–366. Morgan Kaufmann Publishers, Los Altos, CA.

Smith, R. G. (1981) *A Framework for Distributed Problem Solving*. UMI Research Press, Ann Arbor, MI.

Smith, R. G., Davis, R. (1980) Frameworks for cooperation in distributed problem solving. In: A. H. Bond, L. Gasser (Eds.) *Readings in Distributed Artificial Intelligence*, 61–70. Morgan Kaufmann Publishers, Los Altos, CA.

Stefik, M., Bobrow, D. G. (1986) Object-oriented programming: themes and variations. *The AI Magazine*, 6(4), 40–62.

Weld, D., Etzioni, O. (1994) The first law of robotics (a call to arms). In: *Proceedings of the Twelfth National Conference on Artificial Intelligence*, 1042–1047, Seattle, WA. AAAI Press.

Wooldridge, M., Jennings, N. R. (1995) Intelligent agents: theory and practice. *The Knowledge Engineering Review*, 10(2), 115–152.

part 2

Vision
Papers

4 Practical Design of Intelligent Agent Systems

P. C. Janca and D. Gilbert
IBM Corporation

4.1 Introduction

Intelligent agents trace their roots to the artificial intelligence community. Unfortunately, many early customers were 'burned' by their experience with artificial intelligence, and are standoffish when hearing about so-called 'intelligent agents.' Yet several market studies (Janca, 1996) include interviews with successful adopters. These early adopters do have to live with constraints, but universally report that the agent systems save them time and/or money. It is interesting to note that not one of the interviewed early adopters would even consider removing the functioning system.

It is possible to purchase agent-enabled systems today. These systems are typically used by early adopters, who can live with the fact that most such systems:

- Apply to only a single application niche such as electronic mail, or information access, or network management. No currently available commercial agent system can work in more than one such application domain.
- Are free standing and completely self-contained. No building block approach is used, which results in every system being built from zero.
- Require the user to discard a non-enabled application with similar characteristics. If I want to add agents to an existing mail system today, tough luck. I must get rid of the system in favor of a new mail system which includes agents.

None of the above constraints presents a serious problem to the early adopter community. However, moving agent-enabled applications into mainstream[1] use will require support of the following three imperatives:

- Key components (such as engines, interfaces) must become *interchangeable within* an agent system;
- *Interconnection* and *communication* must be available *between* agent systems; and
- Agent systems must *adapt onto* existing, non-agent-enabled systems.

---

[1] Mainstream, as used here, means that a significant portion of the marketplace is aware of the technology, and a measurable quantity is using it.

While research and early adopters are successfully using agent-enabled systems without these attributes today, the general commercial marketplace can only be developed when they are available.

This study information, plus work we have done at IBM with interested customers, has demonstrated that intelligent agent systems are both practical and add value to the systems to which they are attached. While 'early adopter' applications have been introduced over the past few years, commercial, main-stream use is just on the horizon. This chapter will introduce the reader to the current state of commercial agent adoption, will describe the needs of (and problems faced by) current users, will provide a practical model for use in the general marketplace, and will show examples from current research. A companion paper is also available (Gilbert et al., 1996) which describes the technological attributes of agent systems.

4.2   Market State[2]

"Agents will be the most important computing paradigm in the next ten years ... . By the year 2000, every significant application will have some form of agent-enablement." (Janca, 1996)

There are several reasons for this conclusion:

- Desktop applications are becoming so feature-rich that users can master only a small part of their capabilities. Agents mask the complexity and help the user do what he/she wants.
- Sources of information are increasing, and their content is also increasing. Agents help do the data mining – as well as help locate the most productive mines.
- Greater bandwidth means more data can get to you more quickly – but the user still has only 16 hours in the day available to work. Agents help manage the flow, by sending only the information *the user* considers essential.
- Desktops and servers now are getting enough power to easily help users and processes.
- Rapidly increasing use of the Internet and World Wide Web is creating a much more complex computing environment. Many people are beginning to refer to this as 'network-centric' computing. This implies that we are moving from simple connections (i.e., a terminal-to-a-host, or a client-to-a-server) into the complex world of multiple servers and services interconnected like a highway network. Everything is available, but services change by the second, and the

---

[2] Market state information comes from interviews with over 50 vendors of agent enabled applications. Users of these applications were also interviewed. The work and analysis was done by Peter Janca prior to becoming affiliated with IBM.

user has to figure out how to find them. Agents make a cohesive whole out of this stochastic world.

- University and industrial research has now passed the point of mere theory, and experimental systems are freely available and in use on the Internet.
- Early adopters of commercial systems are giving a practical base for future application and commercial development.
- Large custom applications are becoming agent-enabled, further broadening the experience base.

4.3   Just What Are Intelligent Agents?

An agent is software that assists people and acts on their behalf. It is *delegated* to perform some task(s), and given *constraints* under which it can operate. The idea of delegation sets agent software apart: delegation passes some control from the initiator to the agent (similar in concept to asking a concierge to find theatre tickets).

Agents are incorporated within applications such as electronic mail, network management, and personal desktop tools. They differ from any other type of software because of the following characteristics:

- *Delegation:* The user *entrusts* the agent to tackle some or all of an activity. For example, the user may ask the agent to find tickets to the next football game ('entrust'), but not allow the agent to actually 'buy' the tickets.
- *Personalization:* The *user* determines how the agent interacts. In many cases, the agent learns about the user and adapts its actions accordingly (along the lines of a personal assistant). Most agent systems in use today in the early adopter stage do not allow this flexibility.
- *Sociability:* The agent is able to interact with other agents in ways similar to interpersonal communications: This includes some degrees of give and take, flexibility, and goal-oriented behavior.
- *Predictability:* The user has a reasonable expectation of the results.
- *Mobility:* The ability to go out – usually onto the network – to accomplish the delegated task.
- *Cost effective:* The benefits gained by the user (time, information, filtering, etc.) should be of greater value than the cost (monetary, time, re-work, etc.).
- *Skills:* The agent has its own expertise. A simple agent may be capable of only executing a simple command containing no ambiguity ("Turn on the computer whenever I get a message"). On the other hand, the agent could have the ability to deal effectively with the ambiguity in the command, "find the best information about British Telecom". 'Best' is itself an ambiguous term. It may be pre-defined by an information vendor. It may evolve as a result of the agent learning (over time) what the user means. This latter version implies knowledge about the request's context, and the user's need at the time.

- *Living within constraints*: This can be as simple as, "find me the suit, but do not purchase it", or become as complex as, "go only to the most likely information sources, since there is a fee to just access an information source." Some information services, for example, allow the user to set the maximum amount of money to be spent on any search.

To find out how much you know about what is currently being done with agents, try the following short test (answers appear at the end of this chapter):

True or false:

1. Agents are cost-justified today.
2. Agents help people deal with complexity.
3. Agents help businesses reduce labor costs.
4. Agents make it easier to manage a network.
5. Agents enable electronic commerce.
6. Agents handle the mail.
7. Agents find information and present it in an organized way.
8. Agents are found in many applications today.
9. Agents can appear to the user as a cute cartoon icon.
10. Agents are able to work with other agents.
11. Agents can be confusing because every vendor describes them differently.

4.4   Agents – An Introductory Framework

As shown in Figure 4.1, agents can be classified into two broad areas:

- User interface agents; and
- Process agents.

4.4.1 User Interface Agents

User interface agents capture the user's wishes, and translate these into actions for execution elsewhere in the application and/or in the network. This is the part we see when interacting with the little dog in Bob,[3] or the form we use to describe mail-handling rules in cc:Mail (a product of Lotus Development). The face we might see could look like a friendly genie, a stylized mouth (plus eyes, nose), an anthropomorphic representation, or a cartoon character. There is also some research that concludes people do not want any form of character at all. (See work by Ben Shneiderman, University of Maryland. Also see work by Reeves, Stanford

---

[3] A product from Microsoft. Bob was introduced into the consumer market, and featured cartoon characters as interfaces for the user.

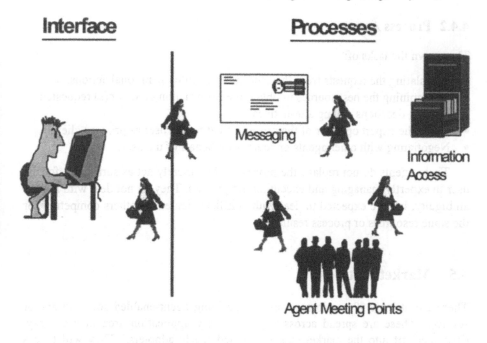

Figure 4.1. A simple agent framework

University. MIT's Media Lab has also done a survey on user preference for agent characteristics (http://www.media.mit.edu.)

User interfaces can be *passive*, such as setting the forms for messaging rules, or they can be *active*, i.e., interact with the user. The passive form is the commonest today, because it produces less ambiguous direction for the rest of the process. Passive forms are more difficult for the user, because he/she must adapt the requests to the rules and syntax required by the interface.

There will be increasing use of the active interface, primarily to support a broader, less-computer-literate audience, but also because the increasingly 'feature-rich' applications are becoming more and more difficult for the user to absorb/use without some help. Increased desktop horsepower makes it possible to support these users with realistic response times.

The user interface – whether active or passive – is critical to the success of the application. It must somehow translate the natural ambiguity in a person's request/ desire into a set of clear, unambiguous statements directed into the process. The interface must also be able to translate the results back into a format desired and understood by the user.

4.4.2 Process Agents

These own the tasks of:

- Translating the requests from the user interface into operational actions.
- Determining the best sources to obtain the information or action(s) requested.
- Making decisions among alternatives.
- Being the expert operator of the process, treating the user as primary client.
- Negotiating with other agents or sources on behalf of the user.

These agents do not replace the process – they merely act as surrogates for the user in expertly managing and executing the process. They do not deal with human ambiguity, but are expected to deal with conflicts created by others competing for the same resources or process results.

4.5   Market State

There are at least 50 vendors currently supplying agent-enabled software and/or services. These are spread across virtually every application area in use today. Customers fit into the market category called 'early adopters.' They will take a niche, (often) technology-centric application, and figure out how to adapt it to their use. Other attributes of today's market include:

- *Self-contained, niche applications:* Each agent-enabled application does its task in its own way. The user must adopt the entire application. For example, to use the agent capability in a messaging system, the user must discard any currently used system and substitute the agent-enabled system in its entirety. A vendor might legitimately argue that this is the whole point of the exercise: Make the agent-enabled product so attractive that a user will buy it to replace a competitor's product.
- *Proprietary formats*: With only a few exceptions (some information access providers, such as SandPoint, provided results via Lotus Notes, rather than a proprietary format), each agent-enabled application today requires the user to adapt to the proprietary format provided by the vendor. This format includes the user interface, the type and flexibility of intelligence mechanism, and the quantity and type of information used for 'rules' of action or behavior for the agent.
- *No standards*: Applications do not interconnect today. The agents used in the leading administrative management system do not work with the agents in the leading messaging system, or the leading information access system.
- *Available in most application areas*, such as:
    - Administrative management,
    - Information access,
    - User interfaces,

- Network management,
- Collaboration.

A recent market study (Janca, 1996) predicted when many people would be using agents, and when the agent-enabled applications would be in widespread use, as shown in Table 4.1.

Table 4.1.

Application area	Many people use	Mainstream
Administrative management	1997	1999
Collaborative	1997	1998
Commerce	1997	2000
Desktop applications	1995	1998
Information access/management	1997	1999
Messaging (e-mail)	1996	1998
Mobile access and management	1996	1998
Network management	1994	1996
User interface	1997	1999

4.5.1 Agents in Information Access

As the data indicates, agents are already in use in such areas as network management (IBM/Tivoli, Hewlett Packard, etc.). However, the area of information access has the largest number of available agent-enabled applications and services today. They range from allowing access via search for specific key words, to searching based on content derived from natural language input. Learning agents (where the agent observes what the user does, and adapts its search template automatically over time) are on the commercial horizon. Assuming standards evolve for interconnection among niche applications, it is likely that an information access application will also include ability to act on the results (such as notify people that their profiles have been selected to be part of a group).

4.6   Agent Design Model

As described above, agent-enabled applications today are closed systems. In this context, the user or vendor develops a system for messaging, information access, or other. The closed system includes appropriate skills (intelligence), knowledge (logic, rules), and a user interface (or other application), see Figure 4.2.

In the model, the three blocks are treated separately, but interconnected.

Agent Design Model

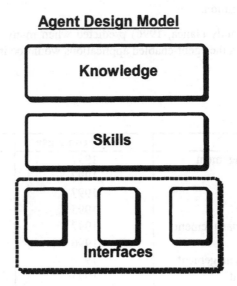

Figure 4.2. Agent design model

4.6.1 Skills

Skill describes what the agent can do, i.e., what can the user expect from the agent. Using the approach described in the model, a user would be able to select the 'best' set of *skills* for the specific application, based on cost, performance, and other tradeoffs. 'Intelligence' is another way to describe this attribute. An agent could have limited skills (i.e., enough to process the request, "get me first class tickets on the 1700 Air France to Paris for 15 June"). Given sufficient instruction or learning, an agent could be much more intelligent (i.e., "get me to Paris for the meetings with the Thompson Group"). The agent already knows when the Thompson Group meetings are being held, knows my preferences for airline, service class, and travel times, and can execute the entire transaction without any further intervention from me.

Although the above is a simple example, in practice there are many styles and capabilities of skills available today – with more possible in the future. Examples include both learning, and inference 'engines.' (When abstracted to the component level as in this Agent System Design Model, skills/knowledge software is often described as an 'engine.')

4.6.2 Knowledge

The user could also select the 'best' *knowledge* representation. This is often described as 'rules' ("... if Tom sends a note, page me"). A rule set could be more complex, and could have inferred conditions ("... if Tom sends a note, first check into my calendar, determine where I am – or was last – and call me"). In general, knowledge should be thought of as information about the user's preferences. This includes information about the groups to which the user belongs. Knowledge about groups can be important. If the agent cannot find a rule or preference to handle a condition, the agent can ask for advice from agents of other members from the same group as the user. Depending upon the situation (and the agent's skills), the agent may then take action, or may notify the user and request confirmation of proposed action(s).

4.6.3 Interface

This set of blocks contains both the *user* and the *application* interfaces.

The *user interface* is what the user sees on the screen. It could be as simple as a form or template of the type used in many e-mail systems today (i.e., "*IF* mail is from Joe, *THEN* put it on the top of the list"). These are clear, deterministic commands. Alternatively, the interface could be something that looks over the user's shoulder, observes how the user handles messages, and builds the agent's own rules to emulate what the user has done. This more sophisticated interface has been researched extensively (Selker, 1994), but is still scarce in commercial applications.

The *application interface* is an entirely new concept. Instead of closed, self-contained agent-enabled applications (as is now the case), the Agent Design Model calls for agents to *connect to any application*. This allows a user to retain a current application which is otherwise satisfactory, but to add agent capability to the extent desired. From early experience, it is clear that some applications are easier to enable with agents than others. However, once an 'adapter' (software that implements the interface between the application and skills utilized) is created for an application, the designer can add any amount of skills and knowledge as described in preceding paragraphs.

4.6.4 Agent Design Model – Experience to Date

IBM has extensive research and product development experience in the field of intelligent agents. IBM is now using the Agent Design Model, and earlier independent applications are now being folded into this. The model enables consistency, re-use of parts, and future flexibility in building new agent-enabled applications. Prior to the company's development and adoption of the Agent

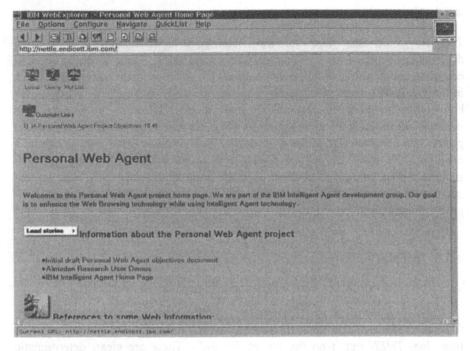

Figure 4.3. A learning agent

Design Model, each agent application was designed independently. New IBM developments are using the model, and we expect this to be quite useful in the industry as well.

The value of an Agent Design Model is broader, of course, than application design. We see the model as the enabler for use of new types of intelligence, skills, and interfaces – from both within and outside IBM. We see this as giving buyers choice as well. We also see this model as simplifying and reducing the costs of support.

4.6.4.1   Example: A Learning Agent

This example (see Figure 4.3) comes from work done at IBM's Almaden Research Center in Northern California. The agent is connected to a World Wide Web browser, and captures information about each page accessed by the user. Over time, the agent learns usage patterns well enough to predict that when page *A* is accessed, the user will typically access page *B* sometime within the next *n* accesses. The result is shown here as a 'Quantum Link,' where the user is advised about the associated page. As the reader can imagine, this technology can be applied in teaching applications, information access, network management .... even electronic mail.

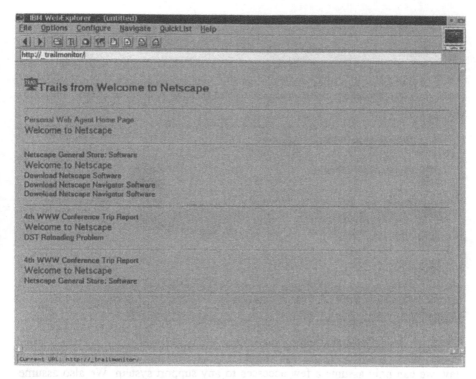

Figure 4.4. An agent with augments user memory

Another use of this technology is in augmenting user memory. How many times have you said, "I remember seeing what I wanted, and it was sometime around the time I also visited the Fly Fishing page." The second example (Figure 4.4) shows this pattern process in action. By searching for all the instances of when I used the 'Welcome to Netscape' page, I can get help in finding the page(s) reached around the same time. The technology has also been applied to generate automatic hot lists, which will order these by analyzing most frequently accessed and most recently accessed pages. Note that the technology is not limited to Web pages: any information source(s) will do.

4.6.3.2 Example: A Simple Learning Application

Agent systems do not have to do complicated things to be useful. Consider an agent enabled system to help a person attending the 1996 Summer Olympics, in Atlanta (see Figure 4.5). Assume that the person will stay about three days, will have two times per day to see sports events, and will probably have free time during the day between events. Assume that the person is a business executive, so may also be interested in news relating to his or her business. Because of the short

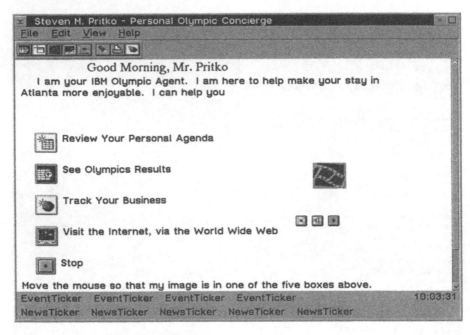

Figure 4.5. A simple learning application

stay, we can only assume a few accesses to any support system. We also assume the person may not be familiar with using a computer, and assume with virtual certainty that the person will have no patience or time to learn any complex syntax. Note the first example is a simple, unobtrusive greeting.

The second example (Figure 4.6) gives the person's schedule and remembers that the person last asked about things to do in Atlanta. It also provides real-time event information, based on knowing the events for which the person has tickets, plus events for which the person expressed interest. It re-orders the help list based on the person's prior selection.

Although only simple learning is used in this example, we have been able to help the person, reduce the time required to learn about events and news, and employ an interface requiring no training. If the person were to use the system more than a few times, we would incorporate more sophisticated learning technology, such as that shown in the first example.

4.7   Commercial Challenges

In addition to solving the problem of component flexibility *within* an agent system, the industry (vendor, developer, and customer support) needs to deal with the following:

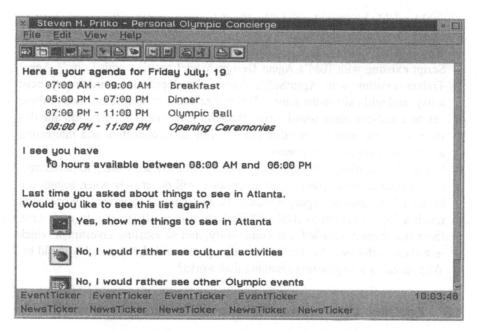

Figure 4.6. A simple learning application – a second example

- **Application paradigm shift to user-centric**: Intelligent agents provide the first software model that is focused from the user's perspective. All other models focus on the application, and require that the user adapt to the application. Although at first this distinction may appear subtle, in fact it requires an 180 degree change in the mind set of the application developer. Agents allow the user to describe any problem the way *the user* wishes (since the agent can translate the user's unique approach into the approach used by the application) – and the developer needs to assure the application can accommodate this approach.

- **Complexity management in a networked world**: Today's networks are largely within the control of a company's network manager (since the company owns/ leases the servers, lines, and software required to provide service to users). With the rapid shift of server resources onto the Internet (as well as software and information distribution), the network manager must now 'manage' a network that may be based largely on services obtained on demand from multiple parties. However, the manager must still somehow assure service. Agents can survey and keep constant track of the network, and can sometimes correct problems or adjust service mix without intervention from the user.

- **Resource consumption:** With agents, it now becomes easy to query an airline reservation system (or any other system) many times over a short period of time. Consider the consequences to servers and networks when all users can do this. Since real resources are consumed with each inquiry, servers and networks could quickly become clogged. The 'free' Internet model will certainly have to change to accommodate this.

- **Heterogeneity:** Multiple agent-enabled models (e.g., General Magic's Tele-Script existing with IBM's Agent Design Model existing with Edify's Agent Trainer existing with AgentSoft's Agent Development Environment) exist today, and will exist in the future. It is not satisfactory to assume each of these can be a self-contained island – even though today's early adopters tolerate this state. A means must be found to easily allow interconnection and interaction among these application systems.
- **Legacy integration:** Although today's early adopters are willing to purchase a closed system, broad commercial acceptance will occur only when agents can be added to existing, legacy systems. In this context, Microsoft Word is as much a legacy system as IBM's OfficeVision (e-mail) system. In each case, there is a trained, satisfied user community, and an existing investment which is still cost-effective. Neither is currently agent-enabled, but possibly could be. Why should a user give up something that works?

4.8 Looking Ahead: Some Sample Agent-Enabled Scenarios

It is often useful to develop sample scenarios to help visualize use of a new technology. Here are several such examples of potential agent-enabled applications:

- **Team share:** This application helps get the team set up by finding the appropriate candidate members. It then builds a profile of team needs, and collects information from internal and outside sources meeting the need profile. It captures the in-process work of the team, and organizes it for retention, retrieval, and presentation. It uses the learned knowledge to contribute to the company's team database, for use in creating and supporting future teams.
- **Meeting on the lake:** This augments the asynchronous meeting metaphor by being able to locate any participant anywhere (even on the lake). The application decides how hard to look for a participant, based on the participant's importance to the team, and the criticality of the need.
- **Watch the trends:** "Keep track of the selling prices and terms for Jeep Cherokee trucks within a 100 mile radius – predict when they are most attractive. I want to buy when I can get the best deal. If need be, check with the Consumer Reports electronic edition to help me select the best vehicle."
- **Personal news today:** This starts with a daily personal newspaper, which includes headlines and summaries for ease of absorption. The application can see which information the user reads first, and can adjust future presentations to match this reading pattern.
- **Build my knowledge:** This feature allows the user to easily flag information of interest, automatically store it for the user, and index it. This allows the user to find it via natural language search. There could be both private and public

sections to this storage, so that the organization could access a portion of the knowledge.

- **Personal research assistant:** This has knowledge of my preferences, as well as my standing requests for information on certain topics. It periodically scans appropriate databases, and delivers summaries on a scheduled or on-request basis. The assistant both understands – and can communicate using – natural language.

- **My man Friday:** This entity senses my arrival (via video and/or oral pattern recognition) and automatically begins execution of my normal startup activities. Friday also negotiates with other agents requesting time on my schedule, and may learn.

- **Find me an expert:** This is similar to engaging a concierge. In this case, the interface tracks down other agents with needed expertise, arranges means to 'talk' with them, and *connects them to me if needed*.

- **The electric aid:** This would be the analog to the unplanned interruptions and information received during the day. For example, it would ensure that my custom morning newspaper includes a quantity of non-requested information that might help me *make serendipitous connections*.

4.8.1 Future Predictions

IBM's vision for agents follows its vision for objects. Open standards must exist that allow the free replacement or extension of components across the computer industry. Future application development will require even more rapid development and ease of tailoring to each user. IBM's agent strategy includes structure, reference implementations of each part of the Agent Design Model, open interconnection to other agent-enabled applications, and rapid inclusion of parts produced from both within and outside IBM. Use of this approach, we believe, will move agents from promise into mainstream use. Readers are encouraged to visit IBM's agent web site at http://www.raleigh.ibm.com/iag/iaghome.

4.9 Test Answers

1. *Agents are cost-justified today.*
True. Administrative applications are the easiest to cost-justify, because they usually result in direct replacement or re-assignment of people. However, every other area studied had shown ways to show cost savings which equalled or exceeded costs.

2. *Agents help people deal with complexity.*
True. Agents can mask the inherent complexity in even a desktop application. They do this by allowing the user to communicate in language natural to the user, then translating the request into the appropriate computer instructions.

3. *Agents help businesses reduce labour costs.*
True. This is clearest in administrative functions.

4. *Agents make it easier to manage a network.*
True. Agents can put more feet and eyes on the streets than a network manager possibly could. They can also react more quickly than their human counterparts.

5. *Agents enable electronic commerce.*
True. Agents assure that you are who you say you are. They also enable rapid closure on sales.

6. *Agents handle the mail.*
True. Check out cc:Mail, Eudora, or virtually any other modern mail package.

7. *Agents find information and present it in an organized way.*
True. Note especially Individual's Hoover, or IBM's insofar.

8. *Agents are found in many applications today.*
True. Had to give one easy question.

9. *Agents can appear to the user as a cute cartoon icon.*
True. Cartoons are often used to keep the user from associating the icon (sometimes called an avatar) with more intelligence than it really has.

10. *Agents are able to work with other agents.*
True. This is (today, at least) as long as the other agents are supplied by the same application. True heterogeneity – where agents from multiple applications can interact – is still several years away.

11. *Agents can be confusing because every vendor describes them differently.*
True. This is partly because agents can apply in so many different ways, and also due to lack of standard models/descriptors (a common condition with start-up technology).

4.10 Further Work

See also the work of Tim Finin at the University of Maryland, Baltimore (finin@cs.umbc.edu), and Oren Etzioni (http://www.cs.washington.edu/homes/etzioni).

References

Gilbert, D. et al. (1996) *The Role of Intelligent Agents in the Information Infrastructure.* IBM.

Janca, P. C. (1996) *Intelligent Agents: Technology and Application.* GiGa Information Group.

Reeves, B., Lombard, M., Melwani, G. *Faces on the Screen: Pictures or Natural Experience?*

Selker, T. (1994) COACH, a teaching agent that learns. *Communication of the ACM*, 37(7), 92–99, July.

Shneiderman, B. *Looking for the Bright Side of User Interface Agents.*

Maes, P. (1994) Agents that reduce work and information overload. *Communication of the ACM*, 37(7), 31–40.

5 Vendors of Intelligent Agent Technologies: A Market Overview

C. Guilfoyle
The Trefoyle Partnership

5.1 Introduction

Intelligent agents sprang into view in the early 1990s. Suddenly the business press and other specialist publications discovered that agents made good stories, and were potentially big business. But varieties of this supposedly new species had been living for years in different habitats.

The primary source of intelligent agent technologies and products was the Distributed Artificial Intelligence (DAI) field. Developers working with complex problems and large knowledge-based systems wanted ways of distributing control and intelligence. Agents as an extension to objects provided an appropriate design model, architecture, and increasingly tools for developing communicating, co-operating intelligent entities. But other disciplines were developing their varieties of agents, sometimes independently, to exploit different strengths in the agent model. Its capacity for intelligent, communications-oriented task automation attracted players in the workflow, groupware, and Computer-Supported Cooperative Work field. Simple agents developed out of macros and scripting, for use with tasks such as email which was rapidly growing in popularity at the same time. Developers working on better user interfaces and interface integration found that the agent model fitted their needs. They could develop personalized interfaces to open products and services to non-technical users. So developers and vendors from a variety of interest groups found that different kinds of agents could support their work. These influences combined, to give a rich, sometimes confusingly rich, range of intelligent agent technologies, tools, and applications, with vast functional differences.

5.2 Agents Hiding Everywhere

The market for tools, products, and services using intelligent agent technologies is potentially very large, but it reflects the development of agents, and is an aggregate of the affected parts of many markets. Figure 5.1 shows the range of disciplines and industry groups that came to promote agent-oriented technologies, products, and services in the first half of the 1990s. By the mid-1990s these had been joined by other vendors, notably those supplying Internet and W3 products and services,

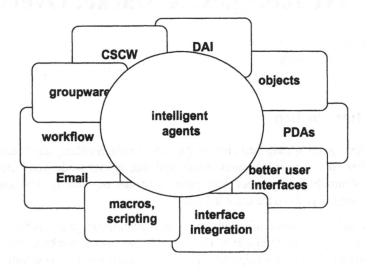

Figure 5.1. Influences on the development of intelligent agents

corporate information retrieval and data mining, and electronics vendors who plan to include embedded agents in products. This variety is to be expected. The agent design model, like the GUI and object-oriented technology, can permeate products from desktop personal productivity tools to global multiservice networks. It can support distributed processing and intelligent co-operation between agents from manufacturing industry to personal information services. The agent design model will affect a large market, and products that do not support it risk being at a disadvantage.

In the longer term we can expect to see wider inter-agent communications standards, so that agents from different vendors can communicate, and at some point cooperate. We are already seeing inter-agent communications languages (more credible now that Java, with its numerous small applet developers, has joined TeleScript as a language that can be used to develop mobile agents, with the General Magic partner programme delivering services so very slowly). The most exciting area for vendors and the mass of users of intelligent agent technology is public networks, where agents hold the promise of making the power of the Internet and W3 easily accessible to non-specialists. As Java and its applets gain ground, suppliers and users can see a language platform that can act as a *de facto* standard for Net-based agents, backed by Netscape's installed base. General Magic has recognized the importance of agent services being available to third party developers, and its repositioning of technologies for Internet server functions, and

Tabriz offering, may realign the company with current requirements. Agent vendors in the Net arena recognize the importance of such services. Cambridge-based AutoNomy plans to license its Agentware technology to Internet service providers, so that they can support personal and customized agents carrying out IR across the Web, for example. The company also plans to publish specifications for agent 'sockets,' so that the agents can take a short-cut in passing information in their agent-speak to Web sites and search engines.

Intelligent agents, then, have the potential to affect a variety of markets, including the fastest-developing information industry areas. But we also have some people saying (reasonably enough) that it's nothing new. We have others asking where the applications are. One is reminded of the position with client-sever systems in about 1989. Initially, few products and tools were clearly intelligent agent products rather than anything else. General Magic and Verity and a handful of others could point to specifically agent-oriented tools. By 1996 we faced the opposite problem. Products and services that claimed to use intelligent agents debased the term, so that customers still did not know what value agents were bringing.

The embryonic market for intelligent agent tools will be dwarfed by the influence of intelligent agents in other markets, none more so than messaging. Table 5.1 gives estimates of the commercial importance of intelligent agents to software products in some of the most important market sectors (Guilfoyle and Warner, 1994).

Table 5.1.

Market area	Importance		
	% 1994	% 1996	% 2000
email/ groupware	1.0	2.0	5.0
public email	0.1	1.0	5.0
PDAs (notepad)	2.0	4.0	8.0
PDAs (pen)	2.0	4.0	8.0
user interface	0.1	0.3	3.0
business desktop	0.1	1.0	3.0
workflow	0.5	1.0	4.0
network management	0.2	1.0	2.0
information retrieval	0.1	0.3	3.0
custom solutions	0.1	0.3	3.0
development tools	10	16	20

Source: Ovum Ltd, 1994

Table 5.2.

Market area	Revenues ($m) in US and Europe-traded market		
	1994	1996	2000
messaging	6	37	780
PDAs	1	3	104
user interface	5	37	460
business desktop	6	84	440
workflow	3	9	76
network management	4	23	70
information retrieval	12	45	680
custom solutions	70	172	650
development tools	11	66	653

Source: Ovum Ltd, 1994

The categories shown above were chosen as markets that would be substantially boosted by intelligent agent capabilities (such as PDAs) or where lack of agent capabilities may prove a barrier. Table 5.2 grosses up these percentages with market sector totals, to give a guide to the commercial importance of intelligent agents in terms of software products and service dollars in the US and Europe.

These numbers were developed in 1994. Some elements have been justified, others overtaken by changes. Most notably, intelligent agents are becoming increasingly important to messaging and information retrieval sectors. PDAs failed to capture the public imagination, but PDA-related agent products and services are beginning to come through a back door, in mobile telecoms, and will be used in set-top boxes for interactive TV.

5.3   Players in the Market

Players in the intelligent agent market are above all varied. This variety reflects the way in which diverse companies, addressing very different markets, have been united by their interest in the agent design model and associated technologies. Already seminars now specify a focus, such as agent messaging, user interface agents, or agents in manufacturing. It is now no longer possible to capture all the commercial activity going under the name of 'intelligent agents' in one comprehensive overview. Appendix A shows more than fifty technology developer or vendor organizations active in intelligent agents, with particular emphasis on agents for the Internet, W3, and related networked applications such as data mining. This list is far from exhaustive.

The 1994 analysis of roles within the market is still valid, however. Organizations form a value chain where:

- technology developers sell tools and license technologies to developers in
- application and product developers in user organizations, systems integrators, value-added resellers, product suppliers, and service suppliers, who sell custom solutions, packaged products, and packaged services to
- end users, who of course ultimately pay for it all.

Table 5.3 shows the position of some of these organizations in the value chain. A single organization may have two roles: for example, Charles River Analytics develops and licenses its own technology, and sells packaged products. BT carries out research and develops its own applications; its initial role in the value chain will be as a user of agent technology, to support complex network management. In the mid-1990s it is investigating agents for service enhancement and to support value-added services.

5.4 Groups Affected by IAGs

The intelligent agent design model, associated technologies, tools and products will affect many players in the IT industry. I believe that in ten years' time most new IT development will be affected, and many consumer products will contain embedded agent-based systems. In the short term, companies active in the intelligent agent market can also be usefully classified according to their background and the reasons for their interest in intelligent agents.

- Many of these companies are 'natural-born AI-ers' who have worked with AI, DAI, and object technologies for years. The Italian company ICON is representative of many AI software specialists who can readily move to using intelligent agents as part of their application development arsenal. Carnegie Group Inc. represents the AI 'gang of four,' as it used to be known. Larger organizations, such as Andersen Consulting, Computer Sciences Corporation, and Logica, can move to intelligent agents as a natural extension of work on AI and object technologies. For these companies, intelligent agents may be no big deal. Their customers may not know or care that their custom systems were developed using agent-based models, technologies, and tools.

Table 5.3.

Organization	Value chain positions		
	Technology developer	Application, product, service developer	End user
Andersen Consulting	◊	♦	
Apple	♦	♦	
Bellcore	♦		
Beyond Incorporated	◊	♦	
BT (British Telecom)	◊	♦	♦
Carnegie Group Inc.	♦	♦	
Charles River Analytics	♦	♦	
D&B Software		♦	
Delphi Internet Services		♦	
Digital Equipment Corp.	◊	♦	
Dow Jones		♦	
ECRC	♦		
Edify	◊	♦	
General Magic	♦		
Hewlett-Packard	♦	♦	
IBM	♦	♦	
ICON		♦	
Logica	♦		
Lotus	◊	♦	
MIT	♦		
Microsoft		♦	
Oracle		♦	
Quasar Knowledge Systems	♦		
Reuters		♦	
SandPoint	◊	♦	
Sun Microsystems	♦	◊	
Synoptics		♦	
Verity	♦	♦	
WildSoft Inc.		♦	
<u>Key:</u>	♦ primary role,	◊ secondary role	

- Other suppliers are driven to provide simple intelligent agents by requirements in their existing vertical markets. Areas where simple intelligent agents can bring immediate benefits include messaging, workflow, and network management. In commercial terms, a not-very-intelligent agent may give a product an important edge over competition where products in any one category are fairly similar. Examples include Beyond Inc's email filtering and routing capabilities, Synoptics' simple agent-based information filtering in its network management products, and the super-macro type agent feature in D&B Software's Smart-Stream workflow package. These application areas are particularly friendly to intelligent agents, as the need and benefits are clear. Customers and suppliers of network management products have been saying for years that they need more intelligent ways of dealing with network traffic, for example. Simple rule-based agent functions such as filtering out excess SNMP messages can bring immediate benefits. The agent terminology of network management may also have made the question 'What is an agent?' redundant in that sphere. There is a danger, however, that customers may be disappointed by the gap between colorful press reports about smart agents handling half the work, and the reality of 'if .. then' rules for message routing.
- The major systems vendors have something in common with both these groups, as they look to intelligent agents as an advanced design model and technology that can deliver useful results, and as a way to solve some difficult problems. Both Apple and IBM have spoken of intelligent agents as the way to deliver the interfaces needed to make computers really usable. Microsoft sees agents as part of its recipe for the home market. As so often, Hewlett-Packard has been doing something simple for years, in this case with the NewWave interface.
- The last group contains smaller suppliers who plan to make their fortunes from agents. General Magic captured the public imagination, and a good supply of capital on its stock market flotation, but its technologies have not yet delivered the level of successful products and services originally expected. Other established contenders include Edify and Verity. Edify has already made quite some ground, and its parentage includes Metaphor, which commercialized agent-like information retrieval and data mining in the late 1980s. Verity, with its background in information retrieval, its InfoAgent development product, and its strong partners (Lotus and Adobe), looks very promising. Newcomers include Agents Inc. (with Pattie Maes' name to back it), AutoNomy, Agent-Soft, and DataMind. Neural networks figure the technologies employed by AutoNomy and DataMind, and a-life techniques which seemed in distant research five years ago are beginning to appear in products. All these suppliers are conscious of the importance of controlling inter-agent communications. The rapid spread of Java will see some Java application start-ups joining the lists of promising newcomers with minimal overheads. Erik Mueller's InfoTicker share price agent springs to mind.

Some of the most commercially interesting developments in agent-based products and services will come at the intersections of these groups. For example,

Lotus already has agent-based products using Notes as an agent platform. If Notes is the agent environment of choice for start-ups offering agent features it could provide an edge over Microsoft, as the latter moves towards better-integrated desktop suites. AT&T may have abandoned its PersonaLink agent-based messaging system, but agents are still much in evidence in systems such as IBM's Intelligent Communications messaging hub proposal, and Oracle's agents for mobile communications. We forget at our peril a final group of suppliers – the 'me-too's. It is hard for the specialist to define, and the non-specialist to understand, what makes software agent software. "Isn't that just objects?" people may ask. "Ah but it's just a macro." Yoav Shoham suggests that

> *agenthood is in the mind of the programmer: What makes any hardware or software component an agent is precisely the fact that one has chosen to analyze and control it in these mental terms.* (Shoham, 1993)

In that sense, anyone can turn round and say that a product is agent-based, or at least suggest it in marketing literature. And some have done so, which encourages just cynicism among potential customers. A comment on the comp.ai Internet newsgroup somewhat rudely suggested apropos Microsoft's 'Bob' that 'Your intelligent agents have no clothes...'. A *Byte* article put it more politely:

> *The buzzword **agent** has been used recently to describe everything from a word processor's Help system to mobile code that can roam networks to do our bidding. The metaphor has become so pervasive that we're waiting for some enterprising company to advertise its computer power switches as **empowerment agents.** (Byte, 1995)*

In these circumstances, publicity is a double-edged sword for the agent software community. It may debase the currency and lead to the kinds of disappointments – and, more importantly, widespread reports of disappointments – which even now dog AI in general. With that thought, I am glad to say that articles about intelligent agents have been getting more sober.

5.5 Current Trends

During the mid-1990s, there has been less glamorous publicity and more tools, which is good news for developers who want to build agent software. The whole area has become more stable, as the idea of intelligent agents loses its novelty, and further products and tools start to appear. Six trends or significant events seem to summarize development in the emerging intelligent agent market in the mid-1990s:

- Continuing press interest and publicity is now beginning to give way to a backlash. The high-profile interface agents and WAN-based agents make good stories, but readers will start to think "So what?" if they cannot describe agents in terms that make sense to them, or buy something that helps them quickly and obviously. Simple task-oriented agents which save real time may seem disappointing after stories of friendly electronic workmates. By about 1997 intelligent agents may well be seen as a disappointment, just as leading software developers in manufacturing and telecoms are starting to field numerous applications that benefit from an agent architecture, and next-generation interfaces and messaging systems routinely use agents for DWIM functionality.

- More languages for mobile agent development appeared, with Java, Tcl, Safe-tcl and Smalltalk Agents joining TeleScript. These languages promised to release a stable mobile agent language to numerous enthusiastic developers through the Internet. This expansion will benefit suppliers by providing choice and suggesting a more mature supply side to potential customers. It may cause problems later unless suppliers can tackle inter-agent communication language issues.

- More commercial tools for agent development are starting to appear, focusing on information retrieval and data mining services (Andersen's Commander Exception Monitor, for example). Charles River Analytics is licensing its intelligent agent technology to third parties for embedding in their products. Verity has released its InfoAgent development product, and lists Lotus and Adobe in its Partner Programme.

- Big players are showing the agent flag – and waving it, though sometimes they end up putting up a white one. AT&T has withdrawn PersonaLink, but as with PDAs, we expect the market for multimedia personal messaging agents to reappear. IBM has numerous projects, including the Intelligent Communications hub and PowerPC interfaces. Microsoft followed its IntelliSense agent feature with demonstrations of the Bob user agent, and plans agent features in its Office97 suite.

- Intelligent agents are beginning to emerge in association with middleware. The ECRC did some research work in this context, and it is an obvious way to use "objects that think." Oracle's Oracle in Motion development platform sees agents providing application and communications integration to mobile workers. Lotus is developing Notes as an agent engine, supporting third-party agent services. Middleware can provide a technically and commercially stimulating area for agents.

- Finally, the commercial world and the press increasingly recognize that the intelligent agent design model will result in very different agent-based systems in different contexts. They recognize different categories, such as user interface agents, information retrieval agents, co-operative planning and scheduling agents, and network management agents. People now talk and write about different kinds of agents, which will reduce confusion, unreal expectations, or unnecessary limits on the potential of intelligent agents.

5.6 Implications of Intelligent Agents for Suppliers

Intelligent agents are potentially very important. They can help customers to use the products they have more effectively, and make real use of the networked information and legacy data sources already available. They can help to overcome the problems of under-used desktop resources and information overload. They can make IT systems attractive to customers, and produce silicon-level intelligence for embedding in manufacturing systems and consumer goods. But developers of application software and products cannot go and buy the perfect intelligent agent to install in their systems. The intelligent agent design model is a high-level metaphor. It describes a way of thinking about design, much like the object-oriented model. Success will depend on the choice of agent functions, and the effort and care expended in developing and marketing the agent-based offerings to wary customers and users. More complex agents are not necessarily commercially better. While some agents can learn, communicate, and cooperate with other intelligent agents, simple agents that provide little more than a macro with 'if .. then' rules can be very useful. The ability of an agent to communicate will often be more important than its intrinsic intelligence.

Suppliers should look now at intelligent agents, and determine how this approach to software and systems design will affect their business.

- They should understand how intelligent agents relate to the technologies and vertical markets they already know. Developers who are comfortable with object technology will see how the agent metaphor works, and AI specialists may already have used agents. Network management and messaging specialists will recognize the value of distributed control, while companies working with user interfaces and business desktop products know the value of macros and scripting languages for task automation.
- They should find out about agents as a whole, and competitive work in parti-cular. Suppliers who ignore intelligent agents do so at their peril in areas such as messaging and workflow. Agent capabilities may become a tick-list item in these markets.
- They should consider how agents relate to their markets. It may be that they want to develop an easy-to-use agent development tool, and become the Lotus Development Corp. of the next decade, for example. It may be that they want to monitor emerging inter-agent communications languages, and ensure their messaging product complies. It may be that their market is not one of those immediately affected, and they wish to adopt a "wait and see" line.
- They should take the highs and lows of agent coverage smoothly. Intelligent agents are already in use in some leading-edge products, services, and user organizations. But these companies are leading-edge, and there is no "killer agent app." visible yet. The press may well turn nasty on agents around 1997, but this is to be expected. The headlines about "double agents" letting users

down will be hard to resist, and it will take quite some time before we have electronic Crichtons in common use.

The market for products and services using intelligent agents will develop in fits and starts, as is to be expected. But the agent design model and associated technologies are already there, usable, useful, with the potential for commercial success. I will finish with a soberly optimistic look towards the future, from Irene Greif, director of workgroup technologies at Lotus:

> ... we believe that agents-centered design can potentially revolutionize UIs and produce usefulness. We also believe they can be built from current technologies, used in new ways and architected to anticipate future advanced in process representation, AI and natural language understanding. We predict enormous benefits from agents delivered in product well before anyone can master and bring to product many of the more ambitious aspects of intelligent agents. (Wayner, 1995)

References

Guilfoyle, C., Warner, E. (1994) *Intelligent Agents: The New Revolution in Software.* Ovum, London.

Shoham, Y. (1993) Agent-oriented programming. *Artificial Intelligence,* 60, 51–92. Robotics Laboratory, Computer Science Department, Stanford University, Stanford, CA.

Wayner, P. (1995) Agents of change. *Byte,* March.

Greif, I. (1994) Desktop agents in group-enabled products. *Communications of the ACM,* 37(7), July.

Appendix: A Selection of Vendor Activities

Organization	Intelligent Agent Activities
Agents Inc.	Personal interface agents, e.g., FireFly music selection
AgentSoft Ltd.	New company focusing on the development and marketing of intelligent agent software products for the Internet and for enterprise Intranet
Agorics Inc.	Joule language for mobile agents
Andersen Consulting	Various including custom developments, Commander Exception Monitor agent-based data mining tool, developed with ComShare; BargainFinder, LifestyleFinder
Apple Computer Inc.	Uses agents in Newton PDA, agent-like querying via HyperCard; also for communications purposes with 'applets,' etc.
AutoNomy Inc.	Agents for information retrieval and other Web-based services
Bellcore Inc.	Research work including message management, agents in information retrieval
BMC Software Inc.	Proving agent input to I2O for Intel
BT (British Telecom Plc.)	R&D work on advanced multi-agent systems; expects to use in network management in future; Jasper agent trial for W3 info management
Carnegie Group Inc.	Uses agent design model in custom work, e.g., with US West
Charles River Analytics	OpenSesame! learning interface product; also licensing technology for embedded intelligence; adding Windows version
Cisco Systems Inc.	Agents in network management strategy for switched Internet; also plans to use Verity agents at Cisco Web site
Crystaliz Inc.	Developing a product called LogicWare for mobile/ communicating agents, with electronic commerce perspective
Geac Computer Corp.	Intelligent agent feature in SmartStream workflow
Dartmouth College	Tcl Agents language for mobile agents
Data Discovery Inc.	Information retrieval agents
DataMind S.A.	NeurOagent for data mining
Delphi Internet Services Corp.	Developing intelligent agents to help users find information on the Internet

Organization	Intelligent Agent Activities
Digital Equipment Corp.	Agent work including Polycenter Path Doctor for network management; Obliq language for mobile agents
Dow Jones	Working on agent-based services
ECRC projects (Germany)	Research including inter-agent languages, middleware, increasingly focusing on mobile agents; Facile language
Edify Corp.	Supplies Electronic Workforce agent environment for workflow task automation, customer service support etc.
Erik Mueller	ThoughtTreasure and InfoTicker real time agent in Java
France Telecom Inc.	General Magic partner; working on agent-based (TeleScript) services, including value-added top-end services accessed through Minitel; also network management applications of agents
FTP Software Inc.	CyberAgent family, e.g., security agent, software development
Fujitsu Laboratories Ltd.	Research includes April – an agent programming language for the Internet
General Magic	Refocusing technologies embodied in Telescript, Magic Cap with Tabriz – more support for Internet, W3 agents
Guideware Corp.	Clearlake Personal Agent products
IBM Corp.	Various projects including REXX agent language, Aglets Library for programming mobile agents in Java; AgentBuilder, a developer's toolkit for building agent-based system
ICL Plc.	Agents in Teamware groupware
ICON CMT Corp.	AI software house developing applications including agent-based credit management
IMAG Grenoble	Map language for mobile agents
Industry.Net Corporation	diffAgent can monitor web sites for specific changes
InText Systems	Object Router Intelligent Agent Toolkit
JavaSoft	New company for Java software
KIMSAC	RACE project using user agents
Lotus Corp.	Agent functions in Notes groupware
MCC Corp.	Includes Java in InfoSleuth work

Organization	Intelligent Agent Activities
Microsoft Corp.	IntelliSense macro type agent feature in several products; Office 97 includes agent overlays
MIT	Several projects on intelligent agents, including task automation and user interface work
Netscape Communications Corp.	High-profile Internet Web start-up; embedding Verity's Topic agent in its Netsite Commerce Server
Nortel	Various agent activities, including agent Orbiter PDA project with agent content summary feature, and mobile information retrieval agent
Novell Inc.	With IBM, one of leaders of Salutation Consortium for equipment connectivity using agents; also agents for network management
Oracle Corp.	Oracle in Motion database client/server offering uses intelligent agents to support wireless infrastructure; ConText linguistic analysis tool to help cope with information retrieved
Personal Agents Inc.	Start-up for agents in electronic commerce
Quarterdeck	WebCompass – creates personalized agents which then use Web search engines to monitor according to your interests
Quasar Knowledge Systems	Sells Smalltalk Agents enhanced version of Smalltalk
SandPoint	Hoover agent-based search program
Sun Microsystems	Various; distributed Java via Internet
Synoptics	Agent-based network management products
System Management Arts Inc.	Using intelligent operations agents to help correlate events, and so automate system-wide problem management
Tenax Software Engineering	Describes its xLabel 5.0 labelling software as based on intelligent agents; for use in Web commerce; at beta test stage
Verity	Developed Topic WebAgents Publishers Toolkit, InfoAgent Developer Kit; partners include Lotus, Adobe; Topic text retrieval tool; agreement with Netscape to embed Topic Agent Server in the Netsite Commerce Server

6   Brokering the Info-Underworld

J. D. Foss
GPT

6.1   Informization in the Global Net

In an increasing global informization, all aspects and commodities of society are becoming represented as information which is stored and accessible from and within the world's networks: business, entertainment, human activities, organizational activities; even activities of the world's communication and information networks themselves (meta-information). There appear to be two main families of information services evolving: (i) information trading and processing, and (ii) group activities (... and probably (iii) the ones we do not yet know about).

The relationship between the telephony network (including the Integrated Services Digital Network – ISDN) and the Internet is increasingly vague. Convergence between communications and information services is inevitable, and could result in a hybrid, heterogeneous global net in which the user perceives a seamless provision of information and communications services products. As more people are empowered with computing and communications capabilities, new and unforeseen services and applications will emerge. The Internet will evolve beyond our current imagination and expectations, so the growth of the global net is unpredictable.

6.1.1   Net Commerce

There is an increasingly urgent requirement for mechanisms to support online commerce. Forrester's analysis (Modahl and Eichler, 1995) concludes Internet revenues will amount to $45.8 billion by 2000, accounting for 1% of the US economy at that time, compared to the current $2.2 billion. They forecast that most of the revenues will occur in financial services and online trade, but state that economic development is currently hindered by unreliable payment mechanisms, lack of user confidence, and 'weak infrastructure.' *The Economist* (1996) raises the issue of the present unclear sales-tax situation on Internet sales – people are hesitant about online business which could result in retrospective tax bills. However, governments are concerned about (tax-free) Internet information transfer, which is replacing traditional courier and information delivery services which would accrue Value Added Tax (VAT). Consequently, the European Commission is requesting research on methods of implementing a 'bit tax' (Ward, 1996).

In the initial stages of the evolution of the global net, online commercial dealings are relatively simple and sparse, and manageable by users, albeit with some suspicion about security. However, the current simplistic service paradigms on the Internet cannot scale to a mature information trading environment, or to the mass of evolving global virtual organisations in an increasingly net-based society. (Foss et al. (1993) and Foss (1995) give a series of scenarios that plot the evolution of information services, especially for commercial services.) The evolving information environment suggests a range of mechanisms – services – to administer and manage information businesses and activities, especially where this environment involves commercial trading. Users of information services require *intermediaries* to assist, navigate, and mediate the invocation of these services. Rudimentary services and tools offer search and retrieval, and so on. More recently, advanced tools have been developed that provide for data-mining (Gardner, 1996) and On Line Analytical Processing (OLAP), e.g., the Fast Analysis of Shared Multi-dimensional Information (FASMI) definition (Pendse, 1995).

A number of functions are required both to serve the administration of info-businesses and to guide users/customers through info-transactions. One of the mechanisms envisaged to provide these functions in an integrated manner is the concept of the *information broker*. A number of broker services are appearing on the WWW. Many of these are 'shopping' agents (especially for compact discs), like the Andersen 'Bargain Finder' (Andersen); the FAST Broker is a purchasing agent from the Information Sciences Institute of the University of Southern California (FAST Broker). Firefly, based on the MIT HOMR, the Helpful Online Music Recommendation service, compares similar client profiles to deduce its recommendations to the enquirer. The Firefly site recently added a CD 'shopping trolley' service, and now also offers communal media services (Firefly). This is an example of the way in which 'new media' services can quickly diversify. Many web sites now offer services that blur the boundaries between a number of services – news, publishing, entertainment, shopping, and other services are seamlessly bundled into entrepreneurial online malls. The significant trend is the speed at which these sites can re-define their service and re-organize their site accordingly. Other agent research at present is aimed at filtering and management functions, including work at Carnegie Mellon University on multi-agent systems for financial portfolio management (Decker et al., 1995).

6.1.2 Extending the Concept of Information Brokerage

In this chapter it is suggested that the concept of brokerage be extended. Here, a broker is considered to be a managed collaboration of any of the above functions, and to act as an intermediary between the customer and a range of information sources. Brokers are not entities that can be rigidly defined – they may operate in a free market as services which – like brokers themselves – are created and managed by independent operators. The broker's position in the trading model (between client and service) may be suitable for administering the legal requirements for information trading – taxation, rights, royalties, and revenues. The broker may often be an independent third party running these services as a business, and obtaining the information functions (probably as agents) from other third party commercial concerns. The broker can operate on behalf of its clients, data mining, proactively marketing, maintaining profiles, and so on. A successfully competitive broker business will continually reconfigure as it adapts to the evolving online information business environment.

We can be confident of an increase in computing power to manage information (at least for the info-aristocracy). At the same time there is an evolving technical capability for users to utilize the network as part of their computing platform – both to acquire application code from the network and to utilize the network for storage. However, *services* are also *users*: they are located and identifiable (e.g., by address) in a network. Successful commercial services are thriving, evolving businesses, increasingly intelligent, dynamically reconfigurable, self-organizing, proactively marketing. They will often be composed of interchangeable core functions, e.g., applications, macros, and agents configured into the best fit for the current task or business phase. As we see the emergence of *net-centric* computing, so we could see the paradigm of *net-centric service provision*. (But note the difference between a network service – as operated by a network operator – and a networked service as operated by an independent third party, over the network).

The global net itself is also a user of services. The network may be managed as separate components, deployed and *brokered* as a range of independently provided entities. These components would be traded or brokered by virtue of their availability, cost, affiliations, licenses, etc., and constructed online, even self-organized into information networks, creating an *info-underworld* of federated distributed heterogeneous information networks (infonets).

Intelligent agents have the characteristics needed to support this dynamic service environment: mobility between a user and other users and across platforms; autonomy to initiate and perform tasks; representation of their owners' interests across a network; flexibility and adaptiveness, customizing their actions to the evolving environment; communicativeness, etc. For the service scenarios described here, agents will need to be able to co-operate in large distributed systems with other agents (possibly federated to other users); to learn and adapt to changing circumstances, re-federations, etc. Some advanced agent research is aimed at these requirements, and the examples of agents listed above indicate the suitability of the technology to networked information services. Consequently, intelligent agents are a fundamental enabling technology for brokerage. The need for intelligent agent technology is discussed later in Section 6.4.

6.1.3 Standards – Why Bother?

Rather than striving for the global standardization of everything, perhaps we should adopt a Darwinian attitude – standards will follow a natural evolution: we can accept that there will always be conflicting standards for many inter-working requirements. New platforms and applications will always be emerging. It would be too restrictive to permanently design for backward or forward compatibility, and in any case technology is now advancing faster than standards bodies can standardize it. Someone somewhere will have a solution for incompatible platforms, especially if it is commercially available. All the consumer has to do is find it, and again this is a broker function.

The remainder of this chapter discusses:

- the underlying concept of information brokering, and the potential constituent services;
- the construction of services (service nodes) in an 'info-underworld' of the global net;
- the requirement for brokers in service construction;
- brokers as evolving, self-organizing services; and
- the requirement for intelligent agents in these scenarios.

6.2 Information Brokerage

Current views of Information Brokerage seem to be limited to search and retrieval functions. However, in the context of the maturing information services and deployment of network resources, information brokering is a *core superset* consisting of all possible intermediary functions required between user (customer) and supplier(s) – the trading parties, see Figure 6.1.

Information brokers mediate a *range* of services operated by *info-specialists* who liaise between *information warehouses,* or *infoware suppliers* and (enquiring) customers. A broker:

- offers an *intermediary range of functions* to aid the customer in his or her dealings with online services;
- can bridge the gap between what is available and what consumers want, e.g., librarians for entertainments (games, video, or audio); travel agents; insurance brokers, etc.;
- can undertake a global trawl of potential information services and suppliers, and assess the suitability of a selection of information products for the client;

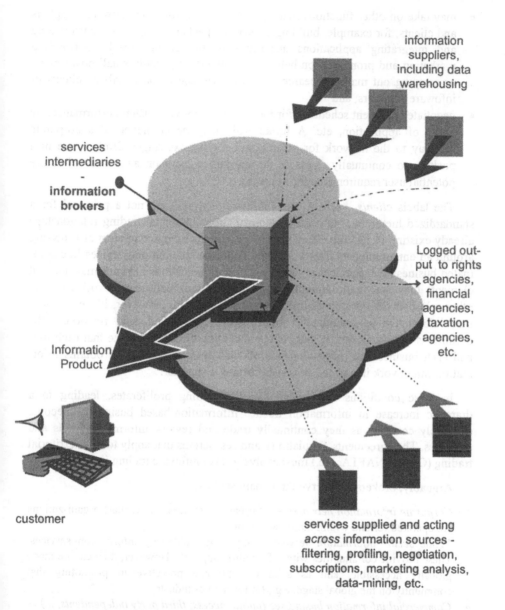

information
suppliers,
including data
warehousing

services
intermediaries
-
information
brokers

Logged out-
put to rights
agencies,
financial
agencies,
taxation
agencies,
etc.

Information
Product

customer

services supplied and acting
across information sources -
filtering, profiling, negotiation,
subscriptions, marketing analysis,
data-mining, etc.

Figure 6.1. Basic model for information brokering. It appears helpful to consider trading events with reference to the traditional trading roles of clients, infoware suppliers, and brokers. Clients want the infoware, infoware suppliers (service providers) have the material *and tools* – they are info-specialists who operate 'info-warehouses' and maintain the repertoire of infoware they are purveying. The broker is the intermediary range of services between the user and the providers. Brokers may be the source of the information, or add value to previously acquired information. They can acquire source material as required, but also acquire the necessary functions to *act across* the source material – filters, negotiation tools, profiling, management tools, information processing tools, etc.

- may take on other functions managing the info-traffic flow between suppliers and clients, for example, building up service packages for clients, customizing and integrating applications according to the client's needs, performing marketing and promotion on behalf of suppliers (especially small businesses), or carrying out market research for their own use or on behalf of clients or infoware suppliers; and
- negotiates payment schedules for the service – by view/listen/performance, by usage of application, etc. A broker role may be employed at a corporate gateway to the network for information service exchanges. Brokers are in a position to continually re-assess the market to maintain awareness of future potential user requirements for infoware.

The labels *clients, brokers,* and *infoware suppliers* are not a proposal for a standardized hierarchy, but a description of the commercial trading relationships already existing in real life. They may be people operating computers or browsing around an entertainments library, or they could be autonomous devices like automated business management systems, e.g., communications network management elements that can trade communications applications between networks, or any other role that fits the client-broker-server relationship. However, if we consider that information is continually sold, resold, repackaged, and reworked, the definitions of *client, server,* and *broker* become blurred. So we see that each user and each business can have elements of each role. A client who obtains information can rework it, and sell it, thus becoming a supplier.

In these conditions it is inevitable that trading proliferates, leading to a dramatic increase in information traffic. Information-based businesses become extremely complex as they continually trade and rework information tools and packages. The agreements, regulations, and restrictions that apply to interterritorial trading (GATT, NAFTA, etc.) must evolve to take infoware trading into account.

Arguably, brokers may serve three main sectors:

- *Corporate information networks* – information services for (virtual) organi-zations are operated for and within the organization.
- *Public sector information services* – e.g., local authority information services. These provide communities with information support. However, they can be made globally accessible, and as such can become proactive in promoting that community on the global stage, e.g., for tourism or industry.
- *Commercial information businesses (public access, third party independents, ...)* – this is the cautious area. All commercial enterprises must be seen to be legal, decent, honest, and truthful. Certainly there need to be legal obligations on commercial information operators to be openly accountable, although this is clearly an area that is wide open for legislation (and exploitation). However, brokers must be viewed as independent entities with trading alliances and affiliations, and as such are open to preferential dealing, albeit within the law.

6.2.1 Information Brokerage – Services and Functions

The services offered by a brokering service may be any of those listed here, below – but not necessarily all of them. This depends on the level of service a broker (probably commercial, probably independent) chooses to offer to any or all of his clientele (clients or infoware suppliers). There is no limit to the number or range of services that an independent party can offer to its clients. Brokers serving a specific field of industry or commerce may provide services that are (near) unique to that sector. Any of these services may be permanently resident within the broker configuration, or available from external sources and bought/rented in as and when necessary.

Some of these services may be:

- **Information search and retrieval**: e.g., search engines on the Internet. Brokers fundamentally provide a mediation of access to any number and type of services. Brokers may also conduct search and retrieval functions themselves. They would also co-ordinate the subsequent processing of the information. This may utilize data-mining methods and tools. Brokerage may include the data-mining processes, or manage (distributed) data-mining on behalf of a client's information base, for example by farming out information processing tasks to data-mining specialists. A broker may take a commercial decision to provide information processing facilities within its own business. A vital broker role here may be to co-ordinate these activities with the profiling, monitoring, and other functions described below.
- **Administration of Information Rights and Revenues (IRR)** – The broker can provide the means for service or information providers to publish their products and collect the appropriate royalties, revenues, etc. Many interested parties are eagerly proposing schemes for protecting rights. The issues related to copyright in an open information network are rather complex, but the broker is in a position to administer rights and revenues mechanisms. See also negotiation.
- **Service selection** – allowing the user (or other brokers) to select from the available services. This could use browsing techniques or relational search, or a combination.
- **Access/hand-off to other brokers** – Brokers should be able to access each other, either transparently or under guidance.
- **Monitoring for events** such as posting of news items of potential interest to the user (compare personalized interactive publishing.)
- **Protecting the user** from undesired intrusive access from other users (or agents); filtering of incoming information.
- **Maintain an *infobase*** on behalf of the user. The information base grows with the user's business experience and may be incremented on a by-transaction basis. Information in the base may be annotated with *credibility ratings* from the previous dealings with business partners, etc. Information imparted to other

users may be qualified with a *confidence factor*. A *satisfaction level* can be derived for the current state of the infobase and used to decide whether more information, updated information, or information from a more reliable source are needed. Such a function implies a self-learning infobase.

- **Profiling** of users according to the infobase. The base can be used to refine searches and to build up knowledge of clients and of suppliers' working practices and preferences: i.e., profiling business associates. The profiles can be utilized and updated in future business transactions.
- **Intelligent prediction** of user requirements for information processes, utilizing the profiles (above).
- **Enabling services to interwork** by providing format translation facilities and conversion services. Includes the definition of standard data formats, and facilities for services to invoke each other.
- **Communications services management** – administration, management, and invocation of communications access and services, e.g., diversion, conferencing facilities, access and user group integrity, etc.
- **Publishing** – **simplifying access** via the net(s), a broker can enable faster and cheaper publishing. Network-stored information can be server-maintained, thus more up-to-date, therefore more valuable.
- **Market research** on behalf of the infoware suppliers. The broker is in a privileged position to accrue information on all transactions he or she conducts, as well as monitoring which suppliers do or do not have various items.
- **Negotiation** between customers and the providers to attain a contracted agreement including costings of sources and services; this may also include rights of future usage of information.
- **Subscription to nets and webs** – independent commercial information services may require contracted subscription access. The broker may provide a negotiated temporary subscription or proxy subscription for non-subscribers to these services and networks.
- **Access, procurement, and integration** of third party services and applications. The broker may add services and applications to a client's working environment (indeed the services mentioned above are examples of this).

These functions may be provided by separate components, e.g., application agents responsible for each of the functions – search engines, negotiation agents (Jennings et al., 1996), trading models, etc. However, some interesting issues are raised by Resnick (Resnick, 1996) relating to collaborative evaluation and filtering, and the risk of censorship. This is based upon work carried out in the GroupLens project (Resnick et al., 1994). Heillmann et al. (Heillmann et al., 1995) also highlight the issues of consumer behavior, and the requirement for user trust in agent-based management information systems.

Broker functionality is also applicable to organizational management – e.g., for browsing of personnel, information library content, etc. The concept of a networked intermediary (such as a brokering service) would offer information management functions required within corporate networks and organizations (especially distributed federations, virtual organizations). In these cases the broker could provide for personnel browsing, document browsing, and management.

As mentioned at the start of this section, the concept of information brokerage is of a *core superset* consisting of all possible intermediary functions required between customer and suppliers. A specific broker business, and a specific task would dictate a specific set of functions to be used. Brokerage, as with any business or service, can cover a wide range of business types, from large global comprehensive combines, down to small niche market services. However, many intermediary functions have yet to be identified for future requirements, and the 'broker model' can serve as a generic architecture. The customers (and suppliers) may need a wide range of intermediary services, and so they must decide whether to employ a broker who can supply all of these specific requirements. If such a broker is not available, it may be preferable (or necessary) to employ the services of a number of brokers. Of course, a broker may 'front' the collective services of a number of sub-contracted brokers. This raises an interesting academic discussion:

- who perceives who – as user;
- who perceives who – as broker;
- who perceives who – as sub-contracted broker;
- who perceives who – as service component;
- who perceives who – as agent; and
- who perceives who – at whatever level – the relations are recursive.

This is discussed further in Section 6.4.

6.2.2 Shopping, from Web Sites to Malls

One of the characteristics of the Internet at present is the free-spirited generosity with which web-site owners invite visitors to hot-link out to another site. Hot-linking visitors to a vast range of external information sources is seen as a useful service. However, in a more commercial future scenario, site owners would surely require visitors to stay within their site to acquire (and so pay for) more services and goods. Does this mean that commercial sites will become more insular? Or will they require mechanisms to provide a full hot-link mechanism to customers while retaining the customers within the site? If so, would an *outer shell* of a broker service provide the necessary consumer services, including hot-linking, while maintaining (and managing) the commercial integrity of the sites within the shell?

The shell may equate to a *mall* operated by the broker who is *trusted* by the site businesses. The broker (aspiring to a high-profile agency) attracts custom from net browsers, and may add value to the browsing environment of a virtual mall – glitzy attractions to entice the public, communal public places, architecture, etc.

The broker may even add ancillary services – selected profiled filtering to reduce the perceived virtual browsers to a recognizable subset that matches each individual's profile, e.g., family and friends. The broker, as mall *service operator* may include federated services for all sites – delivery of physical goods ordered within the mall, etc. For the customers, the *branding* of a mall can be an assurance of quality and familiarity.

The Virtuosi project (Rogers, 1994) is studying the use of information brokering as a commercial venture, and developing broker implementations.

6.3 Service Nodes and the Info-Underworld

To the online user, networked services may have the *appearance* of being delivered from a remote, anonymous location in the network (indeed, if they appear to come from anywhere at all). One of the possible methods of implementing future service nodes is for the node to acquire its necessary functions (applications, agents, etc.) as and when it needs them, or as a continual reassessment of the service's ongoing business trends and requirements. So, initially the node itself may be an empty *shell*, or contain only minimal number of common or essential (life-support) components. The additional service components are then acquired from networked suppliers and integrated to form a composite but self-contained service node (see Figure 6.3). This is basically a virtual private network (telecom terminology: a *VPN*) configured into a service *implementation architecture*. This scenario could be thought of as the deployment of *net-centric service platforms* (also see Foss et al., 1993).

This method of service construction is seen as applicable to many (potentially all) networked services. But here we can consider the role of brokering:

- Broker services may be implemented on net-centric service platforms.
- The construction of services may need broker services to identify and commercially acquire the service components, and also to provide back-up (help) services, etc.

So, for a broker to be constructed, applications and additional services are built in to achieve the functions the broker operating business chooses (or is requested) to offer. In some cases the functions may or may not be permanently resident in a broker business configuration. They may be distributed around the global net and then 'trawled' into the broker service, probably in near real time. Building a broker may involve other brokering services to locate, procure, and integrate the applications for the broker (see Figure 6.2).

The constituent functions that will become the broker services may be independently provided from online applications vendors, agent vendors, etc., i.e., applications software products for sale or rent from other independent retail outlets, or 'information warehouses.'

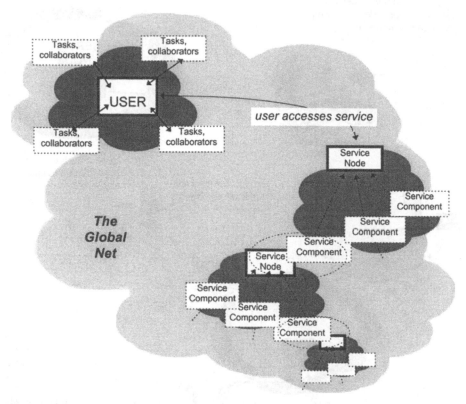

Figure 6.2. A user (who has tasks and collaborators to work with) utilizes a service node, which is itself a user of another service node, etc. Services are built recursively in an underworld of service components and platforms

The service business (e.g., a broker) needs to manage each task it undertakes and to administer local node control functions responsible for business management. Management tasks may include:

- identify the current task (who the client is, what the client wants);
- identify the components and functions needed to perform the task; some of these may already be owned by the broker, others are additional;
- initiate a global search for the additional required components;
- negotiate and procure these components, including payments;
- integrate components into a suitable architecture to perform the service for the client;
- perform the service; and
- disassemble the service components when the service is complete.

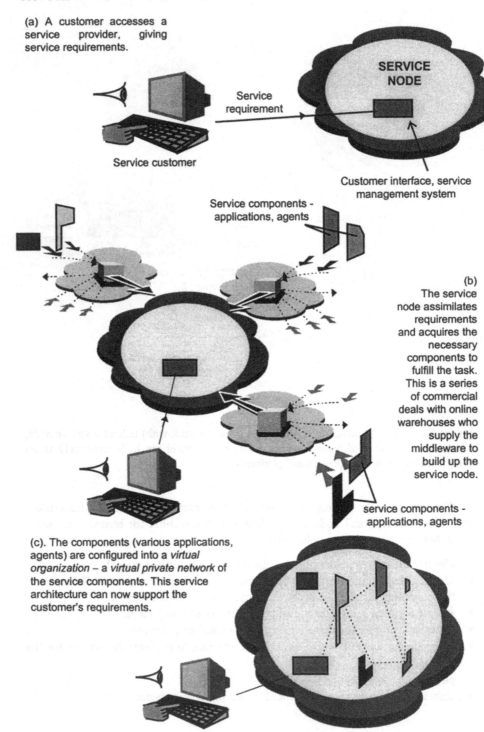

(a) A customer accesses a service provider, giving service requirements.

Service requirement

Service customer

SERVICE NODE

Customer interface, service management system

Service components - applications, agents

(b) The service node assimilates requirements and acquires the necessary components to fulfill the task. This is a series of commercial deals with online warehouses who supply the middleware to build up the service node.

service components - applications, agents

(c). The components (various applications, agents) are configured into a *virtual organization* – a *virtual private network* of the service components. This service architecture can now support the customer's requirements.

Figure 6.3.

Consequently, one of the broker's functions is to analyse the requirements and (virtually) build itself. This requires the broker to locate the distributed functions, so either the broker knows where to look or, if it does not, it enquires from other network-based businesses that do know. This may result in the formation of networked businesses providing the specialized business of *broker support*, i.e., brokers for brokers. The broker as a user in its own right would now be self-organizing, automating its self-building process. The search process may involve the intelligent agents (acting on behalf of the broker) to search for the required functionality.

The service business could also be managed as continual self-reassessment. In this case, the service continually reassesses its business environment (e.g., using online marketing) and reconfigures its component services accordingly.

This scenario continues by considering that *service platforms are recursive*: the platform formed by the network of a number of components could now be a component (with other platforms) to form a platform at a *higher layer*, and so on. Consequently, services at any specific layer are composites of services of lower layers. Many/most/all of these networked services are constructed in a fluid, commercial, self-organized manner from networked components. A broker function is almost essential in this fully mature net-centric service environment.

Among the biggest users of future information services will be the communications and information networks themselves. The network is, effectively, its own user, trading with other networks for resources (e.g., network management agents, protocol handling, communications applications, etc.). Consequently there is a symbiotic relationship between the intelligent information infrastructure and the services that it supports. Given real-time information trawling, self-organization, and service platform creation, there will be a dramatic increase in transaction traffic within the network.

The functions and services being trawled in by the broker (including those for its own construction) are subject to application usage charges, etc. The broker building process thus acquires an information rights and revenues culture all of its own. These charges are of course either absorbed in the brokers' overall business, or are charged as part of the broker's service charge to the client for this specific task. The broker can also raise revenues from advertising or market research and consultancy using information derived from the broker's business. These charges are the business of the broker in a free market.

6.4   The Need for Agents

The specialist nature of an information broker is *not necessarily* to supply the services directly, but to locate, retrieve, and integrate the constituent services from their owners, i.e., information or content owners, and then integrate and customize, if necessary. The broker may have to search and retrieve other services, for example filters, negotiation functions, or management devices, to *act across* the accumulated raw information content. Thus the information product, the *infoware,* is constructed, probably specifically crafted and customized for the end-user. This may utilize the user's direct specifications, or his or her participation, or work with a previously acquired profile of that user (or a mix of any or all of these options).

Intelligent brokers can pre-empt these activities with *intelligent marketing* to predict their users' requirements in their evolving marketplace, and thus a successful broker would reconfigure its own business to support these needs more efficiently and effectively. Otherwise the users may move their dealings to another broker who can provide a higher level of service.

Clearly a number of the functions offered by an information brokering service are either directly serviced by agents, or would be assisted by agent intervention. For example, *wrapper agents* can translate from higher-level search queries into a suitable query language for the target data stores, especially for legacy information sources, by using common syntactic interfaces (Tsvetovatyy and Gini, 1996). Data-mining and information processing are also tasks suited to agent technology, as previously discussed.

6.4.1 Users' Perspectives

Supposing that the global information trading environment is a free market and not governed by standardized architectures for service provision, it is difficult to describe the difference between *what is a broker* and *what is an agent*. A network of collaborating agents may provide a platform for a higher-level user, who *perceives* the platform as a single entity (i.e., a single agent); see Figure 6.4. Agents may also utilize the services of brokers so that they can perform their tasks for their users; and those brokers may in turn be composed of a network of agents. So, in the commercial nature of a free market, there is really no formal hierarchy into which agents and brokers fit; either can be a user of the other. They can also be bought, rented, shareware, contracted under license, etc. This suggests that there may need to be a controlling entity (e.g., an agent) responsible for the location, negotiation, procurement, and integration of the agents into this user's infonet. This controller function takes a view of its world similar to a human user, hence the *underworld* of traded service components. There are inevitable issues about allegiances and loyalty in federated multi-agent systems. Some of the management issues are discussed in (Tsvetovatyy and Gini, 1996). The service components (including agents) are tradable commodities in the lower layers of this service/ agent hierarchy.

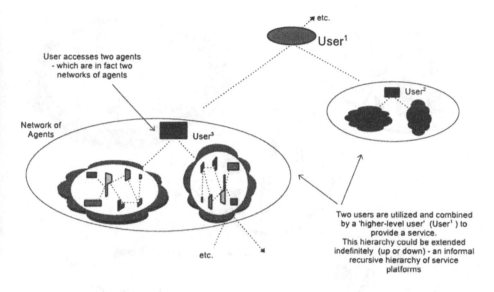

Figure 6.4. Who regards who as the agent? – The 'higher-level' user (user[1]) can regard the 'lower-level users' (users[2,3]) as agents, who similarly view agents of 'lower level' composite infonets, etc.

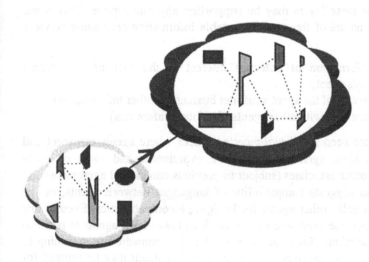

Figure 6.5. Now – suppose the user/customer is another service

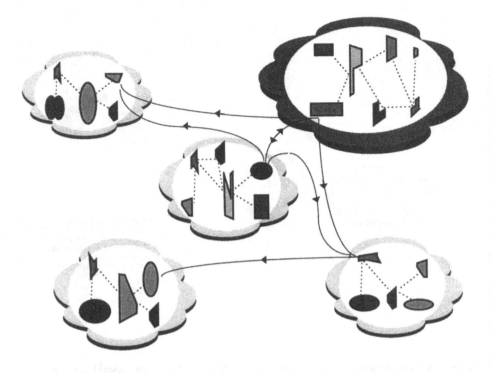

Figure 6.6. One agent in each infonet takes the initiative to browse other (*hitherto* unrelated) infonets. The infonets begin to learn about each other: opportunities, *scavenging* for general information about the common trading environment, marketing activities, etc.

Any number of these layers may be supporting any one service. This is the informal recursive nature of free-market tradable information processing services (including agents):

- trawling for information of potential interest to the user of the infonet represented by this agent;
- *pro-active marketing* of the agent's infonet business to other infonets; and
- serendipitous meetings with other agents (for future references).

This suggests the need for *virtual meeting places* where agents can meet and trade. In these liaisons, agents can compare experiences and swap *or trade* information about other associates (subject to previous contractual agreements and security). This also suggests compatibility of languages between agents, or the ability of agents to enlist other agents for bridging incompatibilities. Even at this level, agents may become users of a sub-network of lower-level agents to perform these inter-agent functions. Such agents may take on a nomadic life, returning to their host periodically for updates. This type of mobile agent may be utilized for policing and monitoring activities in future information environments, checking for abuses of (copy)rights infringements, etc., although society's view of information rights may actually change in this type of environment.

The marketing activities can be used to determine the degree and nature of self-organization of an online business, probably to the point of agents self-writing code. Information businesses can fine-tune (or reconstruct their configuration) according the findings of online marketing, including automated brokering businesses and intelligent agents.

6.5 Summary and Conclusions

A series of scenarios has been presented for the evolution of the global information trading environment. The commercial nature of this environment requires the use of *information service intermediaries* that administer access and selection of a number of information sources that are the basis of *infoware* products for the user. At the same time there is a need to manage and administer information processing activities across the source material to produce the required information product for the customer. Many of these activities amount to *online commerce*, which is causing some understandable misgivings in these early stages. However, potential traders and financiers eagerly anticipate a mature trading mechanism, especially for the administration of some of the legal issues, taxation, rights, royalties, and revenues. This chapter has presented brokerage in the context of a universal trading model in which brokerage is seen as necessary because of the sheer scaling problem as online commerce drastically increases. This chapter has also proposed that brokerage, as an intermediary, can administer the legal and commercial requirements of information trading in a number of market sectors – general public access to community information services, entertainment for domestic users, business users, etc.

Although the concept of information brokerage is not new, this chapter has demonstrated an extension to the basic concept – the broker as a device to administer the commercial construction of service platforms in networks. A scenario has been presented to describe the hierarchical way in which service platforms can be automatically constructed, and to show that this construction is itself subject to brokering for *infoware products*. In this scenario, it is suggested that a free-market online trading environment for service platforms results in an informal recursive hierarchy of service platforms and components, i.e., a net-centric procurement and integration of service components. This scenario has also considered brokerage as a commercial business, and the management of these businesses, and their continual redevelopment in the evolving online trading environment.

In this *underworld* of information processing elements, it appears that agents are necessary to perform automated service construction tasks. In this intensive environment where applications and agents are traded rapidly, brokerage is seen as a user of these services, and also a necessary component to enable scaled trading in this busy underworld.

Given the characteristics of this dynamic environment, intelligent agents are seen as an essential technology. Mobility and autonomy are necessary attributes for service components. It is envisaged that there will be increased activity in co-operative virtual organizations of federated agents, with an increasing emphasis on commercial security. There is a great need for increased research on these types of agent activities. Agents can also represent their 'home' infonets to other infonets in global *ad hoc* browsing exercises to mutual benefit.

Acknowledgements

I am grateful for the help and support from colleagues at GPT: Edwin Ackroyd, Brian Atkin, John Evans, and Kulwinder Garcha.

References

Bargain Finder, Andersen; http://bf.cstar.ac.com/bf/.

Decker, K., Sycara, K., Zeng, D. (1995) Designing a multi-agent portfolio management system; http://www.cs.cmu.edu/~softagents/papers/cikm95.ps.

FAST Broker, Information Sciences Institute of the University of Southern California (ISI); http://info.broker.isi.edu/1/fast .

Firefly; http://www.ffly.com.

Foss, J. D. (1995) Information services and group activities in a national information infrastructure. *Proceedings of the Fifth IEE Conference on Telecommunications*, ICT'95, Brighton, UK., 302–307.

Foss, J. D., Atkin, B. C. M., Ackroyd, E. (1993) The global information trading environment. *Proceedings of the International Symposium of Subscribers Loops and Services*, ISSLS'93, Vancouver, BC., 39–43.

Gardner, C. (1996) IBM data mining technology; http://booksrv2.raleigh. ibm.com:80/cgi-bin/bookmgr/bookmgr.cmd/ BOOKS/datamine/.

Heilmann, K., Kihanya, D., Light, A., Musembwa, P. (1995) Intelligent agents: a technology and business application analysis; http://haas. berkeley.edu/~heilmann/agents/.

Hull, R., King, R., ARPA (1995) Index to the reference architecture for the intelligent integration of information; http://www.isse.gmu.edu/I3_Arch/ X0008_7.Wrapping Services.html.

Jennings, N., Faratin, P., Johnson, M., O'Brien, P., Wiegand, M. (1996) Using intelligent agents to manage business processes. *Proceedings of the First Int. Conference on the Practical Application of Intelligent Agents and Multi-Agent Technology* (PAAM96), London, UK.

Modahl, M., Eichler, S. (1995) Forester report. *People & Technology Strategies*, 2(5), September.

Pendse, N. (1995) The FASMI definition for OLAP; http://www.access.digex. net/~grimes/ olap/fasmi.txt. From: The OLAP Report, *Business Intelligence*.

Resnick, P. (1996) Roles for electronic brokers; http://ccs.mit.edu/paulproj. html.

Resnick, P., Iacovou, N., Suchak, M., Bergstrom, P., Riedl, J. (1994) GroupLens: an open architecture for collaborative filtering of netnews. *Proceedings of ACM 1994 Conference on Computer Supported Cooperative Work*, Chapel Hill, NC: 175–186; http://ccs.mit.edu/CCSWP165.html.

Rogers, A. (1994) Virtuosi – virtual reality support for group working. *BT Technology Journal*, 12(3), July, 81–89.

The Economist (1996) Taxed in cyberspace. *The Economist,* July; http://www.economist. com/issue/13-07-96/wb1.html.

Tsvetovatyy, M., Gini, M. (1996) Toward a virtual marketplace: architectures and strategies. Department of computer science, University of Minnesota; http://www.cs. umn.edu/~tsvetova/paper/paper.html.

Ward, M. (1996) All the world shall be taxed. *New Scientist,* July, 14–15.

7 Personal Agents: A Walk on the Client Side[1]

P. Kearney
Sharp Laboratories of Europe Ltd.

7.1 Introduction

The world is fast becoming a giant heterogeneous information system in which personal electronics products (including Personal Digital Assistants or PDAs, PCs, set-top boxes, etc.) play a key role. For example, PDAs are now seen as communication tools and information access terminals as well as personal data repositories. Sharp's Zaurus PDA is already used in Japan to publish the electronic edition of the *Mainichi* newspaper. The vast number and diversity of the components and uses of the global information system necessitates a decentralized, emergent organization. The agent metaphor offers an attractive route to achieving such an organization. In this chapter, I outline the role of agent software in personal electronics in mediating between the individual user and the available services and project a likely sequence in which personal agent-based products will be successful. I also discuss various standardization and interoperability issues affecting the practicality of agents in this role.

Figure 7.1. Sharp ZR5000 PDA

---

[1] This is a revised and extended version of a paper first presented at the IEE C3 Colloquium on Intelligent agents and their applications, 30th April 1996.

7.2 Agents and Agent Systems

Even (perhaps especially) in the agent research and development community there are regular soul-searching discussions about the nature of agenthood. This is a personal view, but many agent developers would agree with most of it. Central to the definition is the ability of an agent to act autonomously. This implies that an agent receives stimuli from its environment, can perform actions which alter that environment, and decides these actions based upon its own goals whether these are expressed as target states or utility functions or are implicit within reactive behavior rules.

Frequently, an agent's environment will largely be made up of other agents, both human and artificial. Stimuli from, and actions upon these agents takes the form of various acts of communication, which for the sake of simplicity I will call messages. Agents may also influence each other indirectly through their observable effects on other aspects of the common environment.

The recent widespread interest in agents is due to the need:

- to develop software which will make and act upon sensible decisions on behalf of a user or organization, etc., and act upon them reliably;
- to decentralize the management of complex (particularly distributed) systems; and
- to integrate subsystems which previously have been independent, to form a coherent higher-level system.

It needs to be emphasized that the interest in agents is a response to the perceived need for solutions to these problems. Viewing the components of a system as interacting agents with beliefs, desires, intentions, etc., yields useful insight when designing relatively simple systems today, and opens lines of investigation that promise more general and more capable solutions tomorrow. Agent 'technology' is a goal rather than a fact. This is not to say that useful tools and techniques for building agent systems do not exist; they do. They are not definitive solutions, however, nor is it the case that use of such tools defines whether an application is an agent.

In my view, a key goal in studying agents is to learn how to build large-scale systems with beneficial emergent behavior. By this I mean that individual agents are designed independently with behaviors that guide them in pursuit of their own goals and in their interactions with other agents. The properties of the system as a whole are not dictated by the designer, but arise as a result of repeated interactions (Kearney et al., 1994).

7.3 Role of Agents in Personal Electronics

Our view of a personal agent is as software resident on an item of personal electronic equipment that acts as an intermediary between the user and the complexities of electronic services in the widest sense (Gibbins et al., 1994). The purpose of the agent is to provide extra value, flexibility, and functionality to the user while at the same time simplifying operations. The personal agent knows the characteristics, preferences, and habits of its user through a combination of direct instruction, learning by observation, and reinforcement learning. It also knows about infor-mation and other services available across the network, and how to exploit them on behalf of its user, again, through a combination of instruction and observation. The agent can act autonomously, for example acquiring a document it believes its user will want to view and bringing it to the user's attention. It can also carry out instructions, interpreting high-level, user-oriented commands in terms of more specific actions to bring about the desired results.

While single personal agents can certainly provide useful assistance as intelligent intermediaries between users and conventional services, the agent metaphor comes into its own when we provide means of interaction between independent agents, so that the agents themselves form a distributed information system. Many distributed information systems (such as the World Wide Web (Berners-Lee, 1994)) operate on a client-server basis, but it is natural for an agent-based system to be peer-peer. An agent can in general both provide services to other agents and solicit services from them. Broad categories of agents with which personal agents have to interact include:

- *server* agents which act primarily as interfaces to information resources, say;
- *network* agents which provide services related to information transfer (but which may add information value of their own in the process), broking/match-making services; and
- other personal agents.

It is my belief that an important role for personal agents is to support information sharing and other forms of interpersonal cooperation in a flexible way within dynamic and open user communities.

I should say that the mechanism carrying agent-agent interactions is likely to be distinct from those delivering the content services, much as telecommunications systems frequently separate control and data channels. It may be that the current client-server protocols such as the World Wide Web's HTTP protocol act as the content delivery service, and are supplemented by a message service supporting the agent's peer-peer negotiations to agree the desirability and terms of supply of the content (see Figure 7.2).

So the image of an agent-based distributed information system is of a community of peers that provide services to each other on terms which are negotiated to the mutual satisfaction of both agents. The agents evaluate the deals

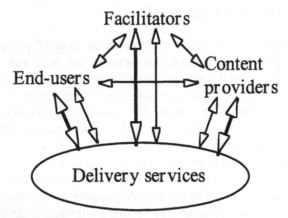

Figure 7.2. Agents represent interested parties

in terms of their own utility functions or the extent to which they contributed to their own goals. For a commercial server agent, the goal may be maximization of the profit to its own organization including optimization of the usage of resources under its control. For a personal agent, the goals may be to:

- provide its user with easy-to-use, timely, and economical access to high-value information (as assessed in the context of that user) while filtering out low-value information; and
- encourage and facilitate (with various degrees of pro-activity) the access of other users to information when it is of value to this agent's user for this to happen.

In many cases it will be of mutual benefit for the agents to assist each other. A good example of this is where agents share their knowledge regarding the location and usefulness of various sources of information (Feynman, 1993). Whether the agents negotiate explicit *quid pro quo* deals, make judgements about the likelihood of reciprocal benefits, or are simply predisposed to help each other unless the requested actions are expensive or prejudicial is debatable.

7.4   Agent-Based Products – A Future History

While there is clearly considerable scope for further research, the current under-standing of intelligent agents and multi-agent systems is sufficiently mature for agent-based products to be developed. We ourselves have built several demon-strator and software prototype systems. Similarly, small computing platforms such as PDAs are now sufficiently powerful to host simple agents. Agents are now poised to make the transition from the research laboratory and speculative popular journalism into the marketplace. Indeed products with the agent label have already started to appear, though purists tend to reject these as not passing the tests of true agenthood. In this section I suggest a sequence of generations of personal agent-based products in the order that they are likely to reach the marketplace.

7.4.1 Automating Actions

Those products currently claiming agenthood tend to automate procedures that normally the user would have to do him or herself. Some are generalizations of the recordable macro, others, such as the agents in IBM's WorkGroup product (Atkinson et al., 1995) are rule-based systems with user-friendly interfaces. Products and prototypes in this class are often aimed at tasks such as automatic categorization and filtering of e-mail, news, etc.

7.4.2 Personal Interface Agents

This generation introduces a degree of genuine autonomy and/or learning capability. The learning may be of the user's habits and characteristics, good sources of selected types of information, etc. A good means of recognizing the semantic content of a document and relating it to the user's interest will be extremely important here. They do not merely execute canned command sequences when triggered by explicitly programmed conditions or user actions, but (to an extent) decide on appropriate courses of action depending on their perceptions of their environment and of the user's long- and short-term goals. These agents may well not communicate with other artificial agents, and their value does not depend on the existence of other compatible agents.

Development of prototype agents in this class is widespread. Perhaps the leading work in this area is being conducted at the MIT Media Labs (see, e.g., (Maes, 1994)). A practical agent product (as opposed to research prototype or demonstrator) must:

- perform a useful task requiring sufficient autonomous behavior to merit using an agent; and
- do so with consistent reliability in all circumstances and without excessively requiring the user to check or confirm actions.

Thus the agent must be able to do things that are not obvious to the user, but are consistent with what the user would do if he or she had the time and knowledge required. The agent must not do things that are contrary to the user's natural way of working or fight against what the user may be trying to achieve independently.

At the current time there are many prototypes which impress by what they can achieve in their 'design case,' but fall short of being fully usable tools by virtue (or should that be vice) of some less than desirable behavior 'off design.' Some genuinely useful agents at the simpler end of the scale are beginning to emerge, however, for example MIT's Remembrance Agent which pro-actively reminds one of relevant documents while one is composing a new document (Rhodes et al., 1996).

7.4.3 Cooperating Personal Agents

The next generation will add to the above an ability to cooperate with other compatible agents, for example to support cooperation between the agent's users. Initially, only agents specifically designed to work together, perhaps produced by the same organizations, will be able to cooperate. The agent communities will be semi-closed, and involve relatively small numbers of agents. This is because issues of building large-scale, open agent systems, standardization, and interoperability have largely not yet been tackled. A simple example of the sort of cooperation that can be useful is the exchange of knowledge of the location of useful documents. Achieving cooperation at this level is already possible.

7.4.4 Ubiquitous Agents

Once the problems of openness/scale and of standardization and interoperability are solved, the way is open to an electronic market mediated and managed by agents. Virtually all 'interested parties' – users, content providers, delivery service providers (e.g., telecommunications companies), and facilitating services – will be represented by agents. These agents will form a dynamic, adaptive, self-organizing, global information system. At this point a critical mass is achieved, and unexpected benefits from synergetic interactions between unrelated agents begin to be observed.

7.4.5 Lift-Off

Things start to get a bit speculative here, but I foresee a situation in which qualitatively new collective properties emerge through a process akin to phase change in physical materials. The dynamic patterns of interaction among the agents become more important than the actions of the agents themselves. In science fiction stories, this is the point where the network becomes sentient and takes over the world. On a more serious note, techniques are needed to encourage beneficial emergent behavior, discourage detrimental behavior, and absolutely forbid pathological behavior. A more likely scenario than the doomsday science fiction one given above is that everything the world has come to rely on simply stops working. I believe current research into systems containing large numbers of very simple agents, artificial life, nonlinear dynamics, and other related subjects can provide important insight.

7.5   Infrastructure, Standardization and Interoperability

As mentioned above, there are factors other than the purely technical that play an important part in agents reaching their full potential. In particular, agent-based products developed by different organizations need to be able to interact in a meaningful way. This section looks briefly at some of the issues involved.

7.5.1 Mobile Agents

Agent systems as currently conceived tend to fall into two broad categories. Firstly, there are the 'mobile' agents such as popularized by the General Magic consortium (White, 1994), which are transmitted from place to place, execute within a secure virtual environment at the remote location to obtain the information sought, then are transmitted back to their home base (see Figure 7.3). Secondly, there are 'static' agents which send declarative messages to each other, often in the form of speech acts (see Figure 7.4). The differences between the two categories should not be over-emphasised, however. Systems employing mobile agents also contain 'static' agents associated with places. The way they dispatch the lighter-weight mobile agents to gather information is analogous to a 'speech act' agent sending a declarative request to a peer containing a high-level description of the information sought. Somewhere in between the two are systems in which agents exchange code fragments, like Java applets.

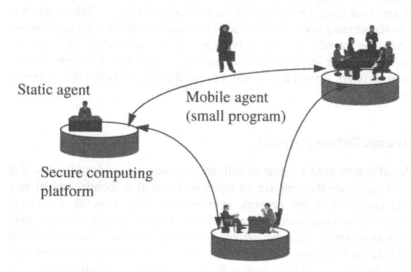

Figure 7.3. Mobile agents

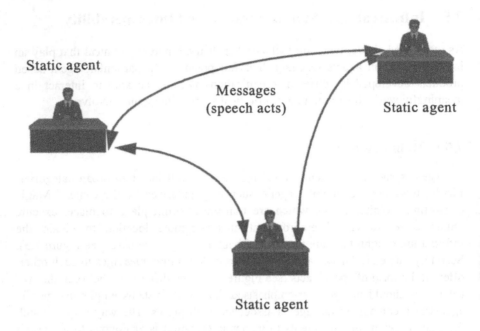

Static agent

Messages
(speech acts)

Static agent

Static agent

Figure 7.4. Static agents

A system using mobile agents requires a common agent execution environment to be used throughout the system (or possibly a small number of compatible ones). Since we are talking about open systems allowing universal access, this requires the emergence of a *de facto* or *de jure* standard. The (relatively) secure execution environments most frequently discussed at the moment as candidate agent platforms are: Java (Sun, 1995), Safe-TCL, and General Magic's TeleScript. It is too early to say whether any of these is likely to become a standard for agent work, though Java has rapidly become established as a widespread platform for distributing code on the Internet. Some recent threads in online discussion forums indicate that there are various moves afoot to meld Java and TeleScript, a trend I find encouraging.

7.5.2 Message Delivery Service

Both styles of system need a means of delivering messages or code to the intended recipient. Many personal agents are on equipment that a) is mobile, and b) may only be in contact with the network intermittently. This requires a message delivery service that operates on a store and forward basis, holding messages until the recipient connects, and that can deliver the message to whichever point on the network the destination agent happens to connect to. The service must work over large geographical areas and must cope with a large number of agents.

7.5.3 Inter-agent Message Language

The language in which speech act messages are expressed also needs to be standardized. Such languages are generally defined in a series of layers. The outer layer specifies the speech act category of the message – whether the body of the message is to be interpreted as a request, a piece of information, etc. In natural language grammatical terms this amounts to an explicit statement of the mood of a sentence. The only candidate standard I am aware of at this level is KQML (Finin, 1994). KQML has a large number of reserved performatives (speech act categories), plus the means of defining others on an application-specific basis. The semantics of performatives is defined in terms of a virtual knowledge base, thus for example the content of the **Tell** performative is in the form of a sentence which is notionally in the sender's knowledge base, though such a knowledge base may not actually exist.

The next layer in is the message content language – in KQML this is the language of the virtual knowledge base. Note that KQML allows applications to use arbitrary content languages, the name of the content language being specified as part of the performative. KQML's 'native' content language is KIF (Genesereth, 1995), a declarative language based on predicate calculus.

The third layer is the ontology, the vocabulary that grounds the abstract grammar of the content language in the real world. It is not practical to define a universal ontology such that all agents can understand all messages about all application domains. Rather, a hierarchy of successively more specific ontologies is required, together with a means for identifying which ontologies a given agent understands. Note that KQML allows an ontology to be named within a performative.

KQML has been widely and successfully used in the building of agent systems. In our own work (e.g., Kearney, 1995; Sehmi et al., 1995) we have used a much simpler set of speech act categories based on the original illocutionary categories proposed by Searle (Searle, 1969; 1974). We relate these to concepts of belief and commitment (Shoham, 1993) rather than to a virtual knowledge base. My personal view is that KQML is not ideal, but is a workable starting point for future discussions. Our own style of message could be adapted to the KQML framework without too much difficulty. I am unsure as to the suitability of KIF as the standard content language, but there is no doubt that this work will contribute useful insight.

A further related issue is the structure of conversations between agents. Whether these be based on social conventions or defined protocols, there needs to be a consistent interpretation of expectations: whether an acknowledgement is required, who initiates the next stage in a negotiation, etc.

7.5.4 Other Issues

Other important issues, particularly for commercial applications include: confidentiality, authentication, secure means of payment, etc. Confidentiality concerns preventing third parties monitoring inter-agent message traffic and other activites of agents, and also circumscribing the accumulation and later use for other purposes of information legitimately obtained during transactions. Encryption techniques can be used to protect message contents, but the fact that there has been traffic between two agents can also be revealing. Authentication concerns the ability to confirm that a message purporting to come from a given agent really did, that it has not been altered along the way, and also that the agent has been given the authority to act on behalf of its owner.

Various means of implementing secure payment are already under investigation, or even being deployed. These range from authorization of credit card payments to schemes involving the electronic equivalent of banknotes and virtual bank accounts. Many believers in freedom of information may object to the introduction of commerce into the global information system. I have sympathy with this view. However, payment supplies an incentive for more people and organizations to make more and better services available. A market mechanism also provides a natural way to balance supply and demand for network resources such as bandwidth, and to discourage profligacy.

7.6 Conclusion

It is likely that agents will play a ubiquitous, pivotal role in the 'Internet of the future.' The huge number and diversity of network-connected items, their volatility, and the variety of services offered mean that a fully decentralized approach will be essential. Rather than imposing an organizational structure from outside, no matter how extensible and flexible it might be, the system needs to be dynamically self-organizing, and this in turn requires a capacity for intelligent behavior associated with each node. To mix contradictory metaphors, intelligent agents are the glue that will hold together the decentralized system of disparate components and also the lubricant that allows it to function smoothly. This chapter has emphasised the role of agent software in personal electronics in mediating between the individual user and the available services.

Before open systems of agents can operate over public networks, a number of infrastructural, interoperability, and standardization issues need to be addressed. Those discussed briefly in this chapter include:

- inter-agent message delivery service;
- secure execution environment for mobile agents and code fragments; and
- inter-agent message language.

An agent standardization initiative called FIPA (Foundation for Intelligent Physical Agents) (Chariglione, 1996) was launched in 1996. This is still in its formative stages, but the areas I have highlighted in this chapter are among those being considered for standardization.

In pursuing the goal of interoperability we must be aware that the study of agents is not a mature subject and techniques are still evolving. I say interoperability here because the goal should not be to enforce uniformity, but to provide a framework in which innovation may flourish. Initial standards must be simple, but designed with the flexibility to be extended in the future. The standards should not lock people in to particular technologies, but allow developers maximum freedom to innovate. Furthermore, evolution of an open market model should go hand-in-hand with the standardization process.

References

Atkinson, B., Brady, S., Gilbert, D., Levine, D., O'Connor, P., Osisek, D., Spagna, R., Wilson, L. (1995) IBM intelligent agents. In: *Proceedings of Unicom Agent Software seminar*, London, April. John Wiley.

Berners-Lee, T., Cailliau, R., Luotonen, A., Nielsen, H. F., Secret, A. (1994) The World Wide Web. *Communications of the ACM*, 37(8), 76–82.

Chariglione, L. (1996) General information on FIPA; http://www.cselt.stet.it/ufv/leonardo/fipa.htm.

Feynman, C. (1993) Nearest neighbor and maximum likelihood methods for social information filtering. MIT Internal Report, December.

Finin, T., Weber, J., Wiederhold, G., Genesereth, M., Fritzson, R., McKay, D., McGuire, J., Pelavin, R., Shapiro, S., Beck, C. (1994) Specification of the KQML agent-communication language (Draft dated February 9th 1994). DARPA Knowledge Sharing Initiative External Interfaces Working Group.

Genesereth, M. R., Fikes, R. E. (1992) Knowledge Interchange Format Version 3.0 Reference Manual. Interlingua Working Group of the DARPA Knowledge Sharing Initiative (see links in http://logic.stanford.edu/kif/).

Gibbins, P. F., Kearney, P. J., Sehmi, A., Smith, R. M. (1994) Intelligent agents in multimedia systems. *Sharp Technical Journal*, 60, December.

Kearney, P. J., Sehmi, A., Smith, R. M. (1994) Emergent behavior in a multi-agent economic simulation. In: A. G. Cohn (Ed.) *Proceedings of 11th European Conference on Artificial Intelligence*, ECAI'94. John Wiley.

Kearney, P. J. (1995) Intelligent agents and personal electronics. In: *Proceedings of Unicom Agent Software seminar*, London, April. John Wiley. Also presented at the IEE Professional Group C10 Colloquium on Developments in Personal Systems, June 1995. Digest No: 1995/140

Maes, P. (1994) Agents that reduce workload and information overload. *Communications of the ACM*, 37(7), July.

Rhodes, B. J., Starner, T. (1996) Remebrance agent: a continuously running automated information retrieval system. In: *Proceedings of the First International Conference on the Practical Application of Intelligent Agents and Multi-Agent Technology* (PAAM96). The Practical Applications Company.

Searle, J. R. (1969) *Speech Acts*. Cambridge University Press.

Searle, J. R. (1975) A taxonomy of illocutionary acts. In: K. Gunderson (Ed.) *Language, Mind and Knowledge*. University of Minnesota Press.

Sehmi, A., Kearney, P. J., Smith, R. M., Gibbins, P. F. (1994) Support for distributed multi-agent systems. In: S. M. Deen (Ed.) CKBS'94: *Proceedings of the Second International Working Conference on Cooperating Knowledge Based Systems*, DAKE Centre, University of Keele.

Shoham, Y. (1993) Agent oriented programming. *Artificial Intelligence*, 60(1).

Sun Microsystems (1995) The Java language: a white paper, available online from http://java.sun.com.

White, J. E. (1994) TeleScript technology: the foundation for the electronic marketplace. General Magic White Paper, General Magic.

part **3**

**Systems and
Their Applications**

8 Rational Software Agents: From Theory to Practice

M. Georgeff and A. Rao
Australian Artificial Intelligence Institute

8.1 Introduction

In today's technological world, computers are increasingly finding application in complex process control, business management, provision of customer service, medical treatment, telecommunications, and so on. These systems often need to carry out quite complex tasks, over some period of time, in a world subject to change and uncertainty. The very scale of an application often prevents complete specification, and even if this could be accomplished, the business and social drivers usually demand changes to the specifications even before the first implementation is rolled out. In the world in which we live, chaos, uncertainty, and change are the norm, not the exception.

Despite this, most designers of complex real-time systems continue to try to apply software technologies and methodologies that were constructed for static, certain, and definable worlds. This invariably leads to huge time and cost overruns, dramatic system failures, and relentless pressure on IT providers to accommodate change and ill-specified functionality.

The Australian Artificial Intelligence Institute's (AAII) focus is on these types of application – dynamic, uncertain, and complex. It aims to investigate and design software architectures suited to these domains and to develop methodologies that allow one to construct systems that can survive uncertainty and change.

To this end, AAII has been conducting research and development on agent-oriented systems (also commonly known as software agents) for the last eight years. Agent-oriented technology is a fundamentally new paradigm for building computer systems that we believe will come to dominate the area of distributed real-time systems.

An agent-oriented system consists of a collection of autonomous software agents (possibly a very large number), each of which responds to events generated by other agents and by the environment in which the agents are situated. Each agent continuously receives perceptual input and, based on its internal state, responds to the environment by taking certain actions that, in turn, affect the environment.

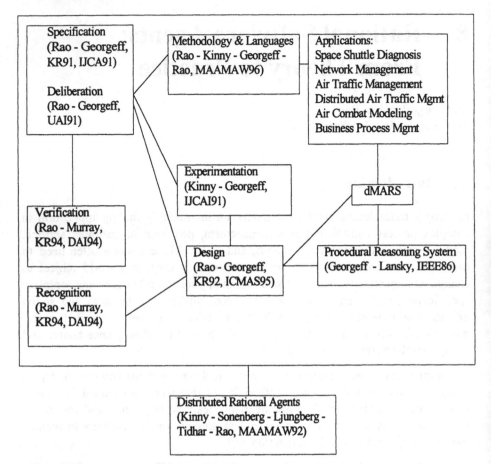

Figure 8.1. Map of AAII research and development

Typically, agents communicate with each other and with the environment using messages. Messages are sent and received asynchronously. No guarantees are given or assumed about the processing of the message once it has reached its recipient.

This design enables each individual agent to be tailored to the subproblem it is solving. It allows for simplicity of design, high robustness, scalability, and fast response to external events.

AAII's research and development work in agent-oriented systems can be divided into three broad categories (see Figure 8.1):

- **Foundations:** This strand of research examines the logical foundations of agent architectures (such as the mental attitudes of beliefs, desires, goals, intentions, plans, commitment, and obligations) and the processes that operate on these mental attitudes (such as deliberation, means-end reasoning, and reconsideration). AAII has actively pursued this area by formalizing various mental attitudes and processes as building-blocks that can be used by others as a framework for extension and refinement.

- **Systems:** This strand involves building tools to assist the design, development, and deployment of software agents. AAII has pioneered the development of agent-oriented systems such as dMARS, a C++ based software development environment for building and testing software agents. The system development effort has been supported by research into areas that bridge the gap between theory and application, such as abstract architectures for building software agents and agent-oriented languages. AAII's agent-oriented technologies have also been continuously refined based on applications that have been built using dMARS as the underlying system.

- **Products and Applications:** This strand involves close interaction with end-users in specific domains – such as air traffic management, business process management, and air-combat modeling – to develop and deploy large-scale agent-oriented applications. AAII has worked with commercial clients to develop application systems targeted for specific problems using dMARS. This has provided important feedback for the further development of dMARS and raised important questions for foundational research.

The success of AAII, both in terms of its fundamental contributions to foundational research and its commercial success in deploying systems for clients, is due to the strong interaction between all the above areas of research and development.

8.2 Agent-Oriented Systems

A number of different approaches have emerged as candidates for the study of agent-oriented systems (Bratman et al., 1988; Doyle, 1992; Rao and Georgeff, 1991a; Rosenschein and Kaelbling, 1986; Shoham, 1993). One such architecture views the system as a rational agent having certain *mental attitudes* of Belief, Desire, and Intention (BDI), representing, respectively, the information, motivational, and deliberative states of the agent. These mental attitudes determine the system's behavior and are critical for achieving adequate or optimal performance when deliberation is subject to resource bounds (Bratman, 1987; Kinny and Georgeff, 1991).

Much work has gone into the formalization (Cohen and Levesque, 1990; Jennings, 1992; Kinny et al., 1994; Rao and Georgeff, 1991a; Singh and Asher, 1990) and implementation (Burmeister and Sundermeyer, 1992; Georgeff and Lansky, 1986; Muller et al., 1995; Shoham, 1993) of BDI-based software agents. However, two main criticisms have been leveled against these endeavors. First, these attitudes are attacked from both directions: classical decision theorists and planning researchers question the necessity of having all three attitudes and researchers from sociology and Distributed Artificial Intelligence critics question the adequacy of these three alone. Second, the utility of studying multi-modal BDI logics, which do not have complete axiomatizations and are not efficiently computable, is questioned by many system builders as having little relevance in practice.

This chapter addresses these two criticisms from the perspectives of the authors' previous work in BDI logics (Rao and Georgeff, 1991a; 1991b; Rao and Georgeff, 1993), systems (Georgeff and Lansky, 1986), and real-world applications (Ingrand et al., 1992; Ljungberg and Lucas, 1992; Rao et al., 1992; Steuart et al., 1996). We argue the necessity (though not the adequacy) of these three attitudes in domains where real-time performance is required from both a quantitative decision-theoretic perspective and a symbolic reasoning perspective. We then show how one can build practical systems by making certain simplifying assumptions and sacrificing some of the expressive power of the theoretical framework. Finally, we describe three implemented agent-oriented systems: an air traffic management system developed for Sydney airport, a business process management system, and an air-combat modeling system.

The primary purpose of this chapter is to provide a unifying framework for this particular type of rational software agent – what we will call a BDI agent – by bringing together various elements of our previous work in theory, systems, and applications. Readers interested primarily in the applications of agent-oriented systems can first read Section 8.7 to better understand the motivations for our approach.

8.3   The System and Its Environment

We first informally establish the necessity of beliefs, desires, and intentions for a system to act appropriately in a class of application domains characterized by various practical limitations and requirements. As typical of such a domain, consider the design of an air traffic management system that is to be responsible for calculating the expected time of arrival (ETA) of aircraft, sequencing them according to certain optimality criteria, reassigning the ETAs according to the optimal sequence, issuing control directives to the pilots to achieve the assigned ETAs, and monitoring conformance.

This and a wide class of other real-time application domains exhibit a number of important characteristics:

1) At any instant of time, there are potentially many different ways in which the environment can evolve (formally, the environment is nondeterministic); e.g., the wind field can change over time in unpredictable ways, as can other parameters such as operating conditions, runway conditions, presence of other aircraft, and so on.

2) At any instant of time, there are potentially many different actions or procedures the system can execute (formally, the system itself is non-deterministic); e.g., the system can take a number of different actions, such as requesting that an aircraft change speed, stretch a flight path, shorten a flight path, hold, and so on.

3) At any instant of time, there are potentially many different objectives that the system is asked to accomplish; e.g., the system can be asked to land aircraft QF001 at time 19:00, land QF003 at 19:01, and maximize runway through-put, not all of which may be simultaneously achievable.

4) The actions or procedures that (best) achieve the various objectives are dependent on the state of the environment (context) and are independent of the internal state of the system; e.g., the actions by which the aircraft achieve their prescribed landing times depend on wind field, operating conditions, other aircraft, and so on, but not on the state of the computational system.

5) The environment can only be sensed locally (i.e., one sensing action is not sufficient for fully determining the state of the entire environment); e.g., the system receives only spot wind data from some aircraft at some times at some locations and thus cannot determine in one sensing operation the entire wind field.

6) The rate at which computations and actions can be carried out is of the same order as the rate at which the environment evolves; e.g., changes in wind field, operational conditions, runway conditions, presence of other aircraft, and so on, can occur during the calculation of an efficient landing sequence and during the period that the aircraft is flying to meet its assigned landing time.

One way of modeling the behavior of such a system, given characteristics (1) and (2), is as a branching tree structure (Emerson, 1990), where each branch in the tree represents an alternative execution path. Each node in the structure represents a certain state of the world, and each transition a primitive action made by the system, a primitive event occurring in the environment, or both.

If we differentiate the actions taken by the system and the events taking place in the environment, the two different types of nondeterminism manifest themselves in two different node types. We call these *decision nodes* and *chance nodes*, representing the options available to the system itself and the uncertainty of the environment, respectively.

In this formal model, we can identify the objectives of the system with particular paths through the tree structure, each labeled with the objective to be realized and, if necessary, the benefit or payoff obtained by traversing this path.

As the system has to *act*, it needs to select appropriate actions or procedures to execute from the various options available to it. The design of such a selection function should enable the system to achieve effectively its primary objectives, given the computational resources available to the system and the characteristics of the environment in which it is situated.

Under the above-mentioned domain characteristics, there are at least two types of input data required by such a selection function. First, given characteristic (4), it is essential that the system have information on the state of the environment. But as this cannot necessarily be determined in one sensing action (characteristics 1 and 5), it is necessary that there be some component of the system that can represent this information and is updated appropriately after each sensing action. We call such a component the system's *beliefs*. This component may be implemented as a variable, a database, a set of logical expressions, or some other data structure. Thus, beliefs can be viewed as the *informative* component of system state.[1]

Second, it is necessary that the system also have information about the objectives to be accomplished or, more generally, what priorities or payoffs are associated with the various current objectives (characteristics 3 and 4). We call this component the system's *desires,* which can be thought of as representing the *motivational* state of the system.[2]

Given this picture, the most developed approach relevant to the design of the selection function is decision theory. However, the decision-theoretic approach does not take into account characteristic (6); namely, that the environment may change in possibly significant and unanticipated ways either (a) during execution of the selection function itself or (b) during the execution of the course of action determined by the selection function.

The possibility of the first situation arising can be reduced by using a faster (and thus perhaps less optimal) selection function, as there is then less risk of a significant event occurring during computation.

Interestingly, to the second possibility, classical decision theory and classical computer science provide quite different answers: decision theory demands that one re-apply the selection function in the changed environment; whereas standard computer programs, once initiated, expect to execute to completion without any reassessment of their utility.

---

[1] We distinguish beliefs from the notion of knowledge, as defined for example in the literature on distributed computing, as the system beliefs are only required to provide information on the likely state of the environment; e.g., certain assumptions may be implicit in the implementation but sometimes violated in practice, such as assumptions about accuracy of sensors, or rate of change of certain environmental conditions.

[2] We distinguish desires from goals as they are defined, for example, in the AI literature in that they may be many at any instant of time and may be mutually incompatible.

Given characteristic (6), neither approach is satisfactory. Re-application of the selection function increases substantially the risk that significant changes will occur during this calculation and also consumes time that may be better spent in acting to achieve the given objectives. On the other hand, execution of any course of action to completion increases the risk that a significant change will occur during this execution, the system thus failing to achieve the intended objective or to realize the expected utility.

We seem caught on the horns of a dilemma: reconsidering the choice of action at each step is potentially too expensive and the chosen action possibly invalid, whereas unconditional commitment to the chosen course of action can result in the system failing to achieve its objectives. However, by adopting an appropriate commitment strategy,[3] it is possible to limit the frequency of reconsideration and thus achieve an appropriate balance between too much reconsideration and not enough (Kinny and Georgeff, 1991). For this to work, it is necessary to include a component of system state to represent the currently chosen course of action; that is, the output of the most recent call to the selection function. We call this additional state component the system's *intentions*. In essence, the intentions of the system capture the *deliberative* component of the system.

8.4   Decision Trees to Possible Worlds

While in the previous section we talked abstractly about the belief, desire, and intention components of the system state, in this section we develop a theory for describing those components in a propositional form. We begin with classical decision theory and show how we can view such a theory within a framework that is closer to traditional epistemic models of belief and agency. In later sections, we will show how this model can then be used to specify and implement systems with the characteristics described above.

Informally, a decision tree consists of decision nodes, chance nodes, and terminal nodes, and includes a probability function that maps chance nodes to real-valued probabilities (including conditional probabilities) and a payoff function that maps terminal nodes to real numbers. A deliberation function, such as *maximin* or *maximizing expected utility*, is then defined for choosing one or more best sequences of actions to perform at a given node.

We can, however, transform such a decision tree, and appropriate deliberation functions, to an equivalent model that represents beliefs, desires, and intentions as separate accessibility relations over sets of possible worlds. This transformation

---

[3]That is, a rule, procedure, or protocol specifying under what recognizable conditions the commitment is maintained or terminated.

provides an alternative basis for cases in which we have insufficient information on probabilities and payoffs and, perhaps more importantly, for handling the dynamic aspects of the problem domain.

We begin by considering a *full* decision tree, in which every possible path is represented (including those with zero payoffs). Given such a decision tree, we start from the root node and traverse each arc. For each unique state labeled on an arc emanating from a chance node, we create a new decision tree that is identical to the original tree except that (a) the chance node is removed and (b) the arc incident on the chance node is connected to the successor of the chance node. This process is carried out recursively until there are no chance nodes left. This yields a set of decision trees, each consisting of only decision nodes and terminal nodes, and each corresponding to a different possible state of the environment. That is, from a traditional possible-worlds perspective, each of these decision trees represents a different possible world with different probability of occurrence. Finally, the payoff function is assigned to paths in a straightforward way. The algorithm for this transformation can be found elsewhere (Rao and Georgeff, 1991c).

The resulting possible-worlds model contains two types of information, represented by the probabilities across worlds and the payoffs assigned to paths. We now split these out into two accessibility relations, the probabilities being represented in the belief-accessibility relation and the payoffs in the desire-accessibility relation. The sets of tree structures defined by these relations are identical, although without loss of generality we could delete from the desire-accessible worlds all paths with zero payoffs.

Given a decision tree and the above transformation, an agent can now make use of the chosen deliberation function to decide the best course(s) of action. We can formally represent this/these selected path(s) in the decision tree using a third accessibility relation on possible worlds, corresponding to the intentions of the agent. In essence, for each desire-accessible world, there exists a corresponding intention-accessible world which contains only the best course(s) of action as determined by the appropriate deliberation function.

Thus, our possible-worlds model consists of a set of possible worlds where each possible world is a tree structure. A particular index within a possible world is called a *situation*. With each situation we associate a set of *belief-accessible* worlds, *desire-accessible worlds*, and *intention-accessible worlds*; intuitively, those worlds that the agent *believes* to be possible, *desires* to bring about; and *intends* to bring about, respectively.

8.5 BDI Logics

The above transformation provides the basis for developing a logical theory for deliberation by agents that is compatible with quantitative decision theory in those cases where we have good estimates for probabilities and payoffs. However, it does not address the case in which we do not have such estimates, nor does it address the dynamic aspects of deliberation, particularly those concerning commitment to previous decisions.

We begin by abstracting the model given above to reduce probabilities and payoffs to dichotomous (0–1) values. That is, we consider propositions to be either believed or not believed, desired or not desired, and intended or not intended, rather than ascribing continuous measures to them. Within such a framework, we first look at the static properties we would want of BDI systems and next their dynamic properties.

The axiomatization for beliefs that we adopt is the standard weak-S5 (or KD45) modal system. We adopt the D and K axioms for desires and intentions; i.e., desires and intentions have to be closed under implication and have to be consistent. We also have the inference rule of necessitation for beliefs, desires, and intentions.

A number of researchers have proposed their preferred axiomatizations capturing the relationships between beliefs, desires, and intentions. However, in other work (Rao and Georgeff, 1991a) we depart from this approach and give a comprehensive family of BDI logics similar in tradition to that of modal logic systems (i.e., KD45 system, S4 system, etc.). The reason for this departure is that we do not believe that there need be a unique and correct axiomatization that covers all interesting BDI agents – one may want to model different types of agents for different purposes.

Static Constraints: The static relationships among the belief-, desire-, and intention-accessible worlds can be examined along two different dimensions, one with respect to the *sets* of possible worlds and the other with respect to the *structure* of the possible worlds. Given two relations four different relationships are possible between them: one being a subset of the other and vice versa, and their intersections being null or non-null. Similarly, as each possible world is a time tree, there are four possible structural relationships that can hold between any pair of worlds: one could be a subworld of the other or vice versa, or the worlds could be identical or incomparable.

Now we can combine the set and structural relationships of the belief, desire, and intention worlds to obtain twelve different BDI systems. Some of these relationships and axiomatizations can be derived from the others. Three of the above relationships and axiomatizations have been considered before under the terms *realism* (Cohen and Levesque, 1990) (if an agent believes a proposition, it will desire it), *strong realism* (Rao and Georgeff, 1991a) (if an agent desires to achieve a proposition, it will believe the proposition to be an option) and *weak realism* (Rao and Georgeff, 1991b) (if an agent desires to achieve a proposition, it will not believe the negation of the proposition to be inevitable).

The choice of BDI system depends also on which other properties are desired of the agent. For example, a number of researchers have proposed requirements concerning the asymmetry between beliefs and other attitudes (Bratman, 1987; Rao and Georgeff, 1991b) and consequential closure principles (Cohen and Levesque, 1990). The first requires that rational agents maintain consistency between their beliefs, desires, and intentions, but not completeness. The second requires that the beliefs, desires, and intentions of an agent must not be closed under the implications of the other attitudes. All the above properties are satisfied by a BDI system in which the pairwise intersections of the belief-, desire-, and intention-accessible worlds are non-null. Other BDI systems in which intention-accessible worlds are subworlds of desire-accessible worlds, which are subworlds of belief-accessible worlds satisfy some, but not all of these properties.

Dynamic Constraints: As discussed earlier, an important aspect of a BDI architecture is the notion of *commitment* to previous decisions. A commitment embodies the balance between the reactivity and goal-directedness of an agent-oriented system. In a continuously changing environment, commitment lends a certain sense of stability to the reasoning process of an agent. This results in savings in computational effort and hence better overall performance (Bratman, 1987; Kinny and Georgeff, 1991; Rao and Georgeff, 1991a).

A commitment usually has two parts to it: one is the condition that the agent is committed to maintain, called the *commitment condition*, and the second is the condition under which the agent gives up the commitment, called the *termination condition*. As the agent has no direct control over its beliefs and desires, there is no way that it can adopt or effectively realize a commitment strategy over these attitudes. However, an agent can choose what to do with its intentions. Thus, we restrict the commitment condition to intentions. An agent can commit to an intention based on the object of the intention being fulfilled in one future path or all future paths leading to different commitment conditions and hence different dynamic behaviors.

Different termination conditions result in further variations in behavior (Rao and Georgeff, 1991a; Rao and Georgeff, 1995; Georgeff and Rao, 1995). For example, we can define a *blindly-committed* agent which denies any changes to its beliefs or desires that would conflict with its commitments; a *single-minded* agent which entertains changes to beliefs and will drop its commitments accordingly; and an *open-minded* agent which allows changes in both its beliefs and desires that will force its commitments to be dropped.

The various forms of termination and commitment can be expressed as axioms of our logic, and semantic constraints can be placed on the dynamic evolution of the accessibility relations. As before, rather than claiming that one particular commitment strategy is *the* right strategy, we allow the user to tailor them according to the application.

The purpose of the above formalization is to build formally verifiable and practical systems. If for a given application domain, we know how the environment changes and the behaviors expected of the system, we can use such a formalization to specify, design, and verify agents that, when placed in such an environment, will exhibit all and only the desired behaviors. Elsewhere (Rao and Georgeff, 1993) we have described how to verify certain behaviors of agents based on their static constraints and their commitment strategies using a model-checking approach. In the next section, we turn to the task of building a practical system based on the above theory.

8.6 Abstract Architecture

While it is not necessary that a system that is specified in terms of beliefs, desires, and intentions be designed with identifiable data structures corresponding to each of these components, the architecture we propose below is based on such a correspondence. The rationale for such a design is that the identification of beliefs, desires, and intentions is useful when the system must communicate with humans or other software agents and can be expected to simplify the building, maintenance, and verification of application systems.

On the other hand, the architecture cannot be simply based on a traditional theorem-proving system, even if extended to handle the temporal, epistemic, and nondeterministic elements of the logic described above. The reason for this is that the time taken to reason in this way, and thus the time taken to act, is potentially unbounded, thereby destroying the reactivity that is essential to an agent's survival. Thus, although we could use a theorem prover to reason 'off-line' about the behavior of an agent-based system, we cannot directly use such a theorem prover to implement the system itself.

The abstract architecture we propose comprises three dynamic data structures representing the agent's beliefs, desires, and intentions, together with an input queue of events. We allow update and query operations on the three data structures. The update operations on beliefs, desires, and intentions are subject to respective compatibility requirements. These functions are critical in enforcing the formalized constraints upon the agent's mental attitudes as described before. The events the system can recognize include both external events and internal events. We assume that the events are atomic and are recognized after they have occurred. Similarly, the outputs of the agent – actions – are also assumed to be atomic. The main interpreter loop is given below. We assume that the event queue, belief, desire, and intention structures are global.

BDI-interpreter
initialize-state()
repeat
    options := option-generator(event-queue);
    selected-options := deliberate(options);
    update-intentions(selected-options);
    execute();
    get-new-external-events();
    drop-successful-attitudes();
    drop-impossible-attitudes();
end repeat

At the beginning of every cycle, the option generator reads the event queue and returns a list of options. Next, the deliberator selects a subset of options to be adopted and adds these to the intention structure. If there is an intention to perform an atomic action at this point in time, the agent then executes it. Any external events that have occurred during the interpreter cycle are then added to the event queue. Internal events are added as they occur. Next, the agent modifies the intention and desire structures by dropping all successful desires and satisfied intentions, as well as impossible desires and unrealizable intentions.

This abstract architecture is an idealization that faithfully captures the theory, including the various components of practical reasoning (Bratman, 1987); namely, option generation, deliberation, execution, and intention handling. However, it is not a practical system for rational reasoning. The architecture is based on a (logically) closed set of beliefs, desires, and intentions and the provability procedures required are not computable. Moreover, we have given no indication of how the option generator and deliberation procedures can be made sufficiently fast to satisfy the real-time demands placed upon the system.

We therefore make a number of important choices of representation which, while constraining expressive power, provide a more practical system for rational reasoning. The system we present below is a simplified version of the Procedural Reasoning System (PRS) (Georgeff-Lansky, 1986; Ingrand et al., 1992), one of the first implemented agent-oriented systems based on the BDI architecture, and a successor system, dMARS.

First, we explicitly represent only beliefs about the *current* state of the world and consider only ground sets of literals with no disjunctions or implications. Intuitively, these represent beliefs that are currently held, but which can be expected to change over time.

Second, we represent the information about the means of achieving certain future world states and the options available to the agent as *plans*, which can be viewed as a special form of belief (Rao and Georgeff, 1992). Intuitively, plans are abstract specifications of both the means for achieving certain desires and the options available to the agent. Each plan has a *body* describing the primitive actions or subgoals that have to be achieved for plan execution to be successful. The conditions under which a plan can be chosen as an option are specified by an *invocation event* and a *context condition*; the invocation event specifies the 'triggering' event that is necessary for invocation of the plan, and the context condition specifies the situation that must hold for the plan to be executable.

Third, each intention that the system forms by adopting certain plans of action is represented implicitly using a conventional run-time stack of hierarchically related plans (similar to how a Prolog interpreter handles clauses).[4] Multiple intention stacks can coexist, either running in parallel, suspended until some condition occurs, or ordered for execution in some way.

The main interpreter loop for this system is identical to the one discussed previously. However, as the system is embedded in a dynamic environment, the procedures appearing in the interpreter must be fast enough to satisfy the real-time demands placed upon the system. One way of tailoring and thus improving the process of option generation is to insert an additional procedure to delay posting events regarding any changes to the intention structure until the end of the interpreter loop. By posting appropriate events to the event queue in this way, the procedure can determine, among other things, which changes to the intention structure will be noticed by the option generator. In this way, one can model various notions of commitment that result in different behaviors of the agent (Rao and Georgeff, 1992).

A number of systems have been implemented using the BDI architecture. Some of them include COSY (Burmeister and Sundermeyer, 1992), INTERRAP (Muller et al., 1995), and GRATE (Jennings, 1993).

8.7 Applications

In this section, we consider three different applications: an air traffic management system, a business process management system, and an air-combat modeling system.

8.7.1 Air Traffic Management

Air traffic worldwide continues to grow, particularly as the economies of the developing countries gather momentum. The direct and indirect costs attributable to air traffic congestion are already enormous, and are predicted to rise to US$10

---

[4]This is an efficient way of capturing all the paths of intention-accessible worlds. In other words, the interpreter does a lazy generation of all possible sequences of actions that it can intend from the plan library.

billion in Europe alone. The challenge is to match the demand with the available capacity.

To assist in solving this problem, AAII has developed a prototype air traffic management system aimed at achieving more efficient utilization of the existing air traffic control infrastructure and relieving air traffic controllers of their extremely high workload. The system, known as OASIS, manages the flow of aircraft arriving at an airport, thus providing significant capacity gains at relatively low cost.

OASIS accurately calculates estimated landing times, determines the sequence of aircraft to land giving the least total delay, and advises air traffic controllers of appropriate control actions to achieve this sequence. It also monitors and compares actual progress of aircraft against the established sequence, and notifies the air traffic controller of significant differences and appropriate action to correct the situation. OASIS is designed to be responsive to sudden changes in environmental conditions (such as meteorological conditions or runway configuration) and changes in user objectives (such as aircraft operational emergencies or requirements).

OASIS gives the air traffic controller more time to concentrate on evaluating alternative control actions. The controller can manually reserve slots in the sequence and, if necessary, issue instructions other than those recommended by OASIS. In this way, the system improves runway utilization and air traffic management, avoiding the inflexibility that accompanies fully automated systems.

In designing a system to fulfill these functions, a number of requirements had to be met. First, the system must predict when an aircraft can be at the runway, considering past performance of that aircraft, its expected future performance, and the winds aloft. It must sequence each incoming aircraft into a landing order that maximizes the utilization of the runway resource. The sequence must be produced in a timely manner, and must be continuously updated to reflect the current, changing, situation.

Once a landing time has been assigned to an aircraft, appropriate controls and instructions for achieving that time must be determined. The appropriateness and effectiveness of instructions depend on the aircraft's position. For example, airborne holding is only appropriate before the aircraft has passed the last holding point, after which only speed instructions and path shortening or stretching can be used. The system should be capable of offering multiple alternative recommendations to the air traffic controller, and must allow its advice to be overridden.

When an aircraft has been instructed to reduce speed or speed up to achieve a particular landing time, the system must monitor progress towards achievement of the intended landing time. It must also react to changes in the environment, e.g., changes in wind direction, and must carry out prolonged chains of goal-directed reasoning, e.g., generating a set of instructions for achieving a landing time. It needs to balance the need for reactivity with this goal-directed behavior.

To satisfy these requirements, an agent-oriented approach was adopted. The system's flexibility results from this co-operative problem solving approach.

The OASIS architecture involves subdividing the air traffic management task into its major parts and designing separate agents to solve each of those sub-problems. Each agent solves its part of the task independently, and co-operates with the others to produce the overall system behavior.

An OASIS implementation comprises one aircraft agent for each arriving aircraft and a number of global agents, including a sequencer, wind modeler, coordinator, and trajectory checker. At any particular time, the system will comprise up to seventy or eighty agents running concurrently, sequencing and giving control directives to flow controllers on a real-time basis. The aircraft agents are responsible for flying the aircraft and the global agents are responsible for the overall sequencing and coordination of the aircraft agents. A detailed description of the system can be found elsewhere (Ljungberg and Lucas, 1992).

Modeling: An aircraft agent is responsible for flying along a certain flight path given by the coordinates of a sequence of waypoints. An example of the chance or uncertainty in the domain is the wind field. If this were the only environmental variable, for each value of the wind velocity at a particular waypoint we would have a corresponding belief-accessible world. The choices available to an aircraft agent include flying along various trajectories between its minimum speed and maximum speed and at an altitude between its minimum and maximum altitude. This can be represented by multiple branches in each of the belief-accessible worlds mentioned above. As the final waypoint is the destination airport, the paths desired by the aircraft agent are those paths where the calculated ETA of the end node is equal to the desired ETA. The desire-accessible worlds can be obtained from the belief-accessible worlds by pruning those paths that do not satisfy the above condition. The intention-accessible worlds can be obtained from the desire-accessible paths by retaining only those that are the best with respect to fuel consumption, aircraft performance, and so on.

Decision Theory and Commitment: The primary objective of the sequencer is to land all aircraft safely and in an optimal sequence. Given the performance characteristics of aircraft, desired separation between aircraft, wind field, runway assignment, and a cost function, the sequencing agent uses a number of different deliberation strategies to compute the best arrival sequence for aircraft and their respective ETAs. On determining a particular schedule, the scheduling agent then single-mindedly commits to the intention; in other words, the scheduling agent will stay committed until (a) it believes that all aircraft have landed in the given sequence or (b) it does not believe that there is a possibility that the next aircraft will meet its assigned ETA. Note that this is not the classical decision-theoretic

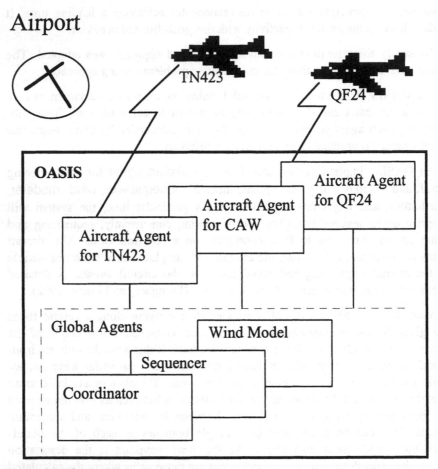

Figure 8.2. The OASIS agent architecture

viewpoint – any change in wind field, for example, should, in that view, cause a recalculation of the entire sequence, even if all aircraft could still meet their assigned ETAs.

Abstract Interpreter: In the implemented version of OASIS, each agent in the system deals only with current beliefs and desires and the options available to the agent to achieve its desires are written as plans. For example, although there may be many different ways of achieving the desired ETA (e.g., flying low at full speed), the plans of the aircraft agents only include as options those trajectories that are maximally fuel efficient.

OASIS was developed using SRI International's Procedural Reasoning System (PRS) as the agent architecture. It can handle in excess of one hundred aircraft agents, each interacting with the various scheduling and coordination agents. The prototype system successfully completed operational tests at Sydney airport in 1995.

AAII is currently developing a commercial version of the Sydney-based prototype system, called HORIZON. HORIZON is based on dMARS and will be suitable for installation at a wide variety of airports. The initial release of this product is expected in late 1997.

8.7.2 Business Process Management

SPOC (Single Point of Contact) is a system developed for Optus Communications (Australia) to assist Customer Service Representatives (CSRs) meet their objective of answering 98% of all customer enquiries at the first point of contact. The system is designed to guide the CSRs through various customer-focused work processes by transparently managing and integrating a large number of product- and function-based legacy applications and data sources.

The SPOC application consists of three major subsystems:

- the presentation subsystem that manages the CSRs GUI screens;
- the reasoning subsystem that guides the CSRs through complex work processes; and
- the infrastructure subsystem that provides a uniform logical access to business objects across the entire organization.

dMARS forms the core of the reasoning subsystem. It is based on a layered architecture with three layers, namely:

- the *system layer*, which consists of a number of system-level agents that maintain the system-level run-time configuration status and implement the particular protocols needed for interacting with back-end services;
- the *team layer*, which consists of team agents that handle the creation and deletion of agents at the user level and maintain team-level performance statistics; and
- the *user layer*, which consists of user agents that handle the work processes for each user and the discourse with the CSR.

The distributed layered architecture facilitates robustness and scalability. The division of agents into those that handle front-end, back-end, and core processes provides modularity of the business processes and assists reuse in different environments (e.g., different customer channels, such as the Internet).

The system is currently being rolled out into the operational environment at Optus. When fully operational, the system will be assisting around 1200 SRs; in this configuration SPOC will be running over 4000 BDI agents on multiple machines.

8.7.3 Air-Combat Modeling

SWARMM (Rao et al., 1992; Steuart et al., 1996) is an air-combat modeling system that allows defense analysts to encode the tactics adopted by pilots in beyond-visual-range (BVR) combat scenarios and build fully-automated surrogate pilot agents that can then participate with real human pilots in simulation studies. The system models both the physical aspects of the aircraft – its performance characteristics, weapons, and sensors, as well as the tactical knowledge and reasoning of the pilot.

The system architecture consists of three subsystems:

- a sophisticated 3D graphics subsystem running on Silicon Graphics that provides a view of all the surrogate pilots from any perspective;
- a physical simulation subsystem that has sophisticated models for different types of aircraft, weapons, sensors, etc., written in Fortran; and
- a pilot reasoning subsystem running on dMARS that models the tactics, reasoning, coordination, and synchronization behavior of pilots.

SWARMM has been designed to scale up to an arbitrary number of surrogate pilots in BVR scenarios. It was deployed in mid-1996 and is currently being used by the Royal Australian Air Force for operational and performance analysis studies involving up to 64 surrogate pilots (32 on each side).

8.7.4 Essential Features

In addition to the above applications, PRS and dMARS have been used in a number of other large-scale applications, including a system for Space Shuttle diagnosis (Ingrand et al., 1992) and telecommunications network management (Ingrand et al., 1992). Others have also used BDI agents to implement real-world applications (Jennings, 1995). These experiences lead us to the firm conviction that the BDI approach is particularly useful for building complex distributed systems involving resource-bounded decision-making.

The essential characteristics which have contributed to the success of our approach can be summarized as follows:

- The ability to construct plans that can react to *specific situations*, can be invoked based on their *purpose*, and are *sensitive to the context* of their invocation facilitates *modular* and *incremental development*. It allows users to concentrate on writing plans for a subset of essential situations and construct plans for more specific situations as they debug the system. As plans are invoked either in response to particular situations or based on their purpose, the incremental addition of plans does not require modification to other existing plans.

- The *balance* between *reactive* and *goal-directed behavior* is achieved by committing to plans and periodically reconsidering such committed plans. The management of such real-time and concurrent activities is done by the system, while still giving the user control in terms of specifying to the system how the balance is to be achieved. As a result, end-users need not be involved in complex low-level programming (a difficult and error-prone activity, even for systems programmers), leading to a *reliable* system.

- The *high-level* representational and programming language has meant that end-users can encode their knowledge directly in terms of basic mental attitudes without needing to master the programming constructs of a low-level language. This has led to *greater flexibility* and *shorter development cycles*. For example, in SWARMM, the use of dMARS plans to represent pilot tactics (instead of a table of condition-action rules as in the earlier simulation system), reduced the average turn-around time for changes to tactics from two months to less than a day.

8.8 Comparison and Conclusion

The BDI architecture draws its inspiration from the philosophical theories of Bratman (Bratman, 1987), who argues that intentions play a significant and distinct role in practical reasoning and cannot be reduced to beliefs and desires. Cohen and Levesque (1990) provided one of the first logical formalizations of intentions and the notion of commitment. Later formalizations include the representationalist theory by Konolige and Pollack (1993) and the work by Singh and Asher (1990).

While the earlier formalisms present a particular set of semantic constraints or axioms as being *the* formalization of a BDI agent, we adopt the view that one should be able to choose an appropriate BDI system for an application based on the rational behaviors required for that application. As a result, following the modal logic tradition, we have discussed how one can categorize different combinations of interactions among beliefs, desires, and intentions.

A number of agent-oriented systems have been built in the past few years (Burmeister and Sundermeyer, 1992; Georgeff and Lansky, 1986; Muller et al., 1995; Shoham, 1993). While many of these appear interesting and have different strengths and weaknesses, none has yet been applied to as wide a class of complex applications as the ones discussed in this chapter.

Currently, there is very little work on bridging the gap among theory, systems, and applications. The work by Bratman (Bratman et al., 1988) describes the different modules of a BDI architecture and discusses the philosophical foundations for each of these modules. However, compared to our abstract interpreter, this model is at a higher level of abstraction and is not useful as a practical system. More recent work by Fisher (Fisher, 1994) on Concurrent Metatem specifies agent behaviors as temporal logic specifications that are directly executed by the system.

However, for applications in which the environment changes at rates comparable with the calculation cycle of the system, such theorem provers are unsuited as system implementations.

The primary contribution of this chapter is in integrating the various aspects of BDI agent research – theoretical foundations from both a quantitative decision-theoretic perspective and a symbolic rational agency perspective, system implementation from an ideal theoretical perspective to a more practical perspective, and applications that rely on the theoretical foundations and are implemented using a practical BDI architecture.

Acknowledgements

This research was supported by the Co-operative Research Center for Intelligent Decision Systems under the Australian Government's Co-operative Research Centers Program. An earlier version of this chapter appeared as 'BDI agents: from theory to practice' in *Proceedings of the First International Conference on Multi-Agent Systems (ICMAS-95)*, 1995.

References

Bratman, M. E., Israel, D., Pollack, M. E. (1988) Plans and resource-bounded practical reasoning. *Computational Intelligence*, 4, 349–355.

Bratman, M. E. (1987) *Intentions, Plans, and Practical Reason*. Harvard University Press, Cambridge, MA.

Burmeister, B., Sundermeyer, K. (1992) Co-operative problem-solving guided by intentions and perception. In: E. Werner, Y. Demazeau (Eds.) *Decentralized AI*, 3. North-Holland, Amsterdam, The Netherlands.

Cohen, P. R., Levesque, H. J. (1990) Intention is choice with commitment. *Artificial Intelligence*, 42(3).

Doyle, J. (1992) Rationality and its roles in reasoning. *Computational Intelligence*, 8(2), 376–409.

Emerson, E. A. (1990) Temporal and modal logic. In: J. van Leeuwen (Ed.) *Handbook of Theoretical Computer Science: Volume B, Formal Models and Semantics*, 995–1072. Elsevier Science Publishers and MIT Press, Amsterdam and Cambridge, MA.

Fisher, M. (1994) Representing and executing agent-based systems. In: *Intelligent Agents: Theories, Architectures, and Languages*, Lecture Notes in Artificial Intelligence 890. Springer-Verlag, Berlin.

Georgeff, M. P., Lansky, A. L. (1986) Procedural knowledge. In: *Proceedings of the IEEE Special Issue on Knowledge Representation*, 74, 1383–1398.

Georgeff, M. P., Rao, A. S. (1995) The semantics of intention maintenance for rational agents. In: *Proceedings of the Fourteenth International Joint Conference on Artificial Intelligence* (IJCAI-95), Montreal, Canada.

Ingrand, F. F., Georgeff, M. P., Rao, A. S. (1992) An architecture for real-time reasoning and system control. *IEEE Expert*, 7(6).

Jennings, N. R. (1992) On being responsible. In: Y. Demazeau, E. Werner (Eds.) *Decentralized AI*, 3. North-Holland, Amsterdam, The Netherlands.

Jennings, N. R. (1993) Specification and implementation of belief, desire, joint-intention architecture for collaborative problem solving. *Journal of Intelligent and Cooperative Information Systems*, 2(3), 289–318.

Jennings, N. R. (1995) Controlling co-operative problem solving in industrial multi-agent systems using joint intentions. *Artificial Intelligence*, 74(2).

Kinny, D. N., Georgeff, M. P. (1991) Commitment and effectiveness of situated agents. In: *Proceedings of the Twelfth International Joint Conference on Artificial Intelligence (IJCAI-91)*, 82–88, Sydney, Australia.

Kinny, D., Ljungberg, M., Rao, A. S., Sonenberg, E. A., Tidhar, G., Werner, E. (1994) Planned team activity. In: *Artificial Social Systems*, Lecture Notes in Artificial Intelligence (LNAI-830). Springer-Verlag, Berlin.

Konolige, K., Pollack, M. (1993) A representationalist theory of intention. In: *Proceedings of the Thirteenth International Joint Conference on Artificial Intelligence (IJCAI-93)*, Chamberey, France.

Ljungberg, M., Lucas, A. (1992) The OASIS air traffic management system. In: *Proceedings of the Second Pacific Rim International Conference on Artificial Intelligence, PRICAI'92*, Seoul, Korea.

Muller, J. P., Pischel, M., Thiel, M. (1995) Modeling reactive behavior in vertically layered agent architectures. In: *Intelligent Agents: Theories, Architectures, and Languages*, Lecture Notes in Artificial Intelligence 890. Springer-Verlag, Berlin.

Rao, A. S., Georgeff, M. P. (1991a) Modeling rational agents within a BDI-architecture. In: J. Allen, R. Fikes, E. Sandewall (Eds.) *Proceedings of the Second International Conference on Principles of Knowledge Representation and Reasoning*. Morgan Kaufmann Publishers, San Mateo, CA.

Rao, A. S., Georgeff, M. P. (1991b) Asymmetry thesis and side-effect problems in linear time and branching time intention logics. In: *Proceedings of the Twelfth International Joint Conference on Artificial Intelligence* (IJCAI-91), Sydney, Australia.

Rao, A. S., Georgeff, M. P. (1991c) Deliberation and its role in the formation of intentions. In: *Proceedings of the Seventh Conference on Uncertainty in Artificial Intelligence* (UAI-91). Morgan Kaufmann Publishers, San Mateo, CA.

Rao, A. S. and Georgeff, M. P. (1992) An abstract architecture for rational agents. In: C. Rich, W. Swartout, B. Nebel (Eds.) *Proceedings of the Third International Conference on Principles of Knowledge Representation and Reasoning*. Morgan Kaufmann Publishers, San Mateo, CA.

Rao, A. S., Georgeff, M. P. (1993) A model-theoretic approach to the verification of situated reasoning systems. In: *Proceedings of the Thirteenth International Joint Conference on Artificial Intelligence* (IJCAI-93), Chamberey, France.

Rao, A. S., Morley, D., Selvestrel, M., Murray, G. (1992) Representation, selection, and execution of team tactics in air combat modelling. In: A. Adams, L. Sterling (Eds.) *Proceedings of the 5th Australian Joint Conference on Artificial Intelligence,* 185–190, World Scientific, November.

Rosenschein, S. J., Kaelbling, L. P. (1986) The synthesis of digital machines with provable epistemic properties. In: J. Y. Halpern (Ed.) *Proceedings of the First Conference on Theoretical Aspects of Reasoning about Knowledge,* San Mateo, CA. Morgan Kaufmann Publishers.

Shoham, Y. (1993) Agent-oriented programming. *Artificial Intelligence,* 60(1), 51–92.

Singh, M., Asher, N. (1990) Towards a formal theory of intentions. In: J. van Eijck (Ed.) *Logics in AI,* Lecture Notes in Artificial Intelligence 478, 472–486. Springer-Verlag, Berlin.

Steuart, S., Murray, G., Tidhar, G., Rao, A. S. (1996) Air mission modeling – an application of artificial intelligence. In: *Proceedings of the First International Simtect Conference,* Melbourne, Australia.

9   Agent-Oriented Techniques for Traffic and Manufacturing Applications: Progress Report

B. Burmeister, S. Bussmann, A. Haddadi, and K. Sundermeyer
Daimler-Benz Research Systems Technology

9.1   Our View of Agent Technology

We view agent-oriented techniques (AOT) as a further development of techniques in object-oriented systems and distributed systems.

- AOT *extend* object-oriented techniques in that the analysis, design, and realization of complex systems are performed on a higher level of abstraction, and in that agents are active, concurrent objects, collectively embedded in a 'society.' Furthermore, agents are a *specialization* of objects in that the internal states of objects are typed by intentional states, for example, and in that messages exchanged among agents are classified by message types (Shoham, 1993).
- AOT can lean upon techniques provided by distributed systems (like sharing resources and synchronization), but they complement these techniques by making subsystems more autonomous and enabling them to co-ordinate their activities actively instead of being co-ordinated by design.

According to this view, there are four ingredients considered as being essential to agents, namely internal/mental states, message types in communication, protocols for co-operation and co-ordination, and roles within organizations. As for mental states, we follow an operational approach which relates the internal states of an agent to its intentionality, especially to notions like beliefs, desires, and intentions (Haddadi and Sundermeyer, 1995).

We foresee a rather broad potential for AOT: Agents might be considered at a conceptual, descriptive, or operational level. AOT can be used for the analysis and design of complex systems, for simulation and planning purposes, for enhancing the autonomy of single systems components, and for realizing new system solutions. AOT are expected to have a significant impact in problem domains where the problem is functionally or geographically distributed into autonomous sub-systems, where the subsystems are situated in a dynamic environment, and where the subsystems have to interact more flexibly. The benefits one gains from AOT are (i) reduction of complexity in systems design due to the concise and natural modeling of the problem domain, and (ii) enhanced robustness and adaptivity due to self-organization of the subsystems.

Research on AOT at Daimler-Benz started in the project COSY with the aim of establishing a methodology for multi-agent systems, in particular, investigating general control and communication strategies appropriate for a large class of applications. The first results of this project were an agent architecture and the DASEDIS tool developed for implementing, testing, and evaluating various multi-agent scenarios. The concepts and tools were tested on various prototypical examples. Our follow-up project VAS is aimed at advancing AOT to meet the requirements of problems in real-life domains such as traffic and manufacturing.

In the next section we describe both the concepts and the tools developed in the COSY project. Sections 9.3 and 9.4 describe previous, current, and future work on applying AOT to traffic and manufacturing problems, respectively. Section 9.5 concludes this chapter.

9.2 Concepts and Tools

The COSY concepts cover in particular an agent model and co-operation protocols. The design of the agent architecture and the DASEDIS test-bed is based on this agent model.

In this model, *behaviors*, *resources*, and *intentions* were identified as the three important elements in the problem-solving of an agent (Burmeister and Sundermeyer, 1992). An agent's behaviors are classified into *perceptual, cognitive, communicative,* and *effectoric* behaviors, each of which are simulated by a specific component in the architecture. Resources are used in a broad sense ranging from *cognitive resources* such as knowledge and belief, via *communicative resources* such as low-level protocols and communication hardware, to *physical resources* such as robot arms. Intentions also cover a broader sense and are divided into *strategic* and *tactical* intentions. While the strategic intentions model an agent's long-term goals, preferences, roles, and responsibilities which in general characterize the agent's motivation for acting, tactical intentions are directly tied to actions, representing an agent's commitment to its chosen plan of actions.

9.2.1 The COSY Agent Architecture

The design of the COSY agent architecture follows a top-down modular approach, with the modules ACTUATORS, SENSORS, COMMUNICATION, MOTIVATIONS, and COGNITION at the top level, as depicted in Figure 9.1. The first three modules are domain specific with their intuitive functionality. The MOTIVATIONS module models an agent's strategic intentions. The COGNITION module evaluates the current situation, and selects and monitors actions of the

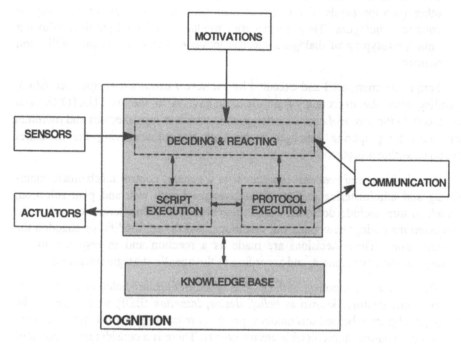

Figure 9.1. COSY agent architecture

agent in that situation. This module is realized as a knowledge-based system and, as shown in Figure 9.1, consists of a *knowledge base*, a *script execution component*, a *protocol execution component*, and a *deciding and reacting component*.

The application specific problem solving knowledge is encoded into plans. Each agent has a library of pre-compiled plans that resides in its knowledge base. Encoded in these plans are some typical courses of actions to achieve certain desired effects. Plans in general have a *header* and a *body*. The header consists of administrative information including the conditions that make them applicable in a given situation. The body of a plan is a tree structure representing some pattern of actions, links representing sequences of actions and branches corresponding to alternative courses of actions. There are two types of plans in the library:

- *Scripts* describe some stereotypical course of actions to achieve certain desired goals. The nodes in the structure of scripts are calls to primitive effectoric behaviors (i.e., actions that can be directly executed by the ACTUATORS), cognitive behaviors (i.e., actions that can be executed internally), calls to other scripts, or calls to co-operation protocols.
- *Co-operation protocols* represent some stereotypical pattern of communication and dialogues (Burmeister et al., 1993). The nodes in the tree represent dialogue states, and links represent transitions from one dialogue state to another.

The root node characterizes the protocol and the other nodes represent calls to other (sub-)protocols. Co-operation protocols provide a systematic way to construct dialogues. They are generic, modular, and configurable, allowing rapid prototyping of dialogues specific to various contexts in the application domain.

Scripts are monitored and executed by the *script execution component* (SEC), handing over the execution of primitive behaviors to the ACTUATORS, and protocols to the *protocol execution component* which in turn executes and monitors protocols by preparing messages to be sent and administering the messages received within a protocol.

The *deciding and reacting component* is a general control mechanism, monitoring and administering the decisions concerned with task and plan selection, which in turn include decisions concerning branches within scripts or protocols. An agent may adopt new goals and intentions, and revise, modify, or abandon the existing ones. These decisions are made as a reaction and in response to the changes in the environment, and according to the agent's strategic intentions.

The cognition component of the COSY agent architecture belongs to a category of agent architectures known as *belief, desire, intention* (BDI) architectures. The principal objective behind this model is practical reasoning, that is reasoning about actions in dynamic, unpredictable environments. There is a considerable amount of theoretical work explaining and investigating the inter-relationship between these attitudes and their input into practical reasoning. The BDI model can be considered as a specialization of the concepts behind the COSY agent architecture. For instance, beliefs are comparable with the cognitive resources; desires and future-directed intentions are specific strategic intentions; and present-directed intentions can be mapped to tactical intentions. The very first implementations of the BDI agent model were the *Procedural Reasoning System* (PRS) (Georgeff and Lansky, 1987) and *Intelligent Resource-bounded Machine Intelligence* (IRMA) (Bratman et al., 1988), both developed for single-agent systems. Since then many other implementations have been reported, especially adapting the model to meet the requirements of agents in multi-agent systems. The description and comparison between these architectures is beyond the scope of this article, but a detailed analysis can be found in an earlier article (Haddadi and Sundermeyer, 1995).

9.2.2 Dasedis

DASEDIS (Development And Simulation Environment for Distributed Intelligent Systems) has two main components (see Figure 9.2): *Simulation* and *Development*. The *simulation component* simulates the MOTIVATIONS, SENSORS, ACTUATORS, COMMUNICATION, and ENVIRONMENT by models specific for each application. The *development component* provides the following tools:

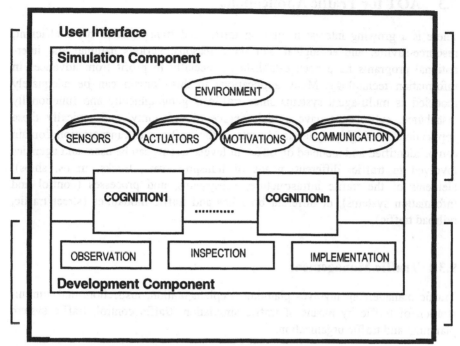

Figure 9.2.   DASEDIS

- A set of tools to implement the application-specific knowledge base of each agent. These tools enable an application designer to implement various data structures such as scripts, co-operation protocols, and the knowledge required to execute these plans.
- A set of tools to monitor problem solving and communication among agents during the execution of the system.
- A set of tools to incrementally inspect agents' knowledge bases. For instance, inspecting what type of general knowledge an agent has and what plans constitute its plan library.

Both the simulation and development component are used under a common graphical user interface which also provides tools for visualization.

The system is started after fixing some initial simulation conditions. During the simulation, the internal status of selected agents' problem-solving and communication can be inspected. At any time during the execution, the simulation may be interrupted, various data structures in the knowledge base of the existing agents inspected, and the simulation re-initiated with new conditions, for example, new agents introduced, some properties of the environment changed, and so on.

9.3 AOT for Traffic Applications

There is a growing interest in making traffic and transportation more efficient, resource-saving, and ecological. For these reasons, various national and international programs have been established especially to profit from advances in information technology. Many applications in this domain can be adequately modeled as multi-agent systems since traffic is geographically and functionally distributed, subsystems have a high degree of autonomy, and typically these applications are highly dynamic. Agents in the traffic and transportation domain can be identified and modeled on different levels: agents can be users and agencies involved in traffic; different means of transport (cars, trucks, trains, ships); elements of the traffic infrastructure, subsystems, and processes (control and information systems); or different branches and traffic modalities (street traffic, railroad traffic).

9.3.1 Traffic Management

Traffic management involves planning, implementation, inspection, and administration of traffic by means of traffic simulation, traffic control, traffic system planning, and traffic organization.

One domain in which AOT can improve existing techniques is in *microscopic traffic simulation* (Burmeister et al., 1996). As we discovered in a joint research project with Daimler-Benz Traffic Research, enhancing the existing systems with agent capabilities leads to a more adequate simulation model. The advantages of the agent-oriented approach are (i) a high-level description of vehicle behavior which is easier to maintain and modify, and (ii) the ability to easily model explicit communication and co-operation between vehicles. In particular, with the recent advances in telecommunications and provision of vehicles equipped with diverse 'telematics' devices, the ability for vehicles to communicate and co-operate promises the modeling of radically new concepts in traffic.

Co-operation of vehicles can improve certain measures in road traffic and consequently increase the throughput of vehicles on the road. Such measures include building up vehicle platoons by electronic coupling, regulation of vehicle distances to optimize route capacity, and co-ordination of velocity and acceleration of vehicles in order to increase the throughput of vehicles at crossings. The high complexity of these scenarios requires tools for modeling and simulation that are flexible to use and easy to enhance and maintain. Such tools can be provided by using AOT.

Another application in this area aims at modeling the planning and decision making in the domain of *traffic organization*. One example is concerned with *traffic markets*, that is, modeling the demand and supply of 'mobility' (of people or goods). AOT can be used to model and simulate this market and study some general patterns of demands for various means of transport and the infrastructure needed. Studying the dynamics of current traffic organization may lead to the modeling and experimental testing of totally new organizational forms.

A small-scale scenario in this application area deals with modeling and simulation of usage and operation of car pooling stations. The system models and simulates the booking of cars by users, and the management of cars at stations. Cars are considered as occupied not only for the duration they are booked for, but also at service, cleaning, and inspection intervals. If a car requested by a user is not available within the desired time interval, the station would offer a different car or an alternative time interval, if possible. Among other issues of interest, this system is used to experiment with different organizational forms and the composition of the fleet in and out of the stations. The goal of these experiments is to optimize the costs of running the stations and arrive at an agreeable arrangement in terms of user benefits and satisfaction.

Finally, as for *traffic control* systems, most present systems are monolithic and have to deal with a huge amount of data gathered by distributed sensors. By identifying and modeling subsystems (possibly associated with groups of sensors) as agents, we will be able to achieve a more flexible, adaptive, and robust system.

9.3.2 Freight Logistics

Freight logistics is an example from the important area of managing capacities and resources, that is, the optimal provision of means of transport under economic, political, and technical constraints. This task can be found in different organizations such as shipping, public transport, and airlines. Typically, resource management involves solving a large variety of subtasks, such as tour and route planning, maintenance planning, and crew scheduling. In principle, each individual task can be solved using mathematical methods from operations research (OR) and can be optimized according to a restricted number of criteria. However, in the presence of dynamic constraints, or when a combination of problems has to be solved, these methods are not very satisfactory.

In a subproject of COSY we analyzed and implemented a scenario of interacting shipping companies. The work was carried out in co-operation with the DFKI, and therefore the scenario resembles the MARS system (Fischer et al., 1993): There is a group of shipping companies whose goal it is to deliver a set of dynamically given orders, satisfying a set of given time and cost constraints. Agents in this scenario are company agents and truck agents. A company agent is responsible for the allocation of transport orders to the company's own trucks. Each truck agent is associated with a particular company from which it receives orders to transport goods. The truck agent does the route planning using its geographical knowledge and informs the transportation company about the deliverance of goods.

Allocating orders to trucks is done in a distributed manner. When a company agent receives an order from a customer, the agent announces the order to its trucks using an enhanced version of the contract net protocol (Fischer et al., 1994). The trucks try to include the order into their local plans and make bids according to the cost of carrying out any additional orders. The company agents could also announce new orders to other company agents. If a bid by another company is better than the bids offered by the company's own trucks, the order will be delegated to that company.

The distributed manner of allocating orders is an elegant way to deal with dynamically incoming orders. However, the main advantage of AOT in this domain is the ability to model co-operating, but autonomous shipping companies. Co-operation among companies is growing in importance, especially in highly competitive markets. Various co-operation methods can be modeled among autonomous agents. Unlike the OR approaches that deal with many depots, company agents can co-operate (for example by sharing orders) without being forced to make all their local information available to the others.

Since each truck is modeled as an agent, it is also possible to easily integrate additional functionalities, (e.g., route planning) into the agent. The autonomy of trucks is also appropriate in dealing with the uncertainty and dynamics inherent in the environment within which they operate. For instance, generally, trucks have incomplete knowledge about the quantity of orders they may be delivering, and naturally about the traffic conditions. Trucks can handle these situations autonomously (for example, by replanning their tour) without having to delegate the decisions to the company.

Different improvements of the existing system may be worked out in the future, for example more sophisticated local planning algorithms (e.g., on the basis of simulated trading), protocols for negotiating about prices for transportation, and integration of OR methods.

9.4   AOT for Manufacturing Applications

Manufacturing control is still an important and active field of research. Even though OR and traditional AI have proposed a large number of solutions to various aspects of manufacturing, in practice many control tasks are solved unsatisfactorily. As part of an international program on *intelligent manufacturing systems* (IMS Report, 1994) which was initiated in 1991, *holonic manufacturing systems* consortium (HMS Report, 1996) has been specifically aimed at investigating these problems and developing the manufacturing control of the 21st century.

The failure of many approaches in practice is mostly due to the dynamic nature of the manufacturing process. Frequent product and process changes demand a high degree of flexibility from the control system in that it should be configurable and scalable. Additionally, constant process disturbances require robust control strategies so that control plans are not outdated once they reach the shop floor. At least the last aspect has to be dealt with before a process can be optimized.

AOT offer methodologies to design manufacturing systems that exhibit the required flexible and robust behavior. The basic idea is that manufacturing components autonomously control their area of responsibility and co-ordinate their actions whenever necessary, for example in the case of material exchange. In this respect, the AOT approach is very similar to the ideas of HMS which also talk of autonomy and co-operation. But in contrast to HMS, AOT already offer the techniques to realize such systems.

The advantages of applying AOT over the previous methods are the following: (i) a distributed approach reduces the complexity of decision making by decentralization and ensures better correspondence of the model with reality, (ii) co-operation techniques allow co-ordination of actions at a high level of abstraction and thus make the system flexible in terms of configuration and size, (iii) different evaluation criteria can be assigned to different agents allowing inconsistencies to be resolved by negotiation, and (iv) the system can adapt to unforeseen events through self-organization.

Within manufacturing, there are at least three levels of abstraction at which the subsystems can be modeled as agents:

- the manufacturing organization level, including distributed manufacturing and plant co-ordination where different plants or components of a plant are considered as agents;
- the level of planning and scheduling activities in a factory, where agents are typically distributed planning and control systems, material flow systems, flexible manufacturing systems, and the like; and
- the process level, where agents are physical units such as manufacturing cells, assembly robots, paint booths, transport units, NC machine tools, and so on.

9.4.1 Flexible Manufacturing

In our studies, we identified four key requirements for manufacturing control systems that are vital in practice: (i) the control system should be able to dynamically incorporate incoming orders; (ii) it should adapt to disturbances concerning orders and resources; (iii) it should exhibit more flexibility when rearranging (the control of) the production process – ideally perform the reorganization itself; and (iv) it should be able to co-ordinate its actions with other control systems.

We believe that AOT can fulfil these requirements. By modeling the manufacturing process as a multi-agent system we can introduce (i) autonomous control for manufacturing components that enables the components to dynamically change their behavior; (ii) active co-operation between components in order to adequately adapt the system behavior to changes; and (iii) self-organization, such as dynamic task delegation, that assures the required flexibility.

To examine whether AOT can really meet the requirements, we designed a prototypical agent-oriented control system that can handle changing orders and process disturbances (Bussmann, 1996). The material flow control of a shop floor was chosen as the application domain because it could easily be isolated from the machine scheduling. The task of this control system is to schedule incoming transport orders dynamically, given a set of transporters. Transport orders are subject to change after their announcement, while transporters may have sudden breakdowns.

The application is designed as a multi-agent system by making each transporter an agent, responsible for the analysis and optimization of its private schedule. Additionally, a co-ordinator agent is introduced for controlling the assignment process and ensuring that the local schedules meet the global criteria given in the application. The co-ordinator agent is the main difference between our work and other contract-net approaches like YAMS (Parunak, 1987). Parunak (1987) argued in the evaluation of the contract-net approach that local scheduling causes sub-optimalities because of incomplete knowledge. Through the introduction of a co-ordinator we were able to achieve global knowledge concerning the loading of transporters while keeping all other advantages of a distributed approach. But the lack of information about which orders may arrive in the future is an inherent characteristic of dynamic problems.

The overall co-ordination process is arranged in four phases and repeated as long as orders have to be scheduled. (1) The co-ordinator chooses from a pool of orders the most urgent ones and announces them to the transporters. (2) Transporters analyse them and respond whether they are able to schedule the orders. (3) Based on the returned results the co-ordinator computes an assignment that maximizes the number of orders assigned. (4) The co-ordinator informs the transporters of the assignment, which in turn compute a detailed local schedule for the assigned orders.

The algorithm developed fulfils the first two requirements stated at the beginning of this section. Because the algorithm is incremental in nature, it can deal with the dynamic input of orders. The adaptiveness can easily be ensured by retracting and re-announcing orders. If an assigned order is changed, it is retracted from the transporters and put back into the pool of incoming orders. Similarly, if a transporter breaks down, its orders are retracted and re-announced by putting them back into the order pool.

The result of this example application demonstrated that AOT are indeed appropriate for modeling and implementing manufacturing control systems. However, AOT should not be applied to all (sub)problems. In the application discussed above, the computation of the assignment, after all the analysis results had been received, turned out to be a partitioning problem for which there exist optimal algorithms in OR. These algorithms can be used within the co-ordinator agent to solve the subproblem of finding an order assignment. In general, AOT should always be combined with other techniques that can perform the domain-specific reasoning.

In the near future, our main effort in the field of flexible manufacturing will be directed towards: (i) designing control systems that cover all aspects of manufacturing control, notably the machine and the material flow scheduling; (ii) combining robustness and flexibility with optimization; and (iii) realizing control systems that run in real production lines.

9.4.2 Plant Control

The strategic control of linked transfer lines, each controlled and optimized autonomously, is still a difficult problem. In the automotive industry, for example, the final steps in producing a car consist of the body construction, the painting of the body, and the assembly of all the parts. Each step is performed with a distinct technology that requires a different control and optimization technique. Nevertheless, despite the (semi-)autonomy in optimization, the production steps are linked together through the exchange of car bodies. And in the case of flow production, any disturbances in one step immediately affect the other steps. Consequently, the optimizations by any of the control subsystems must be co-ordinated across shop boundaries in order to guarantee a smooth flow of car bodies.

In a particular case at a Mercedes-Benz passenger car plant, the assembly is given a certain quota of cars that must be produced on average every day. The present, heuristic approach of linearly distributing the quota over the shifts and towards the preceding process steps has proven to be inappropriate. On the contrary, it is necessary to determine a particular quota per shift for each shop and appropriate actions that are co-ordinated across shops in order to achieve the final quotas. What makes this task difficult is that decisions made in one shop affect the following steps in a complicated way. For instance, in the case of a standstill due to technical problems in a painting booth, the painting shop is able to redirect car bodies to other painting lines in order to make up the number of bodies passed to the assembly on that shift. But not every painting line can treat the same types of cars. Thus, it may be necessary to change the ratio between different types. Such a corrective action may seem optimal to the painting shop control, but it may cause problems in the following assembly shop because parts for the assembly of a certain car type are limited. Therefore, in order to reduce the planning complexity, it is necessary to model the interactions of different plants and their consequences so that shop actions can be optimized while a smooth flow of car bodies is guaranteed. With AOT, each shop can be made an agent that co-ordinates its activities with its neighbours in order to achieve a plant-wide consistent strategy.

Current simulation techniques appear inadequate to solve this problem because the production process changes frequently. At least once a year Mercedes-Benz starts the production of a new car version or changes its production process considerably. In such a case, a standard simulation approach must be reorganized, whereas ideally the program should reorganize itself. Furthermore, the decision-making is also influenced by temporary changes, such as strikes. The user must be able to enter these conditions on a daily basis and the system should adapt itself accordingly. Both aspects, long-term and short-term changes, demand a high level of flexibility from the system.

The first prototype we developed for the control of car plants is a multi-agent system that generates an optimal daily production plan for the whole factory. In this system, each manufacturing center (e.g., the painting booth in building 3 or the assembly line in building 4) is modeled as an agent that autonomously controls the center itself. The flow of car bodies between the centers is co-ordinated through a planning algorithm that propagates production quotas to be produced at the last manufacturing cells back to the very first cells in the production chain. At each production step (e.g., assembly or painting) the requested car bodies, the capacities of the centers, and the flow possibilities are represented as a constraint net. The result of solving the constraint net determines the tasks to be assigned to the machines in that step and the possible production quotas expected of the previous step. This information is propagated back to the previous step which in turn attempts to solve its own constraints and propagates back its requirements to its previous step, and so on. A global solution is found once the algorithm reaches the first step (i.e., each step can fulfil its own requirements and those of its preceding step). A more detailed description of this approach is given in (Baumgärtel et al., 1996).

The prototype was tested at the Mercedes-Benz plant and was run with real data from the production process. The performance of the system was sufficient for strategic use. Response time ranged from one to 20 minutes and was five minutes on average.

Our future work in this field will be to extend the existing prototype to other aspects of strategic control, in particular to the task of disturbance handling. A corresponding project is currently being set up in co-operation with Mercedes-Benz. The goal of the project is to bring the AOT system into operation at the particular plant within a few years.

9.5 Conclusion

This article provided an overview of our approaches to applying AOT to some of the problems in traffic and manufacturing domains. Both domains seem ideally suited for agent-oriented techniques since they are geographically and functionally distributed, have subsystems with a high degree of autonomy, are very heterogeneous with respect to the competence of the subsystems, exhibit complex interactions among the subsystems, and are highly dynamic.

AOT exhibit all the characteristics of a new paradigm in systems analysis and software technology. Naturally, AOT does not provide a solution to all the problems involved. What is needed, but so far has not been understood appropriately, is the coupling of agent techniques with methods from OR, decision theory, or constraint programming.

References

Baumgärtel, H., Bussmann, S., Klosterberg, M. (1996) Combining multi-agent systems and constraint techniques in production logistics. In: *Proceedings of the Int. Conf. in Artificial Intelligence, Planning and Simulation in High Autonomy Systems*, La Jolla, California.

Bratman, M., Israel, D., Pollack, M. (1988) Plans and resource-bounded practical reasoning, *Comput. Intell.*, Vol 4.

Burmeister, B., Sundermeyer, K. (1992) Co-operative problem-solving guided by intentions and perception. In: E. Werner, Y. Demazeau (Eds.) Decentralized AI, 3, *Proceedings of the Third European Workshop on Modelling Autonomous Agents* (MAAMAW-91). North-Holland, Amsterdam.

Burmeister, B., Haddadi, A., Sundermeyer, K. (1993) Configurable co-operation protocols for multi-agent systems. In: C. Castelfranchi, J-P. Müller (Eds.) *From Reaction to Cognition*, (MAAMAW-93), Lecture Notes in Artificial Intelligence 957. Springer-Verlag, Berlin.

Burmeister, B., Doormann, J., Matylis, G. (1996) Agenten-orientierte Verkehrssimulation. *Pre-Proc. 1st Workshop on Multiagent-Systems and Simulation* MASSIM'96, Ulm, Germany (in German).

Bussmann, S. (1996) A Multi-agent approach to dynamic, adaptive scheduling of material flow. In: J. W. Perram, J-P. Müller (Eds.) *Distributed Software Agents and Applications* (MAAMAW'94), Odense, Denmark.

Fischer, K., Kuhn, N., Müller, H. J., Müller, J-P., Pischel, M. (1993) Sophisticated and distributed: the transportation domain. In: C. Castelfranchi, J-P. Müller (Eds.) *From Reaction to Cognition*, (MAAMAW-93), Lecture Notes in Artificial Intelligence 957. Springer-Verlag, Berlin.

Fischer, K., Kuhn, N., Müller, J-P. (1994) Distributed knowledge based reactive scheduling in the transportation domain. In: *Proceedings of the Tenth IEEE Conference on Artificial Intelligence and Applications*, San Antonio, Texas.

Georgeff, M., Lansky, A. (1987) Reactive reasoning and planning. *Proceedings of National Conference on AI* (AAAI 87).

Haddadi, A., Sundermeyer, K. (1996) Belief-desire-intention agent architectures. In: G. M. P. O'Hare, N. R. Jennings (Eds.) *Foundations of Distributed Artificial Intelligence*. John Wiley & Sons, New York.

IMS (1994) Intelligent Manufacturing Systems, Final Report of the International Steering Committee, Hawaii. http://www.ims.org/.

HMS (1996) Holonic Manufacturing Systems Consortium, Press Release, Revision 3.6. http://www.ncms.org/hms/hms.html.

Parunak, H. V. D. (1987) Manufacturing experience with the contract net. In: M. N. Huhns (Ed.) *Distributed Artifical Intelligence*. Pitman/Morgan Kaufman, London/San Mateo, California.

Shoham, Y. (1993) Agent-Oriented Programming. *Artificial Intelligence*, 60. Elsevier.

10 Co-operating Agents: Concepts and Applications

H. Haugeneder and D. Steiner
Siemens AG

10.1 Introduction

In the current discussion the notion of an agent and its descendants, such as agent-based systems, agent software etc., is used in manifold ways exhibiting both similarities and divergences. Our approach to this area stems from Distributed Artificial Intelligence (DAI). The central problem underlying the design of agent based systems from a DAI point of view is characterized by the following question:

> *How can individually motivated, independently designed computational artifacts, i.e., agents, act together to achieve some (at least partial) common goal in a genuinely distributed problem space?*

With this perspective, the emphasis is more on collections of agents and their interaction rather than single agents. The field of multi-agent systems has established itself as one of the two major streams with DAI – the other being Distributed Problem Solving – to design methods and architectures dedicated specifically to this problem area.

This chapter focuses on three issues,[1] which explicate our general approach to constructing multi-agent systems and supporting practical applications. We will present:

- the conceptual design and specification of an agent architecture and the multi-agent language MAI²L for implementation of single agents and co-operative interaction among them;
- a multi-agent environment for constructing co-operative applications based on this model; and
- two application studies in the areas of group scheduling and individualized (road) traffic management.

---

[1] The concepts presented here were developed within ESPRIT Project No. 5362, IMAGINE (Integrated Multi-Agent INteractive Environment) (Haugeneder, 1994), which was supported by the Commission of the European Communities as part of the ESPRIT II framework.

10.2 Co-operating Agents

10.2.1 Agent Architecture

Co-operating agents need to know what they are co-operating about and how to co-operate efficiently. This is achieved by supplying an agent with a *goal* – a description of the world state which it is to achieve. Based upon a set of *actions* it can perform, the agent can construct a variety of *plans* for achieving this goal. The agent *commits* to the 'best' plan by adding the actions called for by the plan to a schedule of events, and *executes* the plan according to the schedule. Co-operation is achieved, not only by carrying out individual actions together, but also by executing shared plans as well as actually planning together.

In order to support this type of co-operation, a variety of capabilities are necessary (Steiner et al., 1990):

- An agent needs to be able to change the world through actions – this is accomplished by the *agent body*
- An agent needs to be able to communicate with other agents – this is accomplished by the *agent communicator*
- An agent needs to have knowledge of how to plan its actions, achieve its goals and co-operate. This is accomplished by the most central agent component – the *agent head*.

Thus, the body represents the basic domain-dependant functionality of the agent, the head represents the problem-solving functionality, and the communicator the message-passing functionality. This architecture is depicted in Figure 10.1.

This agent architecture allows for the easy integration of existing external systems in the agent paradigm by specifying an appropriate head-body interface. Based upon this decomposition the behavior of an agent, as defined in the agent head, can be described in more detail.

The agent head represents the knowledge of how the world can be transformed by executing tasks, and which agents can perform which tasks. It processes this knowledge to find out what tasks, when executed by itself or other agents, will bring about a world state described by one of its goals. This processing is done in accordance with a procedure called the *basic agent loop* of the agent. In the following, we outline the basic loop from a single agent's point of view (Steiner et al., 1993). Figure 10.2 shows how the basis phases of this schema – goal activation, planning, scheduling, execution – fit together: nodes represent processes; labels on arcs represent data passed between processes. This is only a rough sketch of the primary flow of information – all processes can interact with each other via the agent's underlying knowledge.

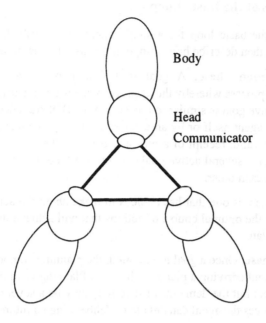

Body

Head
Communicator

Figure 10.1. The structure of a multi-agent system

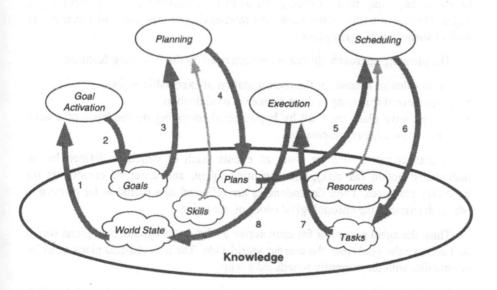

Figure 10.2. Knowledge processing within an agent

10.2.2 Phases of the Basic Loop

The phases of the basic loop for a single agent are described. In the following sections we will then describe how co-operation fits into this framework.

Goal Activation Phase: A goal is a description of a world state. Goal activation is the process whereby the agent recognizes that a particular goal is to be achieved (an active goal is similar to a desire in the BDI framework). This may be triggered by the agent itself or by an external event, e.g., certain conditions on the world becoming valid, receipt of a message from another agent or from the user. An agent may have several active goals at any one time; however, they should be compatible with each other.

A rational agent is one that has choices to make about the actions it may carry out and chooses the optimal course of actions that will achieve its active goals. To do this it must plan.

Planning Phase: Once a goal is activated, the planning component of the agent head may set about deriving a plan to achieve it. Planning is an intrinsic capability of a rational agent but the demands of reactivity may be a severe constraint on the amount of resources the agent can devote to deliberating its future actions.

An agent may use a variety of methods to find a suitable plan. These range from accessing pre-defined, possibly incomplete, plans from a plan library, to automatically creating fully distributed plans. It may use a combination of backward reasoning from desired goals to forward reasoning from current world states. The use of partial plans allows the interleaving of planning and execution as well as shared multi-agent plans.

The planning approach chosen is characterized by the following features:

- Event calculus is used for the representation of executable plans
- Hypothetical reasoning is done by means of abduction
- Co-operative plans are built by hypothetical reasoning on the basis of a temporal knowledge representation.

A plan is represented by a set of events, each of which is defined by an instantiated action (as task), the executing agent, and a set of constraints on necessary resources. Their dependencies are reflected in a partial order of events, which determines the chronological order of execution.

Thus, the agent generates for each active goal a set of hypothetical plans which will achieve the goal from the current world state. The hypothetical plans must be compatible with the currently scheduled events.

Scheduling Phase: In this phase an optimal plan (i.e., one with least cost, according to an appropriately chosen cost function) is chosen from the set of hypothetical plans, and the corresponding tasks are scheduled according to the order of events. (This is equivalent to committing to a plan; a committed plan is similar to an intention in the BDI architecture.) This takes into account

- other already scheduled events of the agent, and
- any resource constraints.

Events of different plans may be interleaved, carried out on a first-in/first-out basis, or scheduled to be executed at specific times (e.g., according to just-in-time principles).

Where a task is to be carried out by, or in coordination with, another agent the relevant synchronization messages are generated by the scheduler. In the case of a reactive plan, the scheduler also inserts the detection of events which trigger the plan into the schedule.

Execution Phase: At the heart of an agent is an executor component that runs the schedules, by calling tasks and handling interrupts according to the schedule events. The tasks may be communicative, in which case they are passed to the agent communicator, or domain-specific, in which case they are passed to the agent body. The interrupts include incoming messages and 'alarm' signals from the body.

Prior to task execution, its preconditions are verified. After successful execution the world state of the agent is updated according to its effects. We mention also that appropriate measures must be taken in case of task failure.

This concludes our discussion of the basic loop of an agent, allowing it to achieve its goal via a plan-based approach.

The situation may arise, however, where an agent cannot achieve a goal on its own – it may not be able to find an appropriate plan or a other agents may be needed in order to execute an optimal plan. This requires co-operation.

10.2.3   Co-operation Between Agents

10.2.3.1 The Need for Co-operation

How can agents co-operate with each other in an efficient and coordinated way? First of all, they need to share a multi-agent plan, just as a single agent needs to plan for coordinating the actions to achieve its goals. The multi-agent plan is similar the single-agent plan in that it deals effectively with interdependencies between actions. But it is more elaborate, since these actions are assigned to different agents and may be communicative in nature.

This leads to the question: how can agents arrive at shared multi-agent plans in a flexible way? Our approach to this is achieved in the following way:

- Agents use co-operation methods to create, maintain, and execute multi-agent plans
- Co-operation methods themselves are abstract multi-agent plan schemas that can be instantiated and thereby customized to fit the problem at hand
- Due to their abstractness, the same set of co-operation methods can be used in a wide class of application domains.

Thus, co-operation is basically the process of distributing goals, plans, and tasks across several agents as shown in Figure 10.3.

The sender of a message must have a sufficient model of the recipient to know the recipient's behavior upon receipt of the message. Exactly this model determines which message the sender sends and correspondingly, the entire co-operative process. Thus, sender and receiver must agree upon the meaning of the exchanged messages. Furthermore, the semantics of the messages vary according to the objects under discussion – the proposal of a goal has a different meaning than the proposal of a plan to achieve the goal. Only if the actual meaning has been determined can agents reason about the messages they send and receive to influence the co-operation.

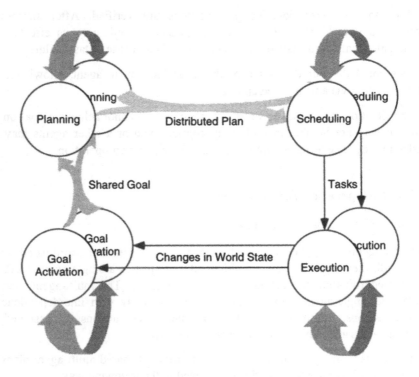

Figure 10.3. Process view of several distributed agents

10.2.3.2 Co-operation Primitives

The basic building blocks for inter-agent co-operation are constituted *by co-operation primitives* (Lux et al., 1993). They are drawn from speech act theory (Searle, 1969). These primitives are composed of *co-operation types* and *co-operation objects*, which are either a goal, a plan, a task, or unspecified information such as results, parameters, or other knowledge. In terms of our architecture co-operation, primitives are basic agent head functions, describing communication between other agents with a specific intention. They are represented as multi-agent actions with specific pre-conditions and effects. These preconditions and effects fix the semantics/intention of the primitives and plan whose plan procedures consist of a call to the head function handling the communication (head-communicator-interface). Thus, the procedure (Proc:) of each co-operation primitive calls the send and receive communication functions on the sender (Speaker) and receiver (Hearer) sides respectively, as shown in Table 10.1.

The core co-operation primitives are shown in Table 10.2; their meaning in the agent context is as follows:

Table 10.1. Co-operation primitives as specific plans

Speaker	Hearer
Pre: *Precondtions*	**Pre:** *Preconditions*
Proc: send (co-op_prim)	**Proc: rccv (co-op_prim)**
Eff: *Effects*	**Eff:** *Effects*

Table 10.2. Co-operation primitives: types and objects

Object/Type	propose	accept	reject	refine	modify	inform	query
Intention						*	
Goal	*	*	*				
Plan	*	*	*	*	*		
Commitment	*	*	*				
Goal breakdown	*	*	*	*	*	*	*
Org. structure	*	*	*	*	*		*
Schedule	*	*	*	*	*	*	*
Task assignment	*	*	*	*	*		
resource alloc.	*	*	*	*	*		
Untyped info						*	*

propose A proposal starts or continues a discussion among agents about a co-operation object. The knowledge transferred by a proposal to other agents is hypothetical as agents sharing this knowledge have not yet committed to it.

accept Indication of commitment to the co-operation object.

refine An agent proposes a further instantiation of the co-operation object.

reject Indication of failure to commit to the co-operation object.

modify A counter-proposal of an altered co-operation object.

query A query for arbitrary knowledge.

inform The answer to a previous information request.

10.2.3.3 Co-operation Methods

As co-operation primitives are represented as plans, they can be further composed to form complex plans, called *co-operation methods*. Co-operation methods are multi-agent plans used to construct and execute domain-specific multi-agent plans. As a consequence they also concern goals, plans, and tasks of the agents involved. The knowledge that the agents have of each other determines the topic of co-operation method. As an example, if an agent has an active goal which it cannot itself handle and if it does not know about the skills of other agents, it must invoke co-operation about the goal. If it has knowledge about which agents could satisfy the goal, it will initiate co-operation about the plan for achieving the goal. Further, if a domain-specific plan is already committed to by agents, they will co-operate about the tasks to be executed.

A high degree of flexibility is essential for the co-operation methods. For instance, a *contract net* (Smith, 1980) is a flexible co-operation method which, in the general case, neither determines the number of agents involved (in fact the number is unlimited) nor prescribes which of the agents will be members of the group.

Obviously, predefined co-operation methods must be freely parameterizable. To simplify establishment of co-operation patterns that are likely to be used frequently, predefined co-operation methods have partly or even completely specified parameters, i.e., they are specialized plans. They allow invoking standard co-operation structures involving the same set of agents and/or the same co-operative links, thereby reducing the usual preliminary negotiations concerning establishment of the co-operation structure. Co-operation methods may be predefined or may be established dynamically. The latter allows for the flexibility required for human agents.

In the extended process view of co-operating agents (as shown in Figure 10.3), local goals of agents become *shared goals* if they are solved in co-operation with other agents. The common planning phase leads to the development of so-called *multi-agent plans*, plans which are executed by more than one agent. During the planning and scheduling process, a multi-agent plan is subdivided – as far as possible – into several single agent plans which can be executed by the agents. The execution of single-agent tasks comprises not only head or body actions but also communicator actions (i.e., sending co-operation primitives) to co-ordinate the behavior of other agents.

The semantics and pragmatics of co-operation primitives are dependent on the current phase and on the co-operation objects involved. The functions $f \in F$ in A have to be extended to react appropriately to the receipt of a co-operation request. The decision whether a co-operation between agents is at all possible made via these functions. The decision process ends either in sending an answer, in executing a body or head action, or in ignoring the received message. Co-operation requests for goals are decided by the function *new_goal*, for plans by the function *find_all_plans*, for schedules by the function *schedule_plan*, and for queries by the function *answer_query*.

Table 10.3. Semantics of goal activation

		Speaker	Hearer
PROPOSE(g)			
	Pre:	$g \in G$	–
	Eff:	$\square$ *proposed(g, H)*	$\square$ *has_goal(S, g)*
ACCEPT(g)			
	Pre:	*has_goal(H, g)* ❖ $g \in G$	*proposed(g, S)* ❖ $g \in G$
	Eff:	–	$\square$ *has_goal(S, g)*
REJECT(g)			
	Pre:	*has_goal(H, g)* ❖ $g \notin G$	*proposed(g, S)* ❖ $g \in G$
	Eff:	✦ *has_goal(H, g)*	–
MODIFY/REFINE(g,g')			
	Pre:	*has_goal(H, g)* ❖ $g \notin G$ ❖ $g' \notin G$	*proposed(g, S)* ❖ $g \in G$
	Eff:	*proposed(g', H)*	$\square$ *has_goal(S, g')*

S, H: co-operating agents (S = Speaker, H = (Set of) Hearer(s)); agent alternate roles when issuing successive co-operation primitives.

$\square$ (x):   abbreviation for $w_c = w_c \cup \{(x)\}$

✦ (x):   abbreviation for $w_c = w_c ☎ \{(x)\}$

As shown in Table 10.3, a number of conditions with respect to the pre-conditions and effects of the sender and receiver of the co-operation primitive can be given. This decision is split according to the agent's basic loop phases and the co-operation objects involved. The preconditions of the co-operation primitives can be seen as applicability conditions. Together with the speech act class and the message type, they yield the semantics of the co-operation primitives. The effects of the co-operation primitives enhance the knowledge of the co-operating agents and trigger functions in the agents' basic loops. Therefore, they can be seen as the pragmatics of the co-operation primitives.

When working in co-operation with other agents, the basic loop becomes distributed (Steiner et al., 1993). This gives rise to a number of conditions that have to be assumed true.

In the goal activation phase, for example, a co-operation is instantiated if an agent cannot find a local plan for the goal or finds a plan which would involve actions to be carried out by other agents. The agent can also propose a goal to a co-operative agent if it thinks that a co-operative plan is cheaper or more effective than a local plan. The proposal of a goal g is answered by the partner after examining the function *new_goal*, as described in Table 10.3.

The semantics of the other basic loop's phases such as planning scheduling and execution can be described in a similar fashion (see (Lux and Steiner, 1995) and (Lux, 1995) for more details).

10.2.4 The Role of Planning in Co-operation

In order to reason about agent actions and to adapt agent actions to changing environments and the actions of other autonomous agents, it is necessary to make explicit the causal relationships of actions; that is, to declare the preconditions and post conditions of each action, and represent the possible beneficial and deleterious interactions between agents. This we do with event calculus, which is an expressive means of describing state changes that can be used to reason efficiently and, most importantly, localizes the effects of actions. The benefit of declaring the preconditions and effects is useful in large open systems, for reasons of software engineering and structured error recovery. We endow the agents with the ability to deliberate about the preconditions and effects of their own actions in order to adapt their actions appropriately to a changing multi-agent environment.

The means by which agents deliberate about their actions is captured through the notion of abduction. That is, the agent tries to derive a new set of actions in Δ that according to its current knowledge will steer it through a future goal. At any one moment an agent may be considering several such Δ's. Abduction provides a means to define agent autonomy, leads to efficient algorithms, and, when used in conjunction with event calculus and negation as failure, leads to a form of event-based default reasoning.

When deliberation occurs amongst several agents a co-operation protocol naturally arises. In our system, the generation of such a protocol is handled in a structured way by the abductive inference process. When an agent would like another to add an action to its Δ it sends a co-operation message of type *propose*. Depending on the proof scheme sketched above, the agent will send an *accept* message if it is possible to find a Δ including the action that leads to its goal, or a reject message if this is not the case. There then follows an exchange of *commitment* messages as the agents reduce the several possible Δ's they are considering to the one that they will actually execute.

10.2.5 A Multi-agent Language

10.2.5.1 The Elements of MAI²L

We now turn our attention to the specific language constructs offered by MAI²L supporting the concepts described above. (MAI²L is implemented in C and is available on UNIX and Windows 95 platforms.) We progress from the low-level knowledge representation and processing aspects via the single-agent aspects to arrive at the multi-agent aspects of MAI²L.

The knowledge base (KB) of an agent consists of tuples, called MAI²L terms, of aspect-value pairs. Some aspects and their values are provided automatically by the system. The KB is structured by contexts which allow for the hypothetical reasoning planning. MAI²L actions and MAI²L plans are special MAI²L terms as they are compiled into executable MAI²L code when they enter the KB. The execution of plans and actions itself is described later on. A value in a plan or an action can be either a constant, a bound variable, or an aspect value. There are some special operators which return frequently used values. The \ operator retrieves the value of a given aspect of a given MAI²L term, the ! operator retrieves the value of a given aspect of the agent itself, !name refers to its name, and the cc operator represents the context in which the plan or action is running. Plans and actions have four aspects which are of particular interest.

Characters (char): The characters represent those agents involved in a multi-agent action or plan. The plan is automatically compiled into separate plans for each character with appropriate synchronization points.

Preconditions (pre): The preconditions contain operations for knowledge access and for setting conditions on that knowledge. Only when the pre-conditions are satisfied, may the action or plan be executed. The following constructs can appear in preconditions:

- Existential queries (get) for MAI²L terms satisfying given constraints on values
- Negation (~) of existential queries using negation-as-failure
- Universal queries (getall) for all MAI²L terms satisfying given constraints on values

- Simple conditions (==, ≡, <, >, <=, >=, in) for comparing two values
- Demons (–>) for specifying additional conditions on the evaluation of the precondition, which is delayed until the demon condition holds. These are used for reacting to changes in the world state immediately without having to plan. (Reactive plans are already in execution waiting for their demons to be triggered.) Demons may also specify time delays, which are useful for message time-outs.

Procedures (proc): An action's procedure consists of a single call to a function, which may be in any language provided there is a suitable interface to MAI²L. Currently, functions may be Prolog C or UNIX calls. The execution of the function takes place either in the body or in the communicator. Arguments to functions are bounded in the precondition, return values in the effects.

Plan procedures allow composing calls to other plans or actions in the following manner:

- Sequential execution of two procedures (... & ...)
- Parallel execution of two procedures waiting until both are finished (... | ...)
- Forking a procedure and continuing without waiting until it's finished (fork ...)
- Mapping over lists (for each ... in ... do ...)
- Conditional execution of a procedure (if ... then ...)
- Looping (while ... do ...).

Effects (eff): the effect of a plan or action is to alter the KB upon successful execution of the procedure. This may be a conjunction of:

- Creation of new terms (+), using local variables to specify aspect values
- Deletion of terms (-)
- Alteration of term by adding new aspect or setting different values for existing aspects.

10.2.5.2 Co-operation in MAI²L

Since MAI²L is designed to be a multi-agent language, it supports distribution of goals, plans and tasks among agents. This is achieved via communication: by means of co-operation primitives at the basic level and co-operation methods at higher levels.

Upon creation, and agent registers with a given Agent Directory Service (ADS) which itself is an agent. The ADS stores information about the communication details of the agents as well as their types and capabilities. The agent communicator then waits for new connections, executing the predefined send and receive actions as scheduled by the head.

Table 10.4. Syntax of co-operation primitives

co-op_msg	:=	msg_type co-op_obj msg_constraints
msg_type	:=	PROPOSE | ACCEPT | REJECT | REFINE | MODIFY | ASK | REQUEST | ORDER | TELL [| SUPPORT | OPPOSE | ...]
msg_constrainsts	:=	reply_constraints other_constraints
reply_constraints	:=	REPLY_WITH {msg_type}*
other_constraints	:=	'list of aspect-value pairs'
co-op_obj	:=	obj_type obj_header obj_body obj_constraints
obj_type	:=	GOAL | PLAN | TASK [| INTENTION | ...]
obj_header	:=	frame_of_reference
obj_constraints	:=	cost | time ...
frame_of_reference	:=	co-op_id co-op_method co-op_context
co-op_method	:=	NIL | method_id
co-op_context	:=	context_id
obj_body	:=	goal_body | plan_body | task_body
goal_body	:=	'MAI^{2}L term'
plan_body	:=	p_name preconditions p_procedure effects
task_body	:=	agent: function resources duration start_time end_time
preconditions	:=	'MAI^{2}L terms'
p_procedure	:=	{task_body}*
effects	:=	'MAI^{2}L' terms'
resources	:=	'list of required resources'
function	:=	'agent body function'
agent	:=	'agent assigned to the task'
duration	:=	'a time interval'
start_time	:=	'exactly scheduled start time'
end_time	:=	'exactly scheduled end time'

```
plan(cnet(TaskType,BestBid),
      chars = Mgr, Bdrs,
      proc = (Mgr:cn_make_proposal(TaskType,Specs) &
              Bdrs:CallForBids = Mgr:propose(Bdrs,Specs) &
              Mgr:(!timeout -> Bids) =
              Bdrs:(refine_bids(Specs,CallForBids\sender,Bids) &
                     refine(CallForBids\sender,Bid)) &
              Mgr:cn_eval_bids(Bids,BestBid,RestBids,TimeOuts) &
              Bdrs:NotifM = Mgr:(accept(BestBid\sender BestBid\object) |
                                   (foreach Bid in RestBids do
                                             reject(Bid\sender,Bid\object)) |
                                   (foreach TOM in TimeOuts do
                                             reject(TOM\sender,TOM\object))) &
              Bdrs:(if (NotifM\mtype = = reject)
                     then uncommit(NotifM\sender)) &
              Mgr:close_connection & Bdrs:close_connection &
              Mgr:new_co-operation(safe_tae(BestBid\sender,TaskType))),
      eff = Mgr:(-cc),Bdrs:(-cc)).
```

Figure 10.4. A MAI²L plan

The **receive** action can be specified with a list of agents and a time-out. The communicator analyses an incoming message and adds the message content (a co-operation primitive) to the corresponding context (creating a new one if necessary) for further processing by the head. The send action accepts either a single agent or a list of agents. The communicator takes care of generating appropriate MAI²L terms for each message to be sent, determines the address of the agent (querying the ADS if necessary) and sends the message.

On the basis of these actions, the co-operation primitives and the co-operation methods can easily be implemented. Some co-operation methods such as ADS registration and tracing, are executed directly by the communicator.

Co-operation primitives, the basic building blocks of co-operation, represent a transfer of knowledge from one agent to one or more agents via MAI²L terms with a specific goal in mind and, as such, are represented as shared multi-agent plans, whose precondition and effects fix the semantics/intentions of the primitive and whose procedures are synchronized calls to the communication actions. A co-operation primitive consists of an explicit performance speech act operating upon a goal, plan, task or arbitrary knowledge; the expressive facilities of co-operation objects are described in Table 10.4.

In addition, the semantics of a co-operation primitive does not rest upon the single message alone, rather also upon the history of exchanged messages and the expected replies, i.e., the entire dialogue must be taken into consideration. Such a dialogue consisting of a sequence of co-operation primitives is called a co-operation method. Co-operation methods are represented as domain-independent multi-agent plans used to construct and execute domain-specific multi-agent plans. An example of contract net in MAI²L is given in Figure 10.4.

10.2.6   A Multi-agent Environment: The MECCA System

10.2.6.1 Implementational Basis

An implementation of MAI²L supporting the agent model described (including a library of agents and co-operation methods) along with tools for developing multi-agent systems comprise *the Multi-agent Environment Constructing Co-operative Applications*, MECCA. An in-depth description of MECCA can be found in (Steiner, 1995).

The MECCA environment is a domain-independent tool for prototyping multi-agent systems based upon a generic agent model. MECCA provides an implementation of MAI²L, an agent head, an agent communicator, a variety of standard agent types and co-operation methods, and some tools for multi-agent system development. MECCA is implemented in IC-Prolog (Chu, 1993), a distributed logic programming language. The IC-Prolog features, which are specifically relevant when viewed as an underlying computational model for multi-agent programming, are multiple threads, a Parlog subsystem, and high-level communication primitives. Multiple threading enables the concurrent execution of independent goals, the Parlog subsystem allows local fine-grained parallelism to be specified, and the high-level communication primitives provide the means for independent IC-Prolog processes on different machines on a network to communicate. The combination of the two logic languages; Parlog, a committed-choice, non-deterministic, concurrent logic language; and ICP, an extended Prolog dialect, offers considerable expressive power since different components of the same application may use either or both of them.

10.2.6.2 Mecca Agents

The agent communicator is implemented as a light weight thread that opens a TCP/IP server port through which it handles message passing of the agent. The communicator also sends trace messages to the monitor agent, and handles alone without involving the head a simple information exchange co-operation with an

Agent Directory Service. Co-operation primitives are implemented as procedures in the communicator, which send messages or wait for one depending on the primitives' semantics. The send and receive procedures can be one-to-one, one-to-many, many-to-one, or many-to-many.

The agent head is a light weight thread which accesses the knowledge base, activates goals, and executes plans and co-operation methods by invoking co-operation primitives. The head is provided with predefined co-operation methods for exchanging knowledge with other agents and for requesting task execution from other agents as well as domain-specific multi-agent plans.

Agent knowledge can be stored, modified, and retrieved in standard ways by the operations **assert, retract, find_any**, or **find_all**. For instance, it is possible to find all known agents having a given skill, or simply to retrieve the agent's information about itself. The agent body is programmed either directly in MAI^2L or in the underlying implementation language, in which cases the head-body interface has to be provided, or it is a separate UNIX process controlled by the head through sockets, pipes, file I/O, or the C interface to MAI^2L.

Within MECCA a number of generic predefining agent types are provided:

- **Agent Directory Service (ADS).** The Agent Directory Service agents are important in MECCA as they play the role of Yellow Page servers throughout the whole network. ADSs can be distributed and allocated a partial responsibility over a portion of the multi-agent system. They are able to communicate with each other to determine the address of a particular agent or to find all agents of a particular type. Thus this information is available to any agent in the system (as it registered with an ADS). They use the co-operation methods **update_data and retract_data** among themselves and with other agents to update their knowledge about the current agents
- **Machine agent.** Machine agents are skeletal agents equipped with a communicator and head. They serve as a basis for constructing more specialized types of agents, as they provide the minimum functionality a MECCA agent must exhibit in order to act in the system
- **Monitor Agent.** Monitor agents display a trace of all communication to and from a given agent. This is realized by a co-operation method directly in the traced agents communicator
- **User Agent (UA).** User agents (Lux and Kolb, 1992) are dedicated to a particular user, providing the interface between the user and the rest of the multi-agent system. They represent knowledge about the user and access the tools a user uses (such as a calendar system) to provide support in executing tasks and co-operating with other humans via their respective user agents
- **User Interface Agent.** User interface agents allow for connecting a variety of different graphical user interface systems to MECCA. They display an agent's knowledge base and receive and process user commands in an agent- and application-specific fashion.

10.2.6.3 Mecca Co-operation Methods

A variety of co-operation methods are provided with MECCA. Some implement low-level co-operation for knowledge exchange and update and are used by all agents. Others, while still domain-independent, require the multi-agent programmer to define certain internal procedures occurring in the method. Domain-dependent multi-agent plans defined for a particular MECCA application must be defined by the MECCA programmer. The following co-operation methods come with MECCA:

- **Request Data** is used by a *Knowledge Seeker* to query a *Knowledge Provider* for information. The co-operation object indicates the type of information requested – either any or all data matching a given pattern. On receipt of the request the recipient may further delegate information retrieval to another agent. The result of the query is passed back to the knowledge seeker
- **Update Data** is used by a Knowledge Provider to assert/retract a fact to/from the Knowledge Recipient's KB. It uses the *order* co-operation type, so that the update is compulsory. Thus, there is no response awaited from the recipient once the order has been sent out. Agents may have domain-dependent behavior upon receiving such an update (e.g., the ADS, when receiving new information about a registered agent, redisplays its graphical presentation of agents)
- **Trial and Error** allows the *Initiator* agent to request the *Recipient* to perform a task. This is done in three steps:

  1. The initiator prepares the task, that is, performs any prerequisite action for the task which it is able to do by itself. It may fail in doing so, in which case the co-operation itself fails (only the initiator knows about it, as it did not yet call another agent).
  2. The initiator sends a message requesting the other agent to perform the rest of the task. The recipient checks if it can execute the task (check of preconditions), if so performs the task and returns the result of the execution to the initiator. If not, the recipient sends a reject message to the initiator.
  3. The initiator evaluates the result.

  A slightly different version of this method, Safe Trial and Error, enables the initiator to first obtain a commitment from the recipient to execute the task.
- **Contract Net** allows a *Manager* to send a request for bids (specifying a task to be performed, criteria for bid evaluation, and a timeout) to a set of *Potential Bidders*. Those potential bidders who refine the proposal (customizing the requirements to what they actually offer, and possibly committing to the task) are referred to as bidders. If there are no bidders, the co-operation fails. Otherwise, the manager sorts the bids according to specified criteria. Based upon the result of this sorting, the set of potential bidders is split in three:

- those who did not answer within the specified timeout;
- the contractor who submitted the best bid with respect to the criteria; and
- the other bidders, known as rejected bidders.

The manager sends a reject to the time-outs and rejected bidders causing them to withdraw their potential commitment to the task. The last part of the co-operation is of the same form as Safe Trial and Error. The manager performs the task according to its bid. The contractor returns the result, which is then evaluated. Note the contractor may still fail in the execution of the task.

- **Extended Contract Net** prevents unnecessary communication in case of failure of contracted task. Here, the manager does not actually reject the bidders until the task is successfully performed. This enhanced version is different from Contract Net in a specific case – when the contractor fails to execute its task, the manager simply awards the task to the bidder with the next-lowest bid and resumes the cycle – preparing the task, ordering the contractor to execute it, and evaluating the result of the execution. This has the disadvantage that the bidders may remain committed longer than they need be, and the bids may become invalid; however, the need for calling Contract Net repeatedly is eliminated.
- **Transfer Bid** allows a potential bidder who cannot make a suitable bid to ask an associated bidder to assume the bid. If this bid is the lowest it will automatically be awarded to the associate by the manager. The associate remembers who sent the bid transfer proposal in order to avoid recursively proposing this bid to the initiator.

10.3 Agent-Based Applications

10.3.1 Assistance in Calendar Management

To support integration and co-operation between humans and machine agents within a uniform multi-agent framework, humans have to be linked to the multi-agent system via so-called personal assistants (PAs). Each human user has his/her own personal assistant.

A personal assistant is an agent – with the same structure as machine agents – which can act on behalf of its associated user. Having the same basic agent model, a PA can interact with other agents using co-operation methods and primitives.

Within a PA, knowledge about a user's goals, plans, capabilities, responsibilities, preferences and so on is represented. Furthermore, a PA has knowledge about the tools, the user is working with. By means of a special graphical interface a PA helps a user in initializing, processing, and managing co-operation processes with other agents – both human (via their respective PAs) and machine agents. A PA resembles a personal secretary, which helps its ordinate within co-operation processes and can act as a representative if the user is not present. A PA acts as an aide, keeping the human up to date on the current state in ongoing co-operation processes, and it advises the user on a variety of ways to co-operate. Thus, a PA, either based on some responsibility attributed to it or after having questioned its user, makes decisions, executes (routine) task such as

- managing and scheduling appointments,
- answering routine requests, and
- filtering and processing mail,

just to mention a few, potentially involving other users' agents. Via a graphical user interface a PA presents co-operation processes to the user; it provides funct-ionalities so that the human does not necessarily have to handle co-operation in terms of low-level messages.

PAs are an extension to concepts like 'Assistant' or 'Apprentice' not only in that they are simple assistants for local work but in that they support a user within complex co-operation processes with other agents. Earlier approaches to the design of PAs – but with different emphasis – were described in, e.g., H≅mm≅inen et al. (1990) and Pan and Tenenbaum (1991).

One of the classical PA tasks, appointment scheduling, will now be considered in more detail. PAs handling that specific task were implemented in the MECCA development environment. The implementation resulted in a prototype system called MAM (MECCA Appointment Manager). Appointment scheduling is an excellent example of how interaction and co-operation of PAs and their users leads to mutual committed multi-agent plans and is therefore a stimulating domain for human-computer co-operation.

The design of MAM started from the observation that users – although equipped with computers – cannot use their individual calendar tool to schedule meetings which are not automatically inserted in their respective calendar files. They can arrange meetings via email message exchange, but it is their own responsibility to find and insert appropriate data and to keep their calendars consistent. At that point, a PA can assist a user not only in automatically scheduling appointments but also in integrating different calendar tools. The core issues approached in MAM are:

- integration of different calendar tools,
- choice between different scheduling strategies, and
- treatment of resource agents as meeting participants.

To bridge this gap between different users' calendar management tools, we have chosen the following approach. The calendar system and the personal calendar data are considered part of an agent, more specifically the instantiation of a PA's body. The PA's head contains functions dealing with different strategies to set up meetings. Also, access to a graphical user interface is provided. This agent based concept allows besides the interoperable use of different calendar management tools for integrating additional resources relevant for meetings – rooms, overhead projectors, etc., can be treated as meeting participants if a calendar file is assigned to them.

In modeling the scenario of automatic appointment scheduling, different types of participants can be distinguished:

- the person who initiates a meeting (called the initiator),
- the persons who ought to attend a meeting (called participants or attendees), and
- resources like meeting rooms, pieces of equipment, etc., which are modeled as machine agents without an interface to set up meetings.

With the integration of machine agents, the scenario of appointment scheduling is extended from mere human-human co-operation to man-machine situations. Compared to machine agents, humans are more sophisticated than resource agents and therefore have a prominent position. For the appointment scheduling domain, this is reflected by the following points:

- only humans can set up meetings,
- humans can have a look at the availability of resource agents, and
- as opposed to humans, resource agents are not allowed to block a free meeting date.

The human participants are linked to each other and to resource agents via their PAs. Each human user's PA behaves like a personal secretary, which – as far as it is possible and as far as authorized – can schedule meetings. Therefore, a PA needs knowledge about the human calendar system, the human's preferences with respect to meeting times, meeting partners, meeting subjects, etc., the human's absence (vacation, conference, official trip, illness, etc.), the names and addresses of the persons the human wants to meet; names and addresses of the machine agents responsible for meeting rooms and equipment, and the format and storage location of the human's personal calendar data. This knowledge is either provided by an Agent Directory Service or is represented locally within the respective PAs.

To schedule and manage an appointment a variety of different conditions have to be considered. The whole spectrum of making appointments has to be supported, ranging from fully specified proposals up to very vague ones. For specification, the following parameters are of special importance:

- *participants*: Two types of participants can be distinguished: human and machine agents. This principal distinction can be further generalized, e.g., mandatory ones and optional ones
- *time*: This attribute is essential for the evaluation procedure. It can be a time point in which case the attribute duration, see below, has to be specified (e.g., tomorrow, 14:00), a continuous time interval (e.g., Tuesday, next week, 14:00–16:00) or a set of distinct time intervals (every day next week in the morning) or even unspecified (e.g., soon, as soon as possible)

- *duration*: In MAM, it is a fixed value specifying the duration in hours or minutes (e.g., one hour); it could also be an interval identifying an approximate duration (e.g., between two or three hours, less than two hours)
- *topic*: The topic may be relevant for a participant's personal assessment of the importance to attend a meeting or not
- *priority*: This value indicates the initiator's personal assessment of the meeting's importance. The priority value is also a measure of how easy it would be to reschedule the meeting.

Following are two of a set of possible strategies in MAM. They are represented as co-operation methods.

Within the *optimistic strategy* the initiator sends a request with a very specific time slot to all specified participants' PAs hoping that they can accept. If all PAs accept within a given time constraint, their users are asked for confirmation of the meeting.

If a user rejects or if she is already occupied at the specified time, the PA rejects the proposal, providing the reason for rejecting. This will cause the initiator to try another schedule.

Table 10.5. Optimistic appointment management

Initiator	Participants
APP_PREPARE_PROPOSAL	
send_app_proposal	
— **PROPOSE** (appointment, exact_time, ...) →	
	receive_app_proposal
	APP_EVALUATE_PROPOSAL
	send_app_reply
← **ACCEPT** —	
← **REJECT** —	
← **MODIFY** —	
receive_app_reply	
APP_EVALUATE_REPLIES	
— **ORDER** (appointment, ...) →	
goto(send_app_proposal)	goto(send_app_reply)

As is more often the case with even a small group of three or four persons, there may be no free time slot. The specific, very constrained meeting proposal has to be relaxed; a more *realistic strategy* has to be tried out by proposing a set of potential time intervals where the meeting could take place. Here, different procedures can be employed; they differ mainly in the point where the actual planning and scheduling of appointments occurs. In a more *centralized* approach, the initiator of a meeting (i.e., the respective PA) collects all information about the free time of the participants and then evaluates it, the other resembles a *circular* which is started by the initiator; here, fixing of an appointment is done successively and locally by each participant by constraining the possible time intervals.

The exchange of messages, the flow of information, and the local reasoning of the agents is shown in Tables 10.5 and 10.6 for the two strategies. For more detail on the MAM approach we refer to (Lux, 1995).

Table 10.6. Realistic appointment management, centralized method

Initiator	Participants
APP_PREPARE_PROPOSAL	
send_app_proposal	
— **PROPOSE** (appointment, rough_time, ...) →	
	receive_app_proposal
	APP_EVALUATE_FREE_TIME
	send_app_info
← REFINE (free_time) —	
receive_app_info	
APP_EVAL_INFO	
send_app_proposal	
— **PROPOSE** (appointment, exact_time, ...) →	
	receive_app_proposal
	APP_EVALUATE_PROPOSAL
	send_app_reply
← **ACCEPT** —	
← **REJECT** —	
← **MODIFY** —	
receive_app_reply	
APP_EVALUATE_REPLIES	
— **ORDER** (appointment, ...) →	
goto(send_app_proposal)	goto(send_app_reply)
goto(app_prepare_proposal)	goto(send_app_info)

10.3.2   Personalized Traffic Guidance

The MECCA/UTS (Urban Traffic Scenario) is another application realized by means of the MECCA system. It targets car park allocation and traffic guidance as specific sub-domains of the whole range of activities that have to be covered in a comprehensive approach for urban traffic control (see Haugeneder and Steiner (1994) for a more elaborate treatment). The system comprises the following two core functionalities:

- **car park allocation** according to specific individual needs, and
- **route guidance** to the selected car park.

The UTS model is based on a market-like competitive scenario, where cars compete for car parks and car parks compete for cars, each ruled by their own private strategy. The initiative for this competition comes from the cars. The route guidance model is based on a distributed problem solving approach for providing optimal paths.

On the highest level of abstraction, the UTS world itself consists of a set of sectors, which form an exhaustive topological partitioning of the overall traffic area; they can be viewed as regions with largely localized traffic-relevant features. On the modeling level, these sectors constitute a local default domain of control interaction. Each of these sectors defines a specific street topology and statically allocated services such as car parks, associated with it. In addition, a dynamically changing set of cars using the streets and provided services are allocated to each sector. Adjacent sectors are linked together via pairs of so-called sources and sinks which are designated by specific locations in their respective street topology. These sources and sinks constitute the connection points between pairs of sectors via which traffic flow from one sector to another can be facilitated.

This leads us to the domain-specific agents employed to model the various entities. Based on the agent architecture described earlier and the domain's ontology, three types of domain agents are provided in the UTS application with the following functionality:

- **Driver's Assistant**. The driver's assistant constitutes the individual car's (semi-) automatic guidance system, it acts on behalf of the driver to provide the required services
- **Parking Assignment System**. The parking assignment system agent is responsible for controlling the behavior of the car park to which it is allocated
- **Traffic Guidance System**. The traffic guidance system agent models the dynamic behavior of one specific sector with which it is associated by providing sector specific services.

In particular, the role of these agent types in the parking allocation process is as follows: The driver's assistant takes the initiative to negotiate on behalf of an individual driver with the car parks' parking assignment system in order to obtain a parking space according to its needs. For the transfer to a successfully booked parking space, the driver's assistant interacts with the traffic guidance system to find optimal routes. The parking assignment system maintains information about its individual car park's resources (free parking spaces) and uses this knowledge to negotiate with the driver's assistants. The traffic guidance system has knowledge about the topology of its associated sector and provides specific services to driver's assistants in the sector, such as route planning. In addition a traffic guidance system comprises the functionality of an generic MECCA agent directory service as described previously.

The behavior of a driver's assistant is defined by its negotiation strategy and cost function. The driver's assistant's cost function can take into account three criteria: the fee of the car park under consideration, the distance to this car park and the car park's booking and reservation policies. Furthermore the driver's assistant selects a co-operation method which defines a certain strategy to lead its negotiation with the car parks. The following three co-operation methods are provided:

- simple contracting,
- contracting with bid maintenance, and
- sequential request with best-first acceptance.

The simple contracting scheme corresponds to contract net with the driver's assistant being the contractor and the parking assignment systems being the bidders. The 'bid maintenance' version of this lets the driver's assistant keep the alternative lower rank bids until a car park has been successfully accessed. This feature is particularly useful if a preferred accepted bid cannot be taken advantage of due to unforeseen events during transfer of the car to the car park. Accidents, traffic jams, etc., are examples of such events. The tentative booking policy of parking assignment systems, as described below, also gives rise to such situations. The third co-operation method, sequential request, does not take into account and evaluate all potentially available car parks; rather the driver's assistant interacts with one car park at a time, checking whether its criteria can be fulfilled.

Two types of parking assignment systems are distinguished according to their behavior in making reservations. On the one hand, there are commitment-based parking assignment systems which try to provide a guaranteed reservation upon request. A parking assignment system with a non-committing reservation policy which only gives a rough indication of the possibility of getting a parking space; however, it does not give a strict guarantee for the availability of the parking space. This limitation in security is reflected by the fee that has to be paid: commitment-based parking assignment systems typically have a higher fee. The difference between commitment based versus non-committed reservation behavior might also be modeled as dynamic parking assignment system-specific behavior which is changed in response to the actual parking situation. Both policies might be offered by a single parking assignment system's differently priced schemes.

Also, the parking assignment system's fees can be modeled as changing with respect to the car with which it is negotiating.

Based on this, parking and guidance can be modeled as multi-agent co-operation. The parking processes are performed between the various types of agents by means of the driver's assistant's co-operation methods. These co-operation methods induce the exchange of knowledge between various distributed agents' knowledge bases, which in turn effects their resulting behavior.

Each parking process is comprised of several phases:

- **negotiation**: calling for all parking space bids in the sector according to the chosen co-operation method (involved agents: driver's assistant and (one or more) parking assignment system(s)),
- **reservation**: making a reservation with the parking assignment system that was awarded the bid (involved agents: driver's assistant and selected parking assignment system),
- **transfer**: moving to the corresponding car park (involved agents: driver's assistant and possibly several (in the case of sector handover) traffic guidance system(s)),
- **registration**: registering with the parking assignment system on arrival at the car park (involved agents: driver's assistant and parking assignment system);
- **parking**: moving to the parking space assigned by the parking assignment system (involved agents: driver's assistant and parking assignment system), and
- **de-registration/payment**: initiative to leave the car park and consequent payment of parking fees (participants: driver's assistant and parking assignment system).

In the multi-dimensional cost-based negotiation phase, which is conducted between a car driver's assistant and the car park's parking negotiation system, the final outcome is a function of the actual negotiation schemes and cost function on the driver's assistant's side and the reservation functionality if the parking and de-registration/payment are performed between the driver's assistant and the parking assignment system selected during the negotiation phase. The transfer phase, however, is the result of co-operation between the driver's assistant and the traffic guidance system, since the traffic guidance provides the route guidance from the car's current position to the car park.

During the negotiation phase, the parking assignment systems of different car parks also form coalitions with other parking assignment systems – even outside the current sector – in order to provide better offers to a driver's assistant or even to be able to provide offers at all in case of shortage of parking spaces. Such coalitions are highly dynamic, i.e., a fully booked car park's parking assignment may leave a coalition, and robust, i.e., the operational unavailability of a member does not disturb the coalition's overall behavior; however, these coalitions may also be defined statically. Functionally, such a coalition acts logically as a single parking assignment system which may offer and provide a car park even in a neighboring sector as long as this conforms with the requesting driver's assistant's cost function (such as sufficient closeness).

The acceptance of such a sector-external offer also includes the transfer of the car to the target sector. This transfer from one sector to another is coordinated by a sector handover mechanism, which again is modeled as an inter-agent co-operation taking place between the traffic guidance systems associated with the neighboring sectors involved. This handover mechanism ensures that an individual car is continuously linked to the responsible sector's traffic guidance system via its driver's assistant when crossing boundaries of the sectors.

During such a transfer phase with sector handover, there is no single component in the system that provides the overall route to the driver's assistant. The originating sector instead provides the route to a suitable sink into the target sector. As this sink is a source for the target sector, its traffic guidance system provides the route from there to the target destination. The logical transfer from the source sector's sink to the target sector's source (which is the same physical location) is performed by de-registering at the source traffic guidance system and registering at the target traffic guidance system. By combining sequences of sector handovers pairwise, arbitrary routes traversing n sectors can be constructed. This mechanism also allows for efficient notification of changes in the optimal routes (e.g., occurrence of a traffic jam).

Thus, within the MECCA/UTS system, parking activities in one sector or among several sectors are guided not by a centralized parking allocation system, but rather by a robust decentralized, sector-oriented control regime which is sensitive to the individual behavior of different driver's assistants and parking assignment systems as well as to the traffic guidance systems routing service. The real origin of its overall functionality comes from the interaction between the various components involved, i.e., their agentified counterparts.

10.4 Conclusion and Outlook

Agent software, although a comparatively young area in software design with many different facets and technical instantiations, has high potential to provide improved solutions for a wide range of applications, two of which were discussed in some detail. We are also witnessing the first steps towards market entry of agent software, both as generic technology and dedicated solutions. Despite this the overall situation of the field is somewhat unsatisfactory due to the diversity of approaches used to create agent-based solutions. The field still shows some lack of standardization. However, there are several dimensions where the initiation of a process of convergence seems both necessary and possible, such as:

- Agent communication and execution models
- A general agent service architecture (agent directory services with suitable agent access policies)
- A format for information exchange between agents – like KIF (Knowledge Interchange Format) and KQML (Knowledge Query and Manipulation Language)
- Agent interaction protocols (high-level, task-driven)
- A generic agent application interface (for easy agentification).

We are convinced that steps towards standardization with respect to these five fields will create another stimulus for technical progress in the field of agent software as a whole as well as for its practical impact. These steps are already being undertaken by the Foundation for Intelligent Physical Agents (FIPA, http://www.cselt.stet.it/fipa/).

Acknowledgements

The authors would like to express their appreciation to Andreas Lux, Michael Kold and Alastair Burt for their substantial contributions to the work presented here.

References

Chu, D. A. (1993) IC.Prolog II: a language for implementing multi-agent systems. In: S. M. Deen (Ed.) *Proceedings of the SIG on co-operation knowledge based systems*. DAKE Centre, University of Keele, 61–74.

Hämmäinen, H., Alasuvanto, J., Mäntylä, R. (1990) Experiences on semi-autonomous user agents. In: J. M. Y. Demazeau (Ed.) *Decentralized AI*. Elsevier Science Publishers, 235–249.

Haugeneder, H. (1994) IMAGINE final project report. IMAGINE Technical Report Series.

Haugeneder, H., Steiner, D. (1994) A multi-agent scenario for co-operation in urban traffic. In: S. M. Deen (Ed.) 1993 *Proceedings of the SIG on Co-operation Knowledge Based Systems*. DAKE Centre, University of Keele, 83–99.

Lux, A. (1995) Kooperative Mensch-Maschine Arbeit – ein Modellierungsansatz und dessen Umsetzung im Rahmen des Systems MEKKA, PhD thesis, Universität Saarbrücken.

Lux, A., de Greef, P., Bomarius, F., Steiner, D. (1993) A generic framework for human computer co-operation. In: M. Huns, M. Papazoglou, G. Schlageter (Eds.) *International Conference on Intelligent and Co-operative Information Systems*. IEEE Computer Society Press, 89–97.

Lux, A., Kolb, M. (1992) Linking humans and intelligent systems or: what are user agents good for? In: *Proceedings of the 16th German AI conference*, 372–385.

Lux, A., Kolb, M. (1995) Understanding co-operation: an agent's perspective. In: *Proceedings ICMAS-95*.

Pan, J. Y. C., Tenenbaum, J. M. (1991) Toward an intelligent framework for enterprise integration. In: *Proceedings 9th National Conference on Artificial Intelligence*. AAAI Press/MIT Press, 206–212.

Searle, J. R. (1969) *Speech Acts*. Cambridge University Press.

Smith, R. (1980) The contract net protocol: high level communication and control in a distributed problem solver. *IEEE Trans. on Computers*, 29, 1104–1113.

Steiner, D. (1995) IMAGINE: an integrated framework for constructing multi-agent systems. In: G. O'Hare, N. Jennings (Eds.) *Foundations of Distributed Artificial Intelligence*. Wiley Interscience.

Steiner, D., Burt, A., Kold, M., Lerin, C. (1993) The conceptual framework of MAI^{2}L. In: *Proc. Fifth European Workshop on Modelling Autonomous Agents in a Multi-agent World*.

Steiner, D., Mahling, D., Haugeneder, H. (1990) Human computer co-operative work. In: M. Huhns (Ed.) *Proc. of the 10th International Workshop on Distributed Artificial Intelligence*. MCC Technical Report ACT-AI-355-90.

Waters, R. C. (1986) The programmer's apprentice: a session with KBEMACS. In: R. C. W. C. Rich (Ed.) *Readings in Artificial Intelligence and Software Engineering*. Morgan Kaufmann, 351–374.

11 Intelligent Agents in Telecommunications[1]

R. Weihmayer
GTE Laboratories Incorporated

H. Velthuijsen
KPN Research

11.1 Introduction

The underlying fabric for communication among intelligent agents will in many cases be provided by telecommunication networks. But telecommunication networks have been seen as a natural domain for the investigation and application of intelligent agents technology as it emerged from the area of Distributed Artificial Intelligence (DAI). Telecommunication network administrations are vast organizations dedicated to operating and managing networks with broad functional segmentations: telephone network outside plant, switching and transmission plants, public network, all supporting different layers of specialized customer or service networks. These networks are organized into multiple physical and logical layers built with large quantities of repeated network elements and subnetwork structures. All these elements need to be configured, monitored, and controlled. In the future, this will preferably be done by automated operation support systems and without substantial human intervention.

Although many recent efforts in applying DAI techniques have come from the telecommunications industry, the legacy information infrastructure that services internal operations in this industry has so far dampened immediate attempts at introducing DAI-based systems in the field. Consequently, the experimental DAI-based systems that have been developed for telecommunications have been primarily aimed at future networks and laboratory environments.

This chapter presents a brief survey of recent efforts in applying DAI to telecommunications including some of our specific experiences with such applications. Applications and domain descriptions thus take precedence over focused analytical study of the corresponding agent systems and their theoretical justifications.

---

[1] This is a condensed and updated version of another paper: Distibuted AI and co-operative systems for telecommunications (Weihmayer and Velthuijsen, 1995).

Our communication engineering and automated 'coarse-grained' co-operative agent perspective leads us to omit treatment of human-computer interaction themes, 'information agents,' etc. Thus, we do not consider here applications based on *mobile* agents and scripting languages such as offered by Java and TeleScript, which lack explicit support for co-operative behavior, even though these types of agents have received a lot of attention in the telecommunications domain over the last couple of years. This is not to say that this technology is not promising. In fact, the commercial application of mobile agents and scripting languages may be closer than that of intelligent, co-operative agents.

Sections 11.2 and 11.3 form the core of our discussion of current applications to telecommunications. Section 11.2 emphasizes general coverage by describing current attempts in connecting DAI and telecommunication problems. Section 11.3 describes four systems in more detail. These systems were chosen because they are the result of sustained domain analysis and justification efforts and of advanced implementation and testbed construction, and because we were familiar with two of them, as major contributors in their development. Section 11.4 assesses the relative success of DAI in telecommunications and speculates on perspectives for DAI applications in telecommunications for the future. This chapter is both a reduced and updated version of a more extensive survey of the field (Weihmayer, 1994).

11.2   Overview of DAI and Telecommunications

After providing the basic rationale for DAI and telecommunications, this section briefly surveys the field with a small classification that also serves to ground the bibliography.

11.2.1   Rationale for DAI in Telecommunications

Inherent distribution and interconnectedness of telecommunication networks and their constituent components provide the basic rationale for DAI approaches to the solution of telecommunication problems. DAI approaches address a number of dimensions of this distribution:

- Along the geographical or functional boundaries of administrative domains, e.g., (Liempd, 1990; Sugawara, 1992b; Weihmayer, 1992).
- Along the functional boundaries of management and operations support tasks, e.g., (Garijo, 1992; Huhns, 1994; Rao, 1990).
- Between the different roles and responsibilities in a hierarchical network management organization, e.g., (Gaçti, 1993; So, 1992)
- Between the physical and/or logical layers of network organizations, such as the network control and transmission layers.

- Between physical network elements and logical network management layers, such as facility agents and customer agents in TEAM-CPS, e.g., (Appleby, 1994; Weihmayer, 1992).

- Between information, knowledge, and capabilities belonging to different entities and roles in a telecommunication system and its environment, such as the service profiles of different users in the negotiating agents approach, e.g., (Griffeth, 1993b).

Distribution is not the only criterion for determining the relevance and appropriateness of application of DAI techniques. DAI can be rationalized in terms of performance, partitioning global information (privacy domains), and requirements for intelligent co-ordination and negotiation between the different agents (users, subscribers, service providers, network operators, etc.) of future telecommunication software infrastructures.

11.2.2   Broad Survey of Applications

DAI techniques have been applied to a wide range of different telecommunication problems. This is illustrated in Table 11.1. First, we recognize the following layering of telecommunication systems: the transmission and switching layer, the network control layer, and the service layer; second, we distinguish between the network development and maintenance tasks of network design, network management, and service management; and third, we single out process support, i.e., systems that support and automate (typical telecommunications) business processes.

We are aware of one application in the **transmission and switching** layer. Nishibe et al. have presented an approach to dynamically allocating channels in an ATM (asynchronous transfer mode) network.

Two applications focus on the **network control** layer: the work by Fletcher and Deen (Fletcher, 1994) on dynamic routing and congestion control; and some of the work by Weihmayer et al. (Weihmayer, 1993), on mediation between control wielded by public network provisioning systems and integrated private network management systems.

One application focuses on the **service** layer. This approach uses DAI techniques to mediate between preferences users may have for the behavior of a telecommunications system and as it is typically implemented by their subscribing to particular service features (Griffeth, 1993); see also Section 11.3. This work builds on an agent-based service execution environment on top of a network. This approach has since been adopted by various others (Busuoic, 1996; Rizzo, 1995; Zibman, 1996). A related approach uses mobile agent technology within the constraints of the Intelligent Network architecture to offer services in a fully deregulated environment (Magedanz, 1996). The work by Gaçti and Pujolle proposes to use DAI techniques to integrate standardized architectural concepts for the areas of service provisioning (in the **service** layer), **service management**, and **network management** (Gaçti, 1993)

Table 11.1. Telecommunication application areas

Process support	Services & features	Service management
(Huhns, 94)	(Gaïti, 93; Griffeth, 93; Magedanz, 96; Rizzo, 95; Zibman, 95)	(Busuioc, 93; Gaïti, 93; Weihmayer, 92)
	Network control (Fletcher, 94; Weihmayer, 93)	**Network management** (Adler, 89; Biron, 92; Conry, 91; Esfandiari, 96; Gaïti, 93; Garijo, 92; Gyires, 96; Rao, 90; Reilly, 96; Silver, 93; Skarmaes, 96; So, 92; Somers, 96; Sugawara, 92)
	Transmission & switching (Nishibe, 93)	**Network design** (Lirov, 91; Liempd, 90)

Service management is furthermore addressed by Weihmayer et al. (Weihmayer et al., 1992) and Griffiths and Whitney in their applications of DAI to distributed service provisioning among service maintenance agents and customer agents.

Network management is the most frequently addressed application area. Three of the more advanced applications in this group are described in more detail in Section 11.3. In network management, a distinction can be made between the traditional network management functions: configuration management, fault management, accounting management, performance management, and security management. Not all of these functions have been addressed by DAI approaches: accounting and security management are, as yet, uncharted grounds, although Reilly has studied in particular the security aspects involved in extending TMN-based network management systems with mobile agent technology.

In several cases, one system combines more than one functionality, e.g., fault and performance management, but most approaches focus on fault management. We mention:

- work on the Multistage Negotiation protocol developed with the task of restoring transmission paths in telecommunication networks in mind (Conry, 1991);

- LODES (Sugawara, 1992) and DBB (So, 1992) for monitoring and diagnosis of faults in coupled, TCP/IP-based LANs;
- MAITE for fault management in the Spanish IBERCOM network of 800 PBXs (Garijo, 1992);
- TEAM-CPS for fault and configuration management of private and public networks that use partially overlapping resources;
- ILS (Integrated Learning System; Silver, 1993);
- work in the 'Réseau Futé (Smart Net)' project on using automated learning technology to create agents for network management (Esfandiari, 1996);
- work by Gyires and Muthuswamy on the 'Statistical Heuristic Search Methodology' for reestablishing virtual paths when connections are interrupted (Gyires, 1996);
- HYBRID for network management of ATM networks (Somers, 1996);
- work on an agent-based architecture for network management (Skarmaes, 1996);
- work by Adler et al. (1989) addressing co-operative agents for fault and performance management;
- the work by Rao and Georgeff (1990) on the Interactive Real-Time Network Management System (IRTNMS) for monitoring, diagnosis, and fault recovery; and finally
- the IDEAL framework (Biron, 1992) which presents a generic framework for building fault management systems.

Two applications are mentioned in the literature for **network design**: one by Lirov and Melamed (1991) where loosely coupled expert systems perform subsequent tasks in finding an optimal network configuration; and one by van Liempd et al. (1990) where blackboard-based nodes are used to configure sections of network connections spanning multiple administrative domains.

The last application referenced in Table 11.1 addresses a **process support** task which is particular to telecommunications, requiring co-ordination among many operations support and database systems.

Several activities studying the application of DAI techniques to telecommunications have abstracted from particular network architectures workflow management for support of provisioning of digital telecommunications services, but others address a particular type of network. TCP/IP-based LANs have been used in a number of applications (So, 1992; Sugawara, 1992), probably because this type of network is readily accessible for experimentation in many research organizations. One application looked at network configuration of a leased-line corporate network (Liempd, 1990). The work by Weihmayer et al. addressed the interplay between a virtual corporate network implemented over a voice/data PBX network with public T1 links (Weihmayer, 1992). The MAITE system was targeted at a network of 800 interconnected PBXs (Garijo, 1992). In (Nishibe et al., 1993), Nishibe et al. describe an application for the ATM network concept.

Present-day public telephony networks have not been the subject of detailed study according to our survey.

11.2.3 DAI Techniques

It may be too early, given how few implementation efforts we have found, to begin a classification according to DAI techniques used. We found that a few well-established DAI techniques are mostly referred to in current applications to telecommunications, for example: blackboard systems in (Adler, 1989; Garijo, 1992; Liempd, 1990); the Contract Net Protocol in (Biron, 1992; So, 1992). Most other references use specialized representations or algorithms for such aspects as agent architecture and organization, negotiation and co-ordination, planning, etc.

11.3 Overview of Four Applications

The significance of the four DAI applications presented in this section lies in the range of DAI techniques used, the underlying domain analysis, and the extent of experimentation work.

11.3.1 'Distributed Big Brother': Campus Network Management

'Big Brother' is a centralized LAN manager operating at the University of Michigan's Computer Aided Engineering Network (CAEN). 'Distributed Big Brother' (DBB) is a research testbed built at CAEN to investigate higher performance and more robust LAN management techniques using a combination of a number of DAI techniques.

The specific domain under consideration is management of campus-level LAN interconnect systems, i.e., multiple LANs connected with bridges, routers, gateways, etc., (spanning less than 10 miles) without intervening WAN. The target functionality is system support, specifically for fault management (So, 1992)

The operational requirements for DBB include maintaining a centralized view of network fault management, improving the robustness of network management processing, and increasing its performance and parallelism. Individual LAN segments and local subnets are loosely coupled in this domain but interdependent inasmuch as they share components, e.g., multiport bridges, and as decisions regarding these components have impact across subnet boundaries. In DBB, those are the entities across which distribution takes place.

The rationale for a DAI approach is to manage a distributed set of homogeneous LAN managers as a dynamically self-reconfigurable organization driven by fault conditions in the campus LAN network. This organization is hierarchical because centralized control remains embodied in a root management agent that maintains a global network view but operates under a delegation of authority scheme to manage distributed manager agents. The intelligence of co-operative agents is thus geared toward maintaining this organization, through organization structuring and hierarchical control; performing load management, e.g., which agents manage what entities in the network; as well as contracting and voting to distribute roles.

DBB agents are fairly large and complex entities loosely coupled in their activities. No single DBB agent, regardless of organizational role or position in the hierarchy, can be a single point of failure. DBB uses the Contract Net Protocol to announce, bid on, and award roles and tasks. Hierarchical control is applied within the context of election procedures, with simple rules to designate agents that officiate election to network management roles.

Agents are structured as interacting communication, contracting, and task processes. They use control problem solving and domain problem solving message types. DBB agents are homogeneous and are implemented as Unix processes in their host workstation. An internal rule base specializes agent behavior based on dynamically assigned roles. Inter-agent communication occurs 'in-band' using UDP over the TCP/IP LANs managed by DBB.

11.3.2 Customer Network Control and TEAM-CPS

TEAM-CPS (Testbed Environment for Autonomous Multi-agent Co-operative Problem Solving; Tan, 1992; Weihmayer, 1992) evolved from a number of communication domains, each requiring distributed problem solving among geographically and functionally distributed problem solvers performing interdependent planning tasks. An industry perspective on this effort is provided in (Mantelman, 1990).

Customer networks are integrated voice/data networks in which switching and transmission facilities can be owned by the customer and/or leased from the public network. A distributed co-operative agent-based architecture for customer network control was developed. Facility provisioning in the public network is assigned to a computer system with the ability to satisfy real-time demand for circuit addition and deletion requests from multiple customer network systems. This is the physical network layer, in contrast to the logical customer network layer.

The DAI approach to this problem models the joint problem solving and co-ordination that the respective network managers go through in resource constrained situations where compromise solutions need to be found to partially or fully restore failed circuits. The problem solvers are by necessity distinct and heterogeneous; the customer manages his logical network layer, which is functionally separated and involves private data and proprietary operations on services, traffic, and usage; the same applies to the public network, which delivers a complex service using a distinct and private infrastructure in a competitive environment. The local problem solving required is in both cases complex and knowledge intensive, and integrates lots of information, e.g., fault management, trunk network design, and provisioning in the public network; and traffic, service, session, and configuration control in the customer network.

TEAM-CPS evolved as a framework for building co-operative agents that are heterogeneous at the domain problem solving level but for which common agent control abstractions can be applied to co-ordinate their problem solving behavior. Customer and public network agents share agent control and problem solving mechanisms but can be endowed with different domain models for planning and problem solving as well as different control policies, represented as rules in agent programs. The TEAM-CPS framework integrates Agent-Oriented Programming (AOP) and classical AI planning as the 'head' and 'body,' respectively, of problem solving agents.

A more flexible and general agent control structure was needed to model plan interactions using higher level knowledge and to deal with pragmatic issues in managing compromise and query dialogues among the agents. Agent-Oriented Programming (Shoham, 1993) is a framework that integrates agent control and communication. In AOP, agents have persistent mental states that use techniques of modal and temporal logic to represent agent beliefs and commitments to other agents. Speech-act models of communication are used to support simple communication to inform, request, and commit about actions.

TEAM-CPS integrates this form of agent control with planning-based problem solving by providing common representation of world states in planning and belief in agent mental states. Agent programs are constructed with simple heuristics to generate proposals and counterproposals. Co-ordination in systems of up to three agents were studied.

11.3.3   LODES: Distributed TCP/IP Fault Management

LODES (Large-internetwork Observation and Diagnostic Expert System) is an expert system for detecting and diagnosing problems in a segment of a local area network (Sugawara, 1992). Different LODES system copies, or instances, can monitor and manage different network segments. LODES is designed in such a way that LODES instances co-operate with each other as agents of a multi-agent system. Co-operation is necessary when it is not clear in which segment the cause of a problem is located, when a problem occurs in a part of the network monitored by more than one LODES agent, or when one agent needs additional information from another agent to perform its own tasks.

LODES was developed for TCP/IP local area networks (LANs) that consist of several constituent networks connected through routers. Each constituent network has its own LODES diagnostic system. LODES addresses connection establishment problems due to unintentional disconnections, slow transmission, and network congestion which arise in such networks.

An expert system approach was taken to overcome these difficulties in the diagnostic task. Furthermore, a distributed approach was chosen over a centralized approach to reflect natural physical and functional distribution of networks, to localize private information, such as passwords, within the boundaries of separate administrative domains, and to increase performance.

The LODES system was primarily developed as a research testbed; however, the system has been tried on real equipment and laboratory-configured networks with some success.

11.3.4 Feature Interaction and the Negotiating Agents Approach

The negotiating agents approach was developed to detect and resolve certain kinds of feature interactions that occur in telecommunications systems (Griffeth, 1993). Features in a telecommunications system provide packages of added functionality to basic communication services (e.g., call-forwarding and caller-ID). The operation of one feature may influence that of another feature. Sometimes such influences, called feature interactions, are intended. However, at other times, these interactions can be unexpected and undesired and need to be detected and resolved.

Features are a way for subscribers to tailor their use of telecommunications services to their specific needs and intentions. However, different parties to a call may have different needs and intentions, which lead to conflicts between the intentions and, analogously, to interactions between the corresponding features.

The negotiating agents approach recognizes that a significant subset of feature interactions are the result of conflicting intentions of different subscribers, who are not necessarily party to the same call. These conflicts may arise over which medium and protocol to use for a call, over the use of shared resources such as terminals and bridges, over what information can be transmitted as part of a call, etc.

The negotiating agents approach uses an agent for each entity that may have an interest in how calls are set up and conducted in a telecommunications system (users, network providers, information providers, etc.). An agent is given information about the intentions of its owning entity and negotiates with other agents to detect and resolve conflicts. The negotiation mechanism was specifically designed for this application to search for win/win solutions and to deal with agents that are not prepared to disclose too much about their preferences. A DAI approach was chosen to separate user preferences and to build on DAI expertise in the area of automated negotiation processes.

The negotiating agents approach has been implemented and tested on top of a multimedia desktop conferencing research prototype.

11.4 DAI and Telecommunications: Where Do We Stand?

Although quite a bit of industrial activity in applying DAI technology to real-world domains has been in telecommunications (Bond, 1992; Durfee, 1991; Jennings, 1994), there are currently no fielded DAI systems in public or private telecommunications. We discuss the issues that have hindered the emergence of fielded DAI systems in telecommunications so far and paint a direction in which we expect real-world applications to come about in the next few years.

11.4.1 Problems with DAI Approaches

There are several reasons why DAI systems are slow to be fielded in mainstream telecommunication systems in spite of the clear rationale and need for their introduction.

One reason is the absence of adequate infrastructure for autonomous agent-based control in present-day communication systems. Another is that the modernization of public networks is a relatively slow process because backward compatibility must be maintained to meet high reliability and availability requirements. DAI adds distribution to the complexity of AI and may thus still be seen as too high a risk.

The technology is still emerging and is only beginning to provide a solid foundation, principled practices, and engineering methodologies required to produce mainstream applications. We note that the basic approach in all four examples in Section 11.3 was to consider a problem for which a co-operative agent solution appears to be the best approach and where there is no 'legacy' system to integrate. Such an approach is suitable for proof-of-concept experimentation and allows a co-operative solution to be built from the ground up. However, it is not conducive to fielded systems. We believe that DAI-based systems will appear along a different path.

Actually, the penetration of expert systems may offer a good predictor for the emergence of DAI-based applications. Good opportunities for the success of DAI in telecommunications will be in network management and operations support for public and private networks. Expert systems are slowly penetrating those areas. Our thesis is that they will provide the intelligent systems infrastructure and potentially the agents of future co-operative systems. Of course, many different AI and reasoning paradigms, not just rule-based reasoning, will provide the intelligence substrate for those mainstream expert systems. In this perspective, we consider the emergence of communication and knowledge sharing between these systems as requiring a DAI technology base that goes beyond basic co-ordination among rule-based inference engines and their knowledge bases.

11.4.2 The Road to Fielded Applications: An Example

Here is an example that illustrates how we believe that fielded DAI applications will emerge in telecommunications. A recent survey (Goyal, 1994) provides information on expert system deployment in various telecommunication domains. One such system, SSCFI (Special Service Circuit Fault Isolation; Goyal, 1994) is an example of advanced deployment of geographically distributed local intelligence.

It is an expert system that is currently being deployed in all the GTE telephone companies in the United States. It functions as an expert test technician that reads and interprets trouble reports on special service circuits; decides to conduct tests and interpret the results of those tests, using in the process a number of remote test and database systems; and, finally, routes the report to the appropriate repair group with the results of its analysis. The first important feature of SSCFI for this discussion is its autonomy. Besides a minimal administrative interface, SSCFI processes operate in the background and have full control over the trouble report queues to which they are initially assigned. SSCFIs are, in a sense, our model of practical, narrow, but intelligent autonomous systems performing their tasks without direct human operational control. These tasks are not to present information to people, but to act within the context of a workflow system where field repair crews are at the receiving end.

The current evolution of SSCFI is pointing toward some form of homogeneous multi-agent task allocation system involving SSCFIs throughout the GTE regions. SSCFIs need fast local access to all the OSSs, database resources, test systems, and test points involved in testing circuits. To maximize throughput, these resources are locally available on their LANs. SSCFIs can do simple load balancing by spawning child processes to jointly handle test loads. The spawning is constrained by the availability of computing resources. DAI begins to come into the picture as load sharing at a national level between all SSCFIs is being considered to exploit time zone differences and sharing of computing resources across regions. Some ideas under discussion include using contracting schemes to have a local SSCFI request other SSCFIs to accept responsibility for testing circuits along with remote control of the resources required to perform those tests and to negotiate the conditions under which this is done.

The above discussion on SSCFI evolution was meant to illustrate our thesis. We believe that naturally distributed systems with strong locality requirements (i.e., need to be close to resources used or operated upon), operating under autonomous control regimes (i.e., with the intelligence to do so), will be the first to require DAI-based approaches. Clearly, our four examples of Section 11.3 also share, albeit in less immediate fashion, these characteristics and are important candidates for the future.

11.5 Conclusion

The notion of intelligent agents is certainly quite pervasive today. A special issue of *Communications of the ACM* (ACM, 1994) shows how intelligent agents are being promoted as the basic building blocks of information systems. If agents are coming, co-operative agents cannot be far.

In telecommunications, requirements for intelligent agents are even more immediate especially since telecommunication networks are canonical distributed systems.

This chapter has thus presented a number of different applications of intelligent agents technology to telecommunication, with a focus on four major systems. These applications are in various stages of conceptualization and development, and clearly the scope of domain specific knowledge engineering taking place shows the rapidly growing maturity of DAI penetration in this field. This makes telecommunications presently one of the more promising application areas for DAI. Even though there are currently no fielded DAI-based systems, we believe that the potential is there for this to happen within the next few years.

References

Adler, M. R., Davis, A. B., Weihmayer, R., Worrest, R. W. (1989) Conflict-resolution strategies for nonhierarchical distributed agents. In: L. Gasser, M. N. Huhns (Eds.) *Distributed Artificial Intelligence*, Vol II, Research Notes in Artificial Intelligence, Chapter 7, 139–161. Pitman, London.

Appleby, A., Steward, S. (1994) Mobile software agents for control in telecommunications networks. *British Telecom Technology*, 12(2), April.

Biron, B., Laasri, H., Rezzouk, J. (1992) A multi-agent framework for diagnosing faults in large telecommunication networks. In: *Proceedings 6th RACE TMN Conference, International Conference on Communications Management for Broadband Networks and Services*, Funchal, Madeira Island, Portugal, September 1-3.

Bond, A. H., Gasser, L. (1992) A subject-indexed bibliography of distributed artificial intelligence. *IEEE Transactions on Systems, Man, and Cybernetics*, 22(6), 1260–1281, November/December.

Busuioc, M., Griffiths, D. (1993) Co-operating intelligent agents for service management in communications networks. In: S. M. Deen (Ed.) *CKBS-SIG Proceedings* 1993, 213–226, University of Keele, September.

Busuioc, M. (1996) Distributed intelligent agents – a solution for the management of complex services. In: *Proceedings ECAI Workshop 'Intelligent Agents for Telecom Applications (IATA '96)'*, Budapest, August 13.

Conry, S. E., Kuwabara, K., Lesser, V. R., Meyer, R. A.(1991) Multistage negotiation for distributed constraint satisfaction. *IEEE Transactions on Systems, Man, and Cybernetics*, 21(6), 1462–1477.

Durfee, E. H. (Ed.) (1991) Special section on distributed artificial intelligence. In: *IEEE Transactions on Systems, Man, and Cybernetics*, 21(6), November/ December.

Esfandiari, B., Deflandre, G., Quinqueton, J. (1996) An interface agent for network supervision. In: *Proceedings ECAI Workshop on Intelligent Agents for Telecom Applications (IATA '96)*, Budapest, August 13.

Fikes, F., Genesereth, M. et al. (1993) KIF – draft specification of the knowledge interchange format. DARPA Knowledge Sharing Initiative Interlingua Working Group, Technical Report.

Finin, T., Weber, J. et al. (1994) KQML – draft specification of the knowledge query and manipulation language. DARPA Knowledge Sharing Initiative External Interfaces Working Group, Technical Report, February 9.

Fletcher, M. (1994) Some further design considerations for the congestion management mechanism MENTHOL, Technical Report, University of Keele, February 20.

Gaçti, D., Pujolle, G. (1993) TMN, IN and DAI. In: *Proceedings TINA'93*, II/111–121, L'Aquila, Italy.

Garijo, F. J., Hoffmann, D. (1992) A multi-agent architecture for operation and maintenance of telecommunications networks. In: *Proceedings Twelfth International Conference on Artificial Intelligence, Expert Systems, and Natural Language (Avignon '92)*, Vol 2, 427–436, Avignon, France.

Goyal, S. K. (1994) Artificial Intelligence in support of distributed network management. In: M. Sloman (Ed.) *Network and Distributed Systems Management*. Addison-Wesley.

Griffeth, N. D., Velthuijsen, H. (1993) Win/win negotiation among autonomous agents. In: *Proceedings 12th International Workshop on Distributed Artificial Intelligence*, 187–202, Hidden Valley, PA.

Griffeth, N. D., Velthuijsen, H. (1994) The negotiating agents approach to runtime feature interaction resolution. In: L. G. Bouma, H. Velthuijsen (Eds.) *Feature Interactions in Telecommunications Systems*. IOS Press, Amsterdam, 217–235.

Griffiths, D. G., Whitney, C. (1991) The role of intelligent software agents in integrated communications management. *British Telecom Technology Journal*, 9(3), 97–105.

Gyires, T., Muthuswamy, K. (1996) Heuristic routing algorithm for re-establishing interrupted connections in telecommunications networks. In: *Proceedings ECAI Workshop on Intelligent Agents for Telecom Applications (IATA '96)*, Budapest, August 13.

Hewitt, C., Inman, J. (1991) DAI betwixt and between: from 'intelligent agents' to open systems science. *IEEE Transactions on Systems, Man, and Cybernetics*, 21(6), 1409–1419.

Huhns, M., Singh, M. (1994) Automating workflows for service provisioning: integrating AI and database technologies.In: *Proceedings 10th IEEE Conference on Artificial Intelligence Applications*, San Antonio, Texas, March 1-4.

Ingrand, F. F., Georgeff, M. P., Rao, A. S. (1992) An architecture for real-time reasoning and system control, *IEEE Expert*, December.

Ishida, T., Sasaki, Y., Fukuhara, Y. (1991) Use of procedural programming languages for controlling production systems. In: *Proceedings IEEE Conference on Artificial Intelligence for Applications (CAIA '91)*, 71–75.

Ishida, T., Sasaki, Y., Fukuhara, Y. (1992) A transaction model for multi-agent production systems. In: *Proceedings IEEE Conference on Artificial Intelligence for Applications (CAIA '92)*, 288–294.

Jennings, N. R. (1994) Co-operation in industrial multi-agent systems. In: *World Scientific Series in Computer Science*, Vol 43. World Scientific, Singapore.

Kuwabara, K., Lesser, V. R. (1989) Extended protocol for multistage negotiation. In: *Proceedings 9th Workshop on Distributed Artificial Intelligence*, 129–161, Eastsound, WA.

Kuwabara, K., Ishida, T. (1992) Symbiotic approach to distributed resource allocation: toward co-ordinated reasoning. In: A. Cesta, R. Conte, M. Miceli (Eds.) *Proceedings MAAMAW'92*, San Martino al Cimino, Italy.

Lesser, V. (1991) A retrospective view of FA/C distributed problem solving. *IEEE Transactions on Systems, Man, and Cybernetics*, 21(6), 1347–1362, November/December.

van Liempd, E. P. M., Velthuijsen, H., Florescu, A. (1990) BLONDIE-III: a distributed implementation of a network configuration problem. *IEEE Expert*, 5(4), 48–55.

Lirov, Y., Melamed, B. (1991) Expert design systems for telecommunications. *Expert Systems with Applications*, 2, 219–228.

Magedanz, T. (1996) Mobile agent-based service provision in intelligent networks. In: *Proceedings ECAI Workshop on Intelligent Agents for Telecom Applications (IATA '96)*, Budapest, August 13.

Mantelman, L. (1990) Orchestrating people and computers in their networks. In: *Data Network Design Strategies*, McGraw-Hill/Data Communications Book Series, Vol 4, 255–266.

Minton, S. et al. (1989) PRODIGY 2.0: The manual and tutorial. Technical Report CMU-CS-89-146, Carnegie Mellon University.

Nishibe, Y., Kuwabara, K., Suda, T., Ishida, T. (1993) Distributed channel allocation in ATM networks. In: *Proceedings IEEE Globecom '93*, 12.2.1–12.2.7, Houston, TX.

Rao, A. S., Georgeff, M. P. (1990) Intelligent real-time network management. In: *Proceedings 10th International Conference on Artificial Intelligence, Expert Systems, and Natural Language (Avignon '90)*, Avignon, France.

Reilly, J. (1996) Security aspects of intelligent agent based extensions to the TMN management framework. In: *Proceedings ECAI Workshop on Intelligent Agents for Telecom Applications (IATA '96)*, Budapest, August 13.

Riecken, D. (Guest Ed.) (1994) Special issue on intelligent agents. *Communications of the ACM*, 37(7), July.

Rizzo, M., Utting, I. A. (1995) An agent-based model for the provision of advanced tele-communications services. In: *Proceedings TINA '95*, 205–218.

Shoham, Y. (1993) Agent-oriented programming. *Artificial Intelligence*, 60, 51–92. Elsevier Science Publishers.

Silver, B., Frawley, W., Iba, G., Vittal, J. (1993) ILS: a system of learning distributed heterogeneous agents for network traffic management. In: *Proceedings ICC'93*, Geneva, Switzerland.

Skarmeas, I. N., Clark, K. L. (1996) Process oriented programming for agent-based network management. In: *Proceedings ECAI Workshop on Intelligent Agents for Telecom Applications (IATA '96)*, Budapest, August 13.

So, Y. P., Durfee, E. H. (1992) A distributed problem solving system for computer network management. *International Journal of Intelligent and Co-operating Information Systems*, 1(2).

Somers, F. (1996) HYBRIRD: intelligent agents for distributed ATM network management. In: *Proceedings ECAI Workshop on Intelligent Agents for Telecom Applications (IATA '96)*, Budapest, August 13.

Sugawara, T., Murakami, K. (1992) A multiagent diagnostic system for inter-network problems. In: *Proceedings INET'92*, Kobe, Japan.

Tan, M., Weihmayer, R. (1992) Integrating agent-oriented programming and planning for co-operative problem solving. In: *Working Notes AAAI Work-shop on Co-operation among Heterogeneous Intelligent Systems*, 129–137, San Jose, CA.

Weihmayer, R., Tan, M. (1992) Modeling co-operative agents for customer network control using planning and agent-oriented programming. In: *Proceedings IEEE Globecom'92*, Orlando, FL, December 6-9.

Weihmayer, R., Ghaznavi, I., Sheridan, P. (1993) A distributed architecture for co-operative management of strategic communication networks. In: *Proceedings IEEE MILCOM'93*, Boston, MA, October 11-14.

Weihmayer, R., Velthuijsen, H. (1995) Distributed AI and co-operative systems for telecommunications. In: J. Liebowitz, D. S. Prerau (Eds.) *Worldwide Intelligent Systems: Approaches to Telecommunications and Network Management*. IOS Press, Amsterdam, Ch. 11, 227–260.

Zibman, I., Woolf, C., O'Reilly, P., Strickland, L., Willis, D., Visser, J. (1995) Minimizing feature interactions: an architecture and processing model approach. In: K. E. Cheng, T. Ohta (Eds.) *Feature Interactions in Telecommunications Systems*. IOS Press, Amsterdam, 65–84.

12 Managing Heterogeneous Transaction Workflows with Co-operating Agents

M. N. Huhns
University of South Carolina

M. P. Singh
North Carolina State University

12.1 Introduction

Business operations, including sales, marketing, manufacturing, and design, can no longer be done in isolation, but must be done in a global context, i.e., as part of an enterprise. A characteristic of such enterprises is that their information systems are large and complex, and the information is in a variety of forms, locations, and computers. The topology of these systems is dynamic and their content is changing so rapidly that it is difficult for a user or an application program to obtain correct information, or for the enterprise to maintain consistent information.

Some of the techniques for dealing with the size and complexity of these enterprise information systems are modularity, distribution, abstraction, and intelligence, i.e., being smarter about how you seek and modify information. Combining these techniques implies the use of intelligent, distributed modules – a distributed artificial intelligence approach. In accord with this approach, we distribute and embed computational agents throughout an enterprise. The agents are knowledgeable about information resources that are local to them, and co-operate to provide global access to, and better management of, the information. For the practical reason that the systems are too large and dynamic (i.e., open) for global solutions to be formulated and implemented, the agents need to execute autonomously and be developed independently. To co-operate effectively, the agents must either *have models of each other and of the available information resources* or *provide models of themselves*. We focus on the latter in this chapter.

For such an open information environment, the questions arise: what should be modeled, where do models come from, what are their constituents, and how should they be used? We discuss the types of models that might be available in an enterprise and how agents can acquire them. We use the ontology developed for the large knowledge-based system, Cyc, for semantic grounding of the models. This provides a common structured vocabulary that all of the agents use and share. We then describe a set of agents for telecommunication service provisioning – a scheduling agent, a schedule-repairing agent, a schedule-processing agent, and an interface agent – and then describe their models and how they use them to co-operate. We also describe the use of actors (Agha, 1986) – one per agent – who manage communications among the agents. Each actor independently maintains the relationship between its agent and the common ontology (in the form of articulation axioms), and updates that relationship as the ontology changes or the agent itself evolves.

12.2 Semantic Inconsistency

A characteristic of all modern enterprises is that they have a lot of information in numerous different forms. A requirement of enterprise information systems is that applications operate correctly and efficiently using all of the information that might be available in the enterprise. One of the major problems in satisfying this requirement is that the information often has different semantics in each of the systems, and the differences must be resolved before the systems can interoperate. There are several types of semantic inconsistencies that can occur among applications and resources, as follows:

- mismatches in units, e.g., '$' versus 'DM'
- mismatches in scale, e.g., 'thousands' versus 'millions'
- mismatches in quantization (granularity), e.g., hotels rated by the *three* categories 'economy,' 'deluxe,' or 'luxurious' in one system, and by the *four* categories '$,' '$$,' '$$$,' or '$$$$' in another
- synonyms, e.g., 'single' versus 'unmarried'
- abbreviations, e.g., 'TX' versus 'Texas' or 'Sep' versus 'Sept.'
- combinations of the above mismatches, e.g., an attribute *cost* with values representing 'dollars,' 'before tax,' and 'for each' versus an attribute *price* with values representing 'francs,' 'after tax,' and 'per dozen'

Inconsistencies such as these need to be resolved in order for applications and resources to interoperate correctly. We believe resolution can be achieved via modeling.

12.3 Modeling

Enterprise information modeling is a corporate activity that produces the models needed for interoperability. The resultant models should describe all aspects of a business environment, including:

- databases
- database applications
- software repositories
- part description repositories

- expert systems, knowledge bases, and computational agents
- business work flows, and the information they create, use, maintain, and own
- the business organization itself

The models provide online documentation for the concepts they describe. They enable application code and data to be reused, data to be analyzed for consistency, databases to be constructed automatically, the impact of change on an enterprise to be assessed, and applications to be generated automatically.

An enterprise might have many models available, each describing a portion of the enterprise and each constructed independently. For example:

- The information present in a database is modeled by the schema for the database, which is produced through a process of logical data modeling.
- The data values present in a database are modeled (weakly, in most cases) by data dictionary information, which is produced through data engineering.
- The information present in an object-centered knowledge base is modeled by the ontology of the objects, which is produced through ontological engineering.
- Process models, possibly in the form of Petri nets or IDEFx descriptions, are produced through logical process modeling.
- STEP (Standard for the Exchange of Product model data) schemas, written in Express, are produced from component and physical process modeling.

Although it might appear that interoperability would require all of these models to be merged into a single, homogeneous, global model, this is *not* the case in our approach. Instead, there are good reasons for retaining the many individual models: 1) they are easier to construct than a single large model; 2) enterprises may be formed dynamically through mergers, acquisitions, and strategic alliances, and the resultant enterprises might have inherited many existing models; 3) because enterprises are geographically dispersed, their resources are typically decentralized; and 4) as enterprises (and thus models) evolve, it is easier to maintain smaller models.

Making use of small individual models means they must be related and reconciled. Unfortunately, the models are often mutually incompatible in syntax and semantics, not only due to the different things being modeled, but also due to mismatches in underlying hardware and operating systems, in data structures, and in corporate usage. In attempting to model some portion of the real world, information models necessarily introduce simplifications and inaccuracies that result in semantic incompatibilities. However, the individual models must be related to each other and their incompatibilities resolved (Sheth and Larson, 1990), because:

- A coherent picture of the enterprise is needed to enable decision makers to operate their business efficiently and designers to evaluate information flows to and from their particular application.

- Applications need to interoperate correctly across a global enterprise. This is especially important due to the increasing prevalence of strategic business applications that require *intercorporate linkage,* e.g., linking buyers with suppliers, or *intracorporate integration,* e.g., producing composite information from engineering and manufacturing views of a product.
- Developers require integrity validation of new and updated models, which must be done in a global context.
- Developers want to detect and remove inconsistencies, not only among models, but also among the underlying business operations that are modeled.

We utilize a mediating mechanism based on an existing common ontology to yield the appearance and effect of semantic homogeneity among existing models. The mechanism provides logical connectivity among information resources via a semantic service layer that automates the maintenance of data integrity and provides an enterprise-wide view of all the information resources, thus enabling them to be used coherently. This logical layer is implemented as a network of interacting agents. Significantly, the individual systems retain their autonomy. This is a fundamental tenet of the Carnot architecture that we developed and deployed (Woelk et al., 1995), which provides the tools and infrastructure for interoperability across global enterprises.

12.4 Semantic Integration via a Common Ontology

In order for agents to interact productively, they must have something in common, i.e., they must be either grounded in the same environment or able to relate their individual environments. We use an existing common context – the Cyc commonsense knowledge base (Lenat and Guha, 1990) – to provide semantic grounding. The models of agents and resources are compared and mapped to Cyc but not to each other, making interoperation easier to attain. For n models, only n mappings are needed, instead of as many as $n(n - 1)$ mappings when the models are related pairwise. Currently, Cyc is the best choice for a common context, because of 1) its rich set of abstractions, which ease the process of representing predefined groupings of concepts, 2) its knowledge representation mechanisms, which are needed to construct, represent, and maintain a common context, and 3) its size: it covers a large portion of the real world and the subject matter of most information resources.

The large size and broad coverage of Cyc's knowledge enables it to serve as a fixed point for representing not only the semantics of various information modeling formalisms, but also the semantics of the domains being modeled. Our system can use models constructed using any of several popular formalisms, such as:

- IRDS, IBM's AD/Cycle, or Bellcore's CLDM for entity-relationship models,
- Ingres, Oracle, Sybase, Objectivity, or Itasca for database schemas, and

- MCC's RAD or NASA's CLIPS for agent models.

Cyc's knowledge about metamodels for these formalisms and the relationships among them enables transactions to interoperate semantically between, for example, relational and object-oriented databases.

The relationship between a domain concept from a local model and one or more concepts in the common context is expressed as an articulation axiom (Guha, 1990): a statement of equivalence between components of two theories. Each axiom has the form

$$ist(G; \phi) \Leftrightarrow ist(C_i; \psi)$$

where ϕ and ψ are logical expressions and *ist* is a predicate that means 'is true in the context.' This axiom says that the meaning of ϕ in the common context G is the same as that of ψ in the local context C_i. Models are then related to each other – or translated between formalisms – via this common context by means of the articulation axioms. For example, an application's query about Automobile might result in subqueries to DB1 about Car, to DB2 about Auto, and to KB1 about car. Note that each model can be added independently, and the articulation axioms that result do not have to change when further models are added. Also note that applications and resources need not be modified in order to interoperate in the integrated environment. The appendix contains a description of the graphical tool, MIST, that we have built to aid in the construction of articulation axioms.

Figure 12.1 shows a logical view of the execution environment. During interoperation, mediator-like agents (Wiederhold, 1992), which are implemented by Rosette actors (Tomlinson ct al., 1991), apply the articulation axioms that relate each agent or resource model to the common context. This performs a translation of message semantics. At most n sets of articulation axioms and n agents are needed for interoperation among n resources and applications. The agents also apply a syntax translation between each local data-manipulation language, DML_i, and the global context language, *GCL*. *GCL* is based on extended first-order logic. A local data-manipulation language might be, for example, SQL for relational databases or OSQL for object-oriented databases. The number of language translators between DML_i and *GCL* is no greater than n, and may be a constant because there are only a small number of data-manipulation languages in use today. Additional details describing how transactions are processed semantically through the global and local views of several databases can be found in (Woelk et al., 1992).

The agents also function as communication aides, by managing communications among the various agents, databases, and application programs in the environment. They buffer messages, locate message recipients, and translate message semantics. To implement message transfer, they use a tree-space mechanism – a kind of distributed virtual blackboard (Tomlinson et al., 1991).

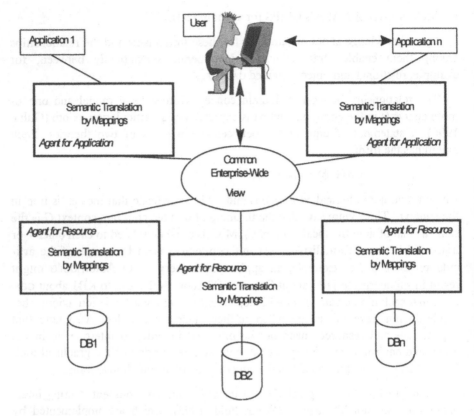

Figure 12.1. Logical view of the execution environment, showing how mediating agents apply articulation axioms to achieve semantic interoperation

12.5 Acquiring and Applying Semantic Metadata

Interoperation requires the semantic translation of not only requests, but also data. The approach taken in (Sciore et al., 1993) is to attach metadata, in the form of a property list, to each data item. The metadata describes a context within which the data item can be validly interpreted. The context can be thought of as a multi-dimensional space, with each property defining one of the dimensions and each data item representing a point in the space. The metadata is then used to construct conversion functions that map the data items among different contexts, or between different points in the space.

Our approach to resolving mismatches in quantization is based on mapping a data item to a finer-grained representation. With such a representation, each data item can be specified unambiguously. For example,

```
create table Hotel (name          char(16) not null,
                    category       char(8) );
insert into Hotel values ('Sheraton', 'deluxe');
insert into Hotel values ('Motel6', 'moderate');
insert into Hotel values ('ShackUp', 'cheap');
```

Articulation Axioms:

Hotel.name   ⇔ Lodging.name (name.arg2 = LispString)
   [Character ⇔ LispString] OK

Hotel.category ⇔ Lodging.cost (cost.arg2 = Money
                 Money.allGenls = ScalarInterval
                 cost.format = IntervalEntry)
   [Character <xx> ScalarInterval] Not OK, so...

   Is Hotel.category an enumerated value? <Yes>
   Are the values enumerable? <Yes>
   List the enumerated values, and indicate their ranges on the following
   scale:

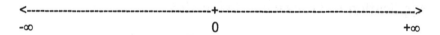

-∞   0   +∞

Resultant Value Maps:

= deluxe   > 100
= moderate 50 <= ... < 100
= cheap   < 50

The mappings used to convert a data item to another representation are called 'value maps' in our system. They are similar to the 'conversion functions' in (Sciore et al., 1993), except that they convert data items into a common ontology, instead of among pairs of data item ontologies.

The use of a common context into which all data items are mapped has several advantages, as follows:

- For n types of data, n value maps are needed, compared to $n(n-1)$ value maps to convert between any pair of n data types.
- An administrator constructing or maintaining value maps needs to consider only his own data types, not those in any other resource or application program. Each value map can be maintained independently of the others.
- Value maps can be associated with each resource and application, and can be applied by mediators that represent each of these.

- There is no ambiguity about which value map to apply to convert a given data item to the common context.

The value maps that are developed are applied to the data returned from queries, to the data that is in updates, and to the data that is part of query specifications. For an example of the last application, consider

select * from Product where cost='125.75'

where 125.75 is in francs, but the Product table stores cost in dollars. In this case, the query cannot be processed until 125.75 is converted to dollars.

The representation to which a data item is mapped must be finer-grained than the data item's own representation, so that information is not lost due to the mapping. This does not guarantee that all operations can be carried out un-ambiguously, but only that they will be unambiguous *whenever possible*. For the above example, suppose the rate for Motel6 is increased by 10%. Applying the value maps yields a cost in the range 55 to 110, but this cannot be translated back into the three-value representation of the database. However, if the rate had been doubled, then it would be in the range 100 to 200, and this could be unam-biguously translated back into the category deluxe.

12.6 Application to Transaction Processing

We have applied our semantic modeling and mediation methodology to achieve relaxed transaction processing in the provisioning of telecommunication services, i.e., the task of providing communication facilities to customers. This task is exe-cuted in a heterogeneous multidatabase environment. It is an example of workflow control, in that it provides control and data flows among transactions executing on multiple autonomous systems (Jin et al., 1993; Tomlinson et al., 1993; Georgako-poulas et al., 1995).

In the extant workflow, a telecommunication company receives a set of paper forms that gives details about the service (DS-1) being ordered. It enters these forms into their system, and tests to determine if certain essential equipment is already in place. If it is, the service can be provided quickly; otherwise, the processing must be delayed until the equipment is installed.

Providing the digital communication service using this workflow takes more than two weeks and involves 48 separate operations – 23 of which are manual – against 16 different database systems. In addition, configuring the operation-support systems so that they can perform such a task often takes several months. This is significant in the company's business environment: many of its competitors were formed in the last decade or so, and they typically have more modern computational facilities than the company's legacy systems.

We sought to reduce this time to less than two hours and to provide a way in which new services could be introduced more easily. Our goals were to develop a prototype workflow management system that could apply to workflows in general, and that would let the company operate as efficiently as its competition without discarding its legacy systems. Our strategy for accomplishing these goals was to interconnect and interoperate among the previously independent systems, replace serial operations with parallel ones by using relaxed transaction processing (Attie et al., 1993; Bukhres et al., 1993; Elmagarmid, 1992; Ansari et al., 1992), and automate previously manual operations, thereby reducing errors and delays.

We defined a distributed agent architecture, shown in Figure 12.2, for intelligent workflow management that functions on top of Carnot's distributed execution environment. The four agents interact as follows to produce the desired behavior. The graphical-interaction agent helps a user fill in an order form correctly, and checks inventories to give the user an estimate of when the order will be completed. It also informs the user about the order's progress. This enables the detection of data inconsistencies early in the process.

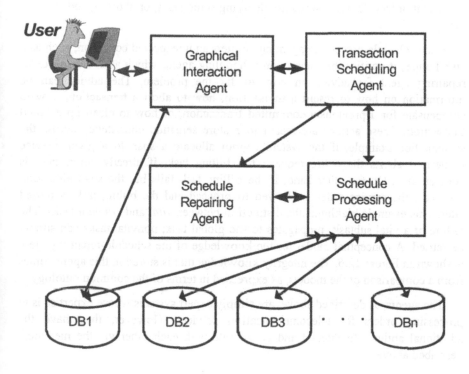

Figure 12.2. Multiagent system for relaxed processing of telecommunication transactions

The transaction-scheduling agent constructs the initial schedule of tasks needed to satisfy an order. The tasks are scheduled with the maximum concurrency possible, while still satisfying all precedence constraints. Some of the rules that implement the scheduling are shown in Figure 12.3. These particular rules, when appropriately enabled, generate a subtransaction to update the database for customer billing. When executing such rules, the transaction-scheduling agent behaves as a finite-state automaton, as shown in Figure 12.4. The resultant schedule showing the commit dependencies among the tasks for all such automata is shown in Figure 12.5.

The schedule-processing agent executes the schedule by invoking tasks as necessary. It maintains connections to the databases involved in telecommunication provisioning, and implements transactions on them. It knows how to construct the proper form for a transaction, based on the results of other transactions. The schedule-processing agent also ensures that different workflows do not interact spuriously. This is akin to the problem of concurrency control in traditional database systems – ensuring that different transactions that access the same data items do not access them in relative orders for which there are no equivalent serial executions (Kamath and Ramamritham, 1996). With a workflow, we need to ensure that subtasks on each database can be serialized in semantically consistent orders. This might require delaying some tasks, or aborting and retrying them.

If the schedule-processing agent encounters an unexpected condition, such as a task failure, it notifies the transaction-scheduling agent, which asks the schedule-repairing agent for advice on how to fix the problem. The advice can be information on how to restart a transaction, how to abort a transaction, how to compensate for a previously committed transaction, or how to clean up a failed transaction. These actions are meant to restore semantic consistency across the system. For example, if the system cannot allocate a span to a given service request, it aborts the entire request; the billing task, if already committed, is compensated. On the other hand, if the billing task fails but the span allocation succeeds, the service order is allowed to proceed and the billing task is retried later. This example highlights the distinction between *vital* and *nonvital* tasks. The failure of a vital subtask propagates to the global task; nonvital tasks can simply be retried. A conceptual model for the knowledge of the schedule-repairing agent is shown in Figure 12.6. The integrity knowledge that is stored in this agent comes from a comparison of the models, as expressed in terms of the common ontology.

The agents, as described above, are simply expert systems whose expertise is in processing orders for telecommunication services. However, they have the additional abilities to interact and co-operate with each other via the mediators described above.

```
; This rule set 1) executes an external program that translates an Access
; Service Request into a command file to update the database for customer
; billing, 2) executes the command file, and 3) checks for completion.
; The scheduling agent, due to its truth-maintenance system, halts this
; transaction whenever an abort of the global transaction occurs.
; ?gtid denotes the global transaction identifier.

Bill-Preparation:
     If        (service-order(?gtid)
               new-tid(?subtid)
               unless(abort(?gtid)))
     then      (do(,run-shell-program "asr2bill"
                              :input "asr-?gtid.out" :output "bill-?gtid.sql")
               bill(?gtid ?subtid)
               tell(GIAgent "task ?gtid BILLING ready"))


Bill-Execution:
     If        (bill(?gtid ?subtid)
               logical-db(?db))
     then      (tell(SchedProcAgent
               "task-execute ?subtid BILL ?db bill-?gtid.sql")
               tell(GIAgent "task ?gtid BILLING active"))


Bill-Completion:
     If        (success(?subtid)
               bill(?gtid ?subtid))
     then      (tell(GIAgent "task ?gtid BILLING done"))


Bill-Failure:
     If        (failure(?subtid)
               excuse(bill(?gtid ?subtid)))
     then      (abort(?gtid)
               tell(GIAgent "task ?gtid BILLING failed"))
```

Figure 12.3. Rules used by the transaction-scheduling agent to generate a workflow
schedule

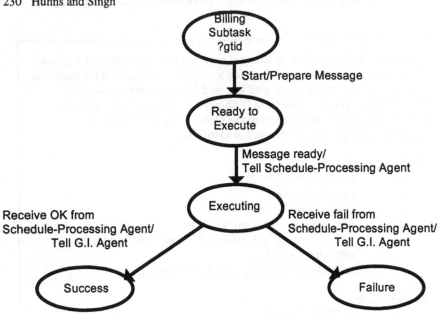

Figure 12.4. Finite-state automation for a DS-1 task assigned by the transaction-scheduling agent

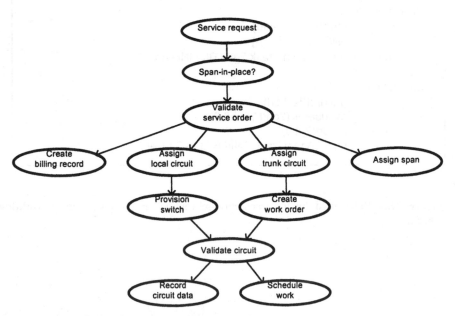

Figure 12.5. Workflow for telecommunication service provisioning generated by the transaction-scheduling agent. Only the default workflow is shown, without any exception paths

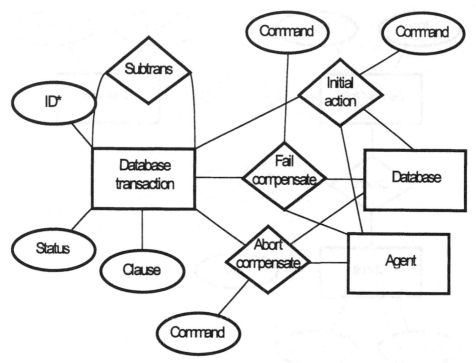

Figure12.6. Semantic model for the schedule-repairing agent

The agents co-operate, at the knowledge level (Newell, 1982), via models of themselves. For example, a conceptual domain model for the graphical-interaction agent is shown in Figure 12.7. An interface form that provides user access and modifications to the knowledge possessed by this agent is shown in Figure 12.8. Entries on the form, or the form's completion, cause queries and transactions to be sent to the other agents or databases in the environment. However, the model does not capture the procedural knowledge necessary to specify the queries and trans-actions; a technique for modeling processes is needed to capture such knowledge. In other words, the models represent the static knowledge of the agents, and not (unfortunately) their dynamics. Nevertheless, they have proven useful in enabling the agents to interact coherently, as we describe next.

Conceptual models for two more agents are shown in Figures 12.6 and 12.9. Each model consists of organized concepts describing the context, domains, or viewpoints of the knowledge possessed by that agent, i.e., the knowledge base of each agent contains rules written in terms of these concepts.

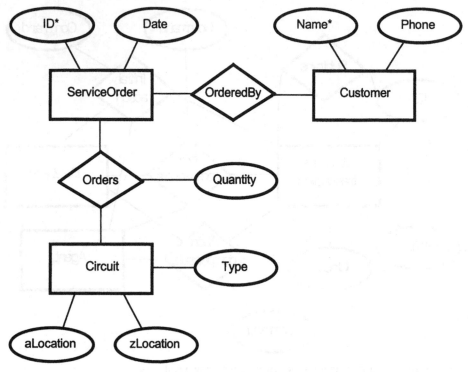

Figure 12.7. Semantic model (simplified) for the graphical-interaction agent

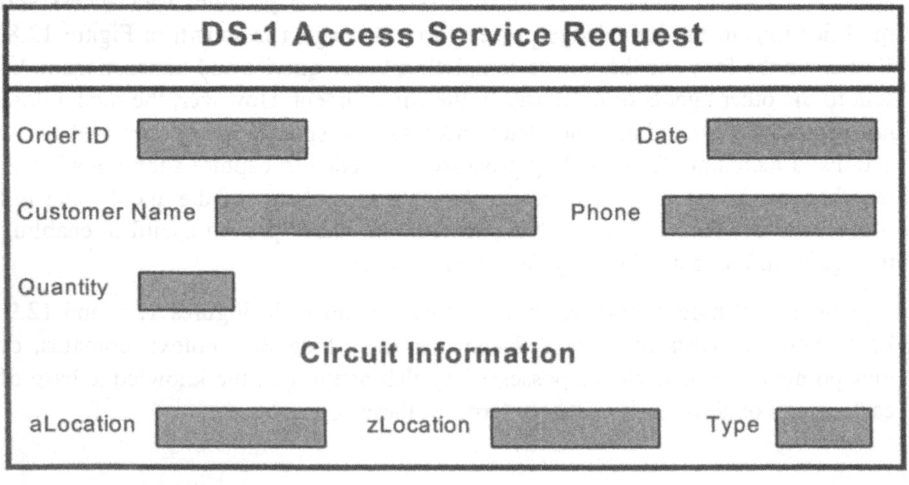

Figure 12.8. User interface form (simplified) corresponding to the declarative knowledge of the graphical-interaction agent

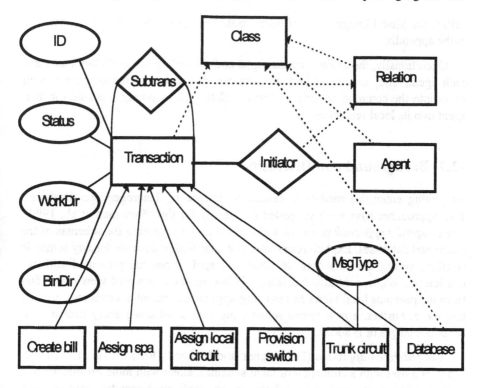

Figure 12.9. Semantic model for the transaction-scheduling agent (dashed arrows indicate instance relationships, and solid arrows indicate subclass relationships)

All of the models in Figures 12.6, 12.7, and 12.9 are related to the common context, and thereby to each other, via articulation axioms. For example, the concept Transaction for the transaction-scheduling agent and the concept DBTransaction for the schedule-repairing agent are each related to the common concept DatabaseTransaction via the axioms:

$ist(Cyc, DatabaseTransaction(?T)) \Leftrightarrow ist(Scheduler, Transaction(?T))$

$ist(Cyc, DatabaseTransaction(?T)) \Leftrightarrow ist(Repairer, DBTransaction(?T))$

The axioms are used to translate messages exchanged by the agents, so that the agents can understand each other. In the above example, the two agents would use their axioms to converse about the status of database transactions, without having to change their internal terminology. Similar axioms describing the semantics of each of the databases involved enable the schedule-processing agent to issue transactions to the databases. The axioms also relate the semantics of the form shown in Figure 12.8 to the semantics of the other information resources in the environment. Such axioms are constructed with the aid of a graphical tool called

MIST, for Model Integration Software Tool. The operation of MIST is described in the appendix.

Operationally, the axioms are managed and applied by the mediators that assist each agent. They use the axioms to translate each outgoing message from their agent into the common context, and to translate each incoming message for their agent into its local semantics.

12.7   Background and Discussion

Integrating enterprise models is similar to integrating heterogeneous databases. Two approaches have been suggested previously for this (Buneman et al., 1990). The *composite approach* produces a global schema by merging the schemas of the individual databases. Explicit resolutions are specified in advance for any semantic conflicts among the databases, so users and applications are presented with the illusion of a single, centralized database. However, the centralized view may differ from the previous local views and existing applications might not execute correctly any more. Further, a new global schema must be constructed every time a local schema changes or is added.

The *federated approach* (Heimbigner and McLeod 1985; Litwin et al., 1990) presents a user with a collection of local schemas, along with tools for information sharing. The user resolves conflicts in an application-specific manner, and integrates only the required portions of the databases. This approach yields easier maintenance, increased security, and the ability to deal with inconsistencies. However, a user must understand the contents of each database to know what to include in a query: there is no global schema to provide advice about semantics. Also, each database must maintain knowledge about the other databases with which it shares information, e.g., in the form of models of the other databases or partial global schemas (Ahlsen and Johannesson, 1990). For n databases, as many as $n(n - 1)$ partial global schemas might be required, while n mappings would suffice to translate between the databases and a common schema.

We base our methodology on the composite approach, but make three changes that enable us to combine the advantages of both approaches while avoiding some of their shortcomings. First, we use an *existing* common schema or context. In a similar attempt, (Sull and Kashyap, 1992) describes a method for integrating schemas by translating them into an object-oriented data model, but this method maintains only the structural semantics of the resources.

Second, we capture the mapping between each model and the common context in a set of articulation axioms. The axioms provide a means of translation that enables the maintenance of a global view of all information resources and, at the same time, a set of local views that correspond to each individual resource. An application can retain its current view, but use the information in other resources.

Of course, any application can be modified to use the global view directly to access all available information.

Third, we consider knowledge-based systems, process models, and applications, as well as databases.

Our use of agents for interoperating among applications and information resources is similar to the uses of mediators described in (Wiederhold, 1992). However, we also specify a means for semantic translation among the agents, as well as an implemented prototype. Other applications of similar agents, such as the Pilot's Associate developed by Lockheed et al. (Smith and Broadwell, 1988), hand-crafted their agents. This is not practical for large 'open' applications: the agents must be such that they can be developed independently and execute autonomously.

Our architecture employs two kinds of computational agents: finer-grained, concurrent actors and coarser-grained, knowledge-based systems. The actors are used to control interactions among the components of the architecture. The knowledge-based agents are used where reasoning is needed, such as in deciding what tasks should be performed next or how to repair the environment when a task has failed. This seems to be a natural division of responsibilities for our example application. However, we took an engineering, rather than a scientific, approach, in that we did not investigate any alternative architectures.

12.8 Conclusion

For years, information-system personnel managed corporate data that was centralized on mainframes. The data was kept consistent, but eventually the amount of data increased to the point that centralized storage was no longer viable. Also, users wanted a way to share data across applications and wanted more direct involvement in the management of the data. So, data began proliferating onto workstations and personal computers, where users could manage it themselves. But this resulted in redundancy, inconsistency, and no coherent global view. Hence, there are now attempts to reintegrate data. Users still need to manage their own data, which remains distributed, but they and their applications need coherent global access, and consistency must be restored.

This chapter describes our approach to enabling interoperation among enterprise information objects, i.e., among suppliers and consumers of information. In this approach, an enterprise information object is integrated based on articulation axioms defined between two contexts: the context of a model of the object and a common enterprise-wide context. The methodology is based on the following principles:

- Existing information resources should not have to be modified and data should not have to migrate.
- Existing applications should not have to be modified.
- Users should not have to adopt a new language for communicating with the resultant integrated system, unless they are accessing new types of information.
- Resources and applications should be able to be integrated independently, and the mappings that result should not have to change when additional objects are integrated.

The above principles are incorporated in an integration tool, MIST, for assisting an administrator in generating articulation axioms for a model, and in a set of agents that utilize the resultant axioms to provide users and applications with access to the integrated resources. They can use a familiar local context, while still benefiting from newly added resources. These systems constitute part of the semantic service layer of Carnot (Cannata, 1991). They help specify and maintain the semantics of an organization's integrated information resources.

Extensions of our work are focused on developing additional information-system applications for agents, including intelligent directory service agents, negotiating electronic data interchange (EDI) agents, database administration agents, and intelligent information retrieval agents. Our most important future work is centered on ways in which agents can acquire and maintain models of each other in order to improve their interactions.

References

Agha, G. (1986) *Actors: A Model of Concurrent Computation in Distributed Systems*. MIT Press, Cambridge, MA, 1986.

Ahlsen, M., Johannesson, P. (1991) Contracts in database federations. In: S. M. Deen (Ed.) *Co-operating Knowledge Based Systems*. Springer-Verlag, London, 293–310.

Ansari, M., Rusinkiewicz, M., Ness, L., Sheth, A. (1992) Executing multi-database transactions. *Proceedings 25th Hawaii International Conference on Systems Sciences*, January.

Attie, P. C., Munindar, P. S., Amit, P. S., Rusinkiewicz, M. (1993) Specifying and enforcing intertask dependencies. *Proceedings of the 19th VLDB Conference*.

Bukhres, O. A., Chen, J., Du, W., Elmagarmid, A. K., Pezzoli, R. (1993) InterBase: an execution environment for heterogeneous software systems. *IEEE Computer*, 26(8), 57–69, August.

Buneman, O. P., Davidson, S. B., Watters, A. (1990) Querying independent databases. *Information Sciences*, 52, 1–34, December.

Cannata, P. E. (1991) The irresistible move towards interoperable database systems. *First International Workshop on Interoperability in Multidatabase Systems*, Kyoto, Japan, April 7-9.

Ceri, S., Widom, J. (1992) Production rules in parallel and distributed database environments. *Proceedings of the 18th VLDB Conference*, Vancouver, British Columbia, Canada, 339–351.

Collet, C., Huhns, M. N., Shen, W. M. (1991) Resource integration using a large knowledge base in Carnot. *IEEE Computer*, 24(12), 55–62, December.

Elmagarmid, A. (Ed.) (1992) *Database Transaction Models*. Morgan Kaufmann Publishers Inc., San Mateo, CA.

Georgakopoulas, D., Hornick, M., Sheth, A. (1995) An overview of workflow management: from process modeling to workflow automation infrastructure. *Distributed and Parallel Databases*, 3(2), 119–152, April.

Guha, R. V. (1990) Micro-theories and contexts in Cyc part I: basic issues. MCC Technical Report Number ACT-CYC-129-90, Microelectronics and Computer Technology Corporation, Austin, TX, June.

Heimbigner, D., McLeod, D. (1985) A federated architecture for information management. *ACM Transactions on Office Information Systems*, 3(3), 253–278, July.

Jin, W. W., Ness, L., Rusinkiewicz, M., Sheth, A. (1993) Executing service provisioning applications as multidatabase flexible transactions. Bellcore Technical Report (unpublished).

Kamath, M., Ramamritham, K. (1996) Bridging the gap between transaction management and workflow management. In: *Proceedings of the NSF Workshop on Workflow and Process Automation in Information Systems: State-of-the-Art and Future Directions*, May.

Lenat, D., Guha, R. V. (1990) *Building Large Knowledge-Based Systems: Representation and Inference in the Cyc Project*. Addison-Wesley Publishing Company, Reading, MA.

Litwin, W., Mark, L., Roussopoulos, N. (1990) Interoperability of multiple autonomous databases. *ACM Computing Surveys*, 22(3), 267–296, September.

Newell, A. (1982) The knowledge level. *Artificial Intelligence*, 18(1), 87–127, January.

Sciore, E., Siegel, M., Rosenthal, A. (1992) Context interchange using meta-attributes. *First International Conference on Information and Knowledge Management*.

Sciore, E., Siegel, M., Rosenthal, A. (1994) Using semantic values to facilitate interoperability among heterogeneous information systems. *ACM Transactions on Database Systems*, 19(2), 254–290.

Sheth, A. P., Larson, J. A. (1990) Federated database systems for managing distributed, heterogeneous, and autonomous databases. *ACM Computing Surveys*, 22(3), 183–236, September.

Siegel, M., Madnick, S. E. (1991) A metadata approach to resolving semantic conflicts. *Proceedings of the 17th International Conference on Very Large Database Systems*, Spain, September.

Smith, D., Broadwell, M. (1988) The pilot's associate – an overview. *Proceedings of the SAE Aerotech Conference*, Los Angeles, CA, May.

Sull, W., Kashyap, R. L. (1992) A self-organizing knowledge representation scheme for extensible heterogeneous information environment. *IEEE Transactions on Knowledge and Data Engineering*, (4)2, 185–191.

Tomlinson, C., Scheevel, M., Singh, V. (1991) Report on Rosette 1.1. MCC Technical Report Number ACT-OODS-275-91, Microelectronics and Computer Technology Corporation, Austin, TX, July.

Tomlinson, C., Attie, P., Cannata, P., Meredith, G., Sheth, A., Singh, M., Woelk, D. (1993) Workflow support in Carnot. *IEEE Data Engineering*.

Wiederhold, G. (1992) Mediators in the architecture of future information systems. *IEEE Computer*, 25(3), 38–49, March.

Woelk, D. et al. (1995) The Carnot prototype. In: O. A. Bukhres, A. Elmagarmid (Eds.) *Object-Oriented Multidatabase Systems*, Prentice-Hall, Englewood Cliffs, NJ.

Woelk, D., Shen, W. M., Huhns, M. N., Cannata, P. E. (1992) Model-driven enterprise information management in Carnot. In: C. J. Petrie Jr. (Ed.) *Enterprise Integration Modeling: Proceedings of the First International Conference*. MIT Press, Cambridge, MA.

Appendix:
The Development of Articulation Axioms

We have developed a graphical tool, the Model Integration Software Tool (MIST), that automates the routine aspects of model integration, while clearly displaying the information needed for effective user interaction. The tool produces articulation axioms in the following three phases:

1. MIST automatically represents an enterprise model in a local context as an instance of a given formalism. The representation is declarative, and uses an extensive set of semantic properties.
2. By constraint propagation and user interaction it matches concepts from the local context with concepts from the common context.
3. For each match, it automatically constructs an articulation axiom by instantiating axiom templates.

MIST displays enterprise models both before and after they are represented in a local context. MIST enables a global knowledge base, representing a common enterprise-wide context, to be browsed graphically and textually to allow the correct concept matches to be located. With MIST, a user can create frames in the common context or augment the local context for a model with additional properties when needed to ensure a successful match. MIST also displays the articulation axioms that it constructs. The three phases of articulation axiom development are described next in more detail.

In the model representation phase, we represent the model as a set of frames and slots in a context created specially for it. These frames are instances of frames describing the metamodel of the schema, e.g., Relation and Database-Attribute for a relational schema.

In the matching phase, the problem is: given a representation for a concept in a local context, find its corresponding concept in the common context. The two factors that affect this phase are 1) there may be a mismatch between the local and common contexts in the depth of knowledge representing a concept, and 2) there may be mismatches between the structures used to encode the knowledge. For example, a concept in Cyc can be represented as either a collection or an attribute (Lenat and Guha, 1990, pp. 339ff).

If the common context's knowledge is more than or equivalent to that of the local context's for some concept, then the interactive matching process described in this section will find the relevant portion of the common context's knowledge. If the common context has less knowledge than the local context, then knowledge will be added to the common context until its knowledge equals or exceeds that in the local context; otherwise, the common context would be unable to model the semantics of the resource. The added knowledge refines the common context. This does not affect previously integrated resources, but can be useful when further resources are integrated.

Finding correspondences between concepts in the local and common contexts is a subgraph-matching problem. We base subgraph matching on a simple string matching between the names or synonyms of frames representing the model and the names or synonyms of frames in the common context. Matching begins by finding associations between attribute/link definitions and existing slots in the common context. After a few matches have been identified, either by exact string matches or by a user indicating the correct match out of a set of candidate matches, possible matches for the remaining model concepts are greatly constrained. Conversely, after integrating an entity or object, possible matches for its attributes are constrained.

In the third phase, an articulation axiom is constructed for each match found. For example, the match between a relational attribute phone in model AAA and the Cyc slot phoneNumber yields the axiom

$$ist(Cyc\ phoneNumber(?L\ ?N)) \Leftrightarrow ist(AAA\ phone(?L\ ?N))$$

which means that the phone attribute definition determines the phoneNumber slot in the common schema, and vice versa. Articulation axioms are generated automatically by instantiating stored templates with the matches found.

13 Software Technologies for Building Agent Based Systems in Telecommunication Networks

M. Plu
France Telecom

13.1 Introduction

To allow multiple corporations to provide more and more sophisticated information and electronic commerce services to many customers, telecommunication operators build infrastructure integrating these services with telecommunication networks. This chapter presents some software technologies used for this purpose.

We will consider pieces of software that provide services using this infrastructure as software agents for the following reasons. Firstly, they are generally under the control of different authorities. Secondly, they may be developed with various technologies by people working in different domains, having various development tools, and embedded in heterogeneous computer environments. The agent concept should help to integrate these heterogeneous services in a single system and to isolate the various autonomous control policy entities in this system.

This service integration is necessary to provide common access to all services, common use of generic services like client or services global directories, central control of user access, and technological support to establish various consumer-provider relationships between humans or software entities. These relationships are needed between end-user and service provider, but also between service providers when a service uses services from other providers. This kind of relationship is needed to offer more and more integrated services and to avoid developing specific services already available. More global or complete services will have to integrate the results of several services. Providing simple services like room reservation, car rental, and travel ticket reservation can be greatly improved by aggregating their results. The added value of a service can be seen as a key point in service competition. Added value services can include information cross checking through different sources, information filtering according to user profiles, or simply uniform presentations of heterogeneous information.

Among the numerous issues concerning service integration, this chapter will present agent-oriented software techniques used in telecommunication companies to deal with the following problems:

- multiple authority co-operation,
- interoperation with heterogeneous information managed by heterogeneous software, and
- physical distribution of computation.

The presentation of these problems will be conducted according to some international standard recommendations to analyze open distributed systems. These recommendations have been defined by an ISO (International Standardization Organization) group called ODP (Open Distributed Processing). These recommendations are of great importance in many telecommunication domains. They will be briefly presented in Section 13.3.

13.2 Overview

Most of the components of a system that integrates various service providers and their consumers behave according to their own policy. For example, consumers will try to get the best services offer at the lowest price whereas service providers will try to offer the required services in a way that maximizes their profit. In spite of potential conflict between these policies, these entities have to establish relationships in order to reach their goal. A contractual definition of the relationships between these entities, and some policy rules, defining what is allowed or prohibited, may be useful to specify what kind of services can be actually provided. The use of conceptual agents to provide these kinds of descriptions will be presented in Section 13.4.

Multiple partnerships between service providers also raise the problem of software interoperability. This problem can be solved by implementing a specific adaptation layer in each piece of software for each specific partnership they are involved in. But this approach lacks flexibility, robustness, and openess. Partnerships between involved service providers may change during design time and may evolve during service operation. A service is unavailable or incomplete as soon as one of the needed services in a given partnership becomes unavailable, although the same needed service may be offered by another provider. All potential providers of a needed service are not known at design time and new ones can become available continually through the integration infrastructure. Consequently, fixed partnerships cannot take advantage of all the available possibilities or improvements of incoming new services. The basis of an application-independent communication protocol to allow interoperation between heterogeneous software will be introduced in Section 13.5. The basis of such a protocol in network management will be presented.

In such an integrated service framework, service computation is physically distributed over various networked heterogeneous computers. Distributed computing raises many specific problems. Concurrency, asynchronism, information delay, and no shared memory are examples of such problems. Thus, distributed programming needs some specific features in programming languages. At present, two main paradigms have been proposed: Remote Procedure Call (known as RPC) and remote programming. Remote programming using the attractive metaphor of smart mobile agents will be more specifically presented in Section 13.6.

Before going into detail on specific pieces of software technology, it may be useful to specify and justify the use of an agent-oriented approach.

13.3   Agents as a New Way of Thinking About Software

This section deals with the following question: Why is it useful to call a piece of software that offers services an agent?

It is obvious that software systems are offering more and more sophisticated services. This make them more and more complex. For an ease of use, this complexity must be hidden. That is why computer science uses programming abstraction. Roughly speaking, evolution steps among programming languages can be sketched by the new abstractions they included starting from assembler code, followed by high-level programming instructions and procedure or function calls, up to object encapsulation.

With assembler code, a programmer had to deal with the different resources of a machine such as processor registers, memory, input-output device access, or interruption. The first programming languages, like the famous BASIC, delivered the programmer from these constraints. A program was then defined by its instruction steps. Procedure or function calls allow programmers to define data processing units by their input parameters and output results. A program is then defined by flows of data between these processing units. Objects brought a new structuring level to programs. Each object integrates a set of functions called methods and their related data. The public functions of an object define its interface. Computation is then defined by object interactions with message passing between objects. The object-oriented approach is currently being used in more and more application domains and particularly in the telecommunication industry.

Agents bring a new level of abstraction which is close to objects in such a way that agents can be seen as a specialization of objects. In a network environment, agents can be defined as autonomous, truthworthy, distributed, communicative, persistent objects in an open system. We shall now describe these object properties.

13.3.1   Agents' Autonomy

Agents are autonomous in the sense that they embed their own control policy. This policy is defined by the authority they represent in a computer system. As remarked in Section 13.1, service consumer agents and service provider agents have different policies. Service provider agents are free to refuse a request addressed to them, to set the cost of a service, or to choose the resources to be allocated in order to offer a specific service. In the same way, a consumer agent is free to choose the service provider that it believes to be the best compromise between quality of result and cost of a service with regard to its user needs. Agent autonomy also means that these decisions are made by the agent on its own. This latter cannot rely on the human authority it represents, since this person might not be available or might not want to be disturbed. With mobile agents, for example, as they will be presented in Section 13.6, once a user agent is sent into the network, the user may decide to turn off his or her terminal and to retrieve the agent result later in his or her mailbox. Then, the user will not be available to give more information for the agent to achieve its task. Therefore, an agent has to embed all the knowledge it needs to cope with any problem that might occur and make the right decision.

13.3.2 Agents' Trustworthiness

For an agent to make a decision on behalf of its authority, it must be trustworthy. Letting your agent automatically pay for some services with your credit card gives an idea of the level of trust you must have in your agent's capabilities. That means, firstly, that agents must be able to guarantee a well defined quality of service. Secondly, the service they offer must match the required service. Of course, in order to obtain such a trust level, you do not want your agent to give you all the details of what it is actually doing. You will not be able to understand it or even to evaluate whether it is appropriate. The description level needed is related to the kinds of service this piece of software can offer you. It should tell you the guarantee you have, the conditions under which the result is guaranteed, what compensation you may receive if the guarantee has not been fulfilled, what it costs, when it is available, within which time limit you obtain the result, how you can get these services, etc. This description does not need to specify what computation the service involves, what kind of information it needs, or how it is implemented in a specific machine architecture or computing environment. Information security or client anonymity are also important matters. Once again this kind of information can be useful for a human end-user as well as for a service provider who wants to make some partnership with other service providers. It can help users to understand the autonomous behavior of the agents they use. This understanding can engage them to customize their agent by, for example, disabling some untrusted capabilities. The description of the agent behavior must then be made with explicit representations that make sense for users. Thus, common sense concepts like intention, beliefs, or commitments, usually assigned to people, are sometimes used to describe the behavior of a software agent.

This point of view on software description will be developed in Section 13.3.

13.3.3 Agents' Distribution

Agents in network environments are bound to be physically distributed over different interconnected machines. Hence they include network-related components such as communication protocols which they have to deal with. As they are distributed, they cannot share local information with one another. Some information might be duplicated and inconsistencies may appear. Communication between agents depends on the network availability. Failure or overload of the network may imply broken functionality or over-delayed information. Communication over a network also raises some confidentiality and security issues. Agent distribution also implies that a global clock might be difficult to obtain. Thus asynchronism between agents is most often a reasonable hypothesis. Agent distribution problems will be discussed further in Section 13.6.

13.3.4 Agents' Communication

To co-operate, agents have to communicate efficiently, which means that they have to understand each other. Using common concepts to understand each other is a good basis for such communication efficiency. In a highly heterogeneous and open system such as a service infrastructure, application-independent communication protocols and communication languages must be shared by all the agents in order to communicate. These protocols include formally well-defined types of messages that agents exchange to communicate, in order to update their internal state. Such protocols will be presented in Section 13.5.

13.3.5 Agents' Temporal Continuity

To be able to offer their services at any time and to keep track of their evolving environment, agents also have to be persistent. This implies that they may run concurrently and need available computing resources at any time. As they are able to execute any task at any time, they may also send a request at any time. They cannot afford to stop to wait for the result of their request as they may have other tasks to achieve or requests to process. Thus in most cases, communication between agents is asynchronous. Persistence also means that they have to continue to exist across changes of context over a long period of time (ITU-T X 901). During the agent's lifetime, its environment inevitably changes. For example, its resources may fail, its capabilities may be updated, its information will become obsolete. Agents have to deal with this problem and adapt their service capabilities according to the current status of their environment. To achieve this, they must be kept aware of all these evolutions. When possible, they will try to react to some events by changing the state of their environment in such a way that they will still be able to offer their services correctly.

13.3.6   Agents as Objects

Agents are objects in the sense that they encapsulate data, capabilities, resources, and various knowledge. Like objects, they are accessible through an interface, but the level of this interface is more specific for an agent than for any other kind of object. An agent interface describes services. Let us look at this distinction in more detail.

Firstly, services are oriented towards external users whereas methods are more oriented towards internal computation. Agent-internal computation comes from the computational nature of an agent. Software agent computation can be achieved by many objects, in the same way as human life comes from the activity of many cells (Tokoro, 1993). The border between internal and external can be defined by homogeneity and policy control. Software or libraries are often designed by a homogeneous team of developers with the same development environment, framework, and background concepts. This homogeneity limit of an agent defines the begining of heterogeneity. Outside an agent, the previously noticed problem of efficient communication between agents appears and generic communication protocols are needed. The limit can also be the applicability limits of the agent control policy defined by the agent authority. This limit raises potential conflicts between agent goals and interests. Outside an agent, interaction may be unstable and unreliable, whereas inside the agent, computation seems to be stably coordinated. It is important to notice that homogeneity and interaction stability can be measured according to different granularities. A granularity defines the level of abstraction to consider. At another level of abstraction, heterogeneity and instability can be found inside an agent. Agents can thus be seen as being themselves made of agents. This aspect is inherent to the recursive nature of some programming concepts.

Secondly, as previously noticed while discussing agent's trustworthiness, service-level description has to define some guarantees such as security, consistency, reliability, fairness, honesty, etc. This kind of guarantee does not concern all object interfaces whereas it concerns all agent services.

Thirdly, agent services define the user access to a piece of code. Once again, the term user includes end-user, developer, or software as well.

When a developer tries to reuse a software component made of many objects, it is not always easy for him or her to know what kind of object he or she is going to specialize, or what object method he or she is going to call for his or her own use. Public method interface distinction can be specific to other objects from the library, and is not always appropriate for general use. For the end-user, graphical interfaces tend to offer more and more choices through more and more menus or icons.

Users may have some problems matching their needs with all of these graphical widgets. The agent role is to reduce all the available possibilities and to offer only the needed services. These services can be negotiated online, personalized through profile definition, or defined by appropriate media such as speech, or natural language text. Software access to other software is ensured through a specific interface that we may call the service interface. This service interface integrates standard communiation protocols.

13.3.7   Agents in Open Systems

Finally, network agents interoperate in an open system. In such systems things change in an unpredictable way. Communication capabilities can break down. Needed services can become unavailable at any time. During the agent life, all kinds of heterogeneous system components and services arrive in the system offering new facilities and new possibilities. To be efficient and competitive, an agent must take into account the best offer available in the system. Flexibility in its partnership with other agents, adaptability to unforseen events, awareness of new available facilities, and learning how to take advantage of new incoming services are challenges for network agents to meet in order to remain useful to users. Trader or matchmaker software, information translation, learning techniques, self-organization properties, are software techniques that become more and more important in such open systems.

13.3.8   In Summary

To summarize this new way of thinking about software, the agent concept tries to capture the following behavior of a piece of software:

- it acts automatically, on its own on your behalf, or it offers services according to its authority policy;
- the services a network agent is able to provide depend on its evolving capabilities, its resource boundedness, its previous commitment, and also on the availability of other agents;
- it tries to match intelligently what is possible for it with what you need;
- it tries to provide only the services you need;
- it tries to engage a user to trust its secure services by ensuring some guarantee;
- it is available as often as possible;
- it keeps track of new features of its environment; and
- it tries to remain competitive and to provide the best possible services.

We now look at some pieces of software technology used by telecommunication companies to make these network agents operational in a service integration architecture.

13.4 Service Integration Architecture

The need to build a system that integrates multiple services has been explained above.

An architecture defines a set of concepts and principles to be applied during system design and construction (Berndt, 1994). The architecture of open distributed systems is precisely defined by an ISO (International Standardization Organization) group named ODP (Open Distributed Processing). Even if standardization is slow and has required a long term effort, this is extremely important for telecommunication companies since the systems they build may be used worldwide. ODP recommendations are used by telecommunication consortia like IUT-T (International Communication Union) (IUT-T X.901) or TINA-C (Telecommunication Information Networking Architecture Consortium) (Dupuy, 1994).

Here is a brief overview of the ODP framework.

ODP provides a framework for describing a complete distributed system called the ODP Reference Model (RM-ODP). It suggests system analysis along five, loosely to strongly related, viewpoints (ITU-T X 901):

- an enterprise viewpoint,
- an information viewpoint,
- a computational viewpoint,
- an engineering viewpoint, and
- and a technological viewpoint.

The enterprise viewpoint describes the system from the perspective of the value delivered to an organization. It provides organization members with a description of the various requirements and objectives of the system it aims to satisfy. It is specified in terms of roles played, activities and obligations of the system, and business and management policy statements about the system. At this level of system description, the agent concept is very useful, as we will see in Section 13.5.

The information viewpoint models the information structure and flow of the system. Rules and constraints that govern the manipulation of information are also identified. Section 13.6 will present a language and some communication primitives to define this level of description.

The computational viewpoint provides application designers with a view on programming functions and data types that is independent of the computer systems and networks on which they run.

From the engineering viewpoint, the visible objects are control and transparency mechanisms, processors, memory, and communication networks that together enable programs and data distribution. Mobile agents, presented in Section 13.7, deal with this viewpoint and with part of the computational viewpoint.

Finally, the technology viewpoint provides persons in charge of the configuration, installation, and maintenance of a distributed system a view of the artefacts with which the system is built, including hardware and software: the local operating system, the input-output devices, storage, access point to communications, etc.

13.5 An Agent-Oriented Enterprise Viewpoint

In the ODP Reference Model agents are used to define the enterprise viewpoint of a system. Again, the distinction between this level of description and the four others gives some precision as to the kind of abstraction an agent provides and what it is good for. It is not appropriate for showing information structures and flow or for describing computation. It does not explain the use of memory, processor, or networks, or the operating system or devices needed. But an agent is appropriate to show the added value it can provide to users, applying policy and playing specific roles in a community.

In an enterprise viewpoint specification language, an agent is defined as 'an object which initiates performative actions' as (ITU-T X 903). It is distinguished from an artefact, which does not initiate performative actions.

Five fundamental types of performative actions are defined:

- an agent incurs an obligation to another agent;
- an agent fulfills an obligation to another agent;
- an agent waives an obligation to another agent;
- an agent gets permission from another agent to perform some action it was not previously permitted to perform; and
- an agent is not allowed to perform an action it was previously allowed to perform.

Obligation, permission, and prohibition are types of policies. A policy is a prescriptive relation between one or more objects and some defined behavior which establishes a norm for the correctness of the behavior of these objects.

Behaviors of agents are thus directed by policies. Policies fulfilled by agents depend on their roles in a community. A community is a composition of objects formed to meet an objective. This objective is expressed as a contract. A contract is an agreement between the community which defines obligations of objects involved. A contract may include:

- a specification of the different roles (identifier of a behavior) that objects involved in the contract must assume;
- quality of service attributes, such as information transfer rate, the latency, the probability of a communication being disrupted;
- indication of duration or periods of validity; and

- indication of behavior which invalidates the contract, and also penalties assigned to agents having this misbehavior, or compensation obtained by agents having to support the consequences of this misbehavior.

In the enterprise language definition, it is also noticed that in an enterprise specification, an ODP system and the environment in which it operates are represented as a community. But at some level of description of that community an ODP system is represented as an agent. Once again, this shows the recursive nature of an agent that can itself be described as a community of agents.

13.5.1   An Enterprise Viewpoint Example

To better understand how agent abstraction helps to integrate services involving multiple providers and consumers, let us consider an example of an enterprise viewpoint specification.

The system we will describe is called a trader. Its enterprise viewpoint specification is given in a committee draft document issued by the ISO Open System Inteconnection, Data Management and Open Distributed Processing group (ISO 21-N-9122).

A trader is defined as a means for offering a service and discovering services that have been offered. In its enterprise specification, seven agent roles are identified in the trading community:

- the trader role registers service offers made by exporter agents and returns service offers to importer agents according to some constraints;
- the exporter role sends service offer descriptions to the trader agent;
- the importer role obtains from the trader service offers satisfying some constraints;
- the service provider role provides a service described in an exported service offer;
- the service user role uses a service described in an imported service offer;
- the trader policy maker defines and manages the trader policy of the trader agent; and
- the trader administrator role enforces the trader policy of the trader agent.

These roles may be played by five agents as shown in Figure 13.1. An agent that needs a service may first play a service importer role with the trader agent to obtain a service offer. It will later play a service user role with the service provider agent to use this service. In the same way, an agent that wants to provide a service first plays an exporter role with the trader agent to register its service. It will later play a service provider role with user agents that require this service.

All these agents are directed according to the policy of their role in the community. Here are some of the most interesting policies from an agent point of view:

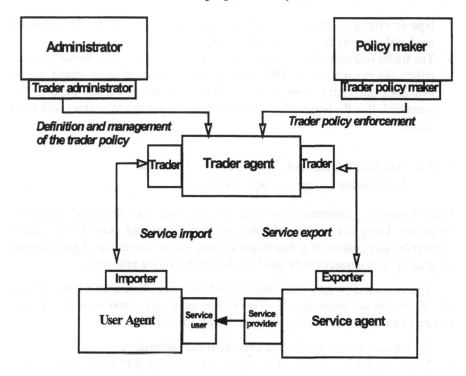

Figure 13.1. Trading community

- The importer policy defines required services including preferred and manda-tory attributes.
- The exporter policy of an agent defines the services it can offer, and may define preferred and mandatory attributes about agents to be allowed to import these services. The exporter agent is responsible for the accuracy and the quality of services it offers.
- Security policy of the trader agent defines permitted and prohibited interactions that may occur between the trader agent and importer, exporter, and admini-strator agents.
- The service offer acceptance policy of the trader agent defines how it decides to accept or refuse to register a service offer. This selection can be based on criteria such as service type, cost, expiry date, or trustworthiness of a service. For example, a service offer acceptance policy may require an expiry date for service offers. A trader agent is allowed to remove expired service offers. It may also be compelled to ensure the timely removal of stale service offers.
- The import request acceptance policy defines how the trader agent restricts the set of service requests that it will accept. Restriction based on the importer agent's identity is prohibited. These restrictions must be based only on service

type or offer properties. For example, returning service offers that cannot be used at the import date may be prohibited.

- The trader referee policy regulates by a set of rules conflicts between importer policy and exporter policy. Offers answered by the trader to an import request that does not verify constraints considered mandatory by the importer are permitted. It is the importer's responsibility to decide not to interact with these offers.

13.5.2 An Agent-Oriented Approach for a Formal Enterprise Language Specification

Most frequently, enterprise viewpoint specifications are described in natural languages. Using a more formal language to simulate and evaluate the various agent roles and policies of a distributed system can be interesting. Agent-oriented programming languages can be good candidates for such a purpose.

Agent-oriented programming was defined by Yoav Shoham as a specialization of object-oriented programming. The following points summarize the specialization of an object provided by an agent (Shoham, 1993):

- Agents have a more precise and structured state definition.
- Agent interfaces are defined using an application-independent term by state transitions of the receiver agent message expected by the sender agent message or by state transitions effectively achieved by the receiver agent message.
- Agents have a default behavior (state transition) and declarative control mechanism to specialize this behavior for specific purposes.

An agent state is defined by its capabilities, the information it believes to be true or false at a given instant, and commitments it has towards itself or other agents. Commitments between agents can be seen as established contracts between them.

A time parameter is included:

- in the state and behavior description;
- in commitments to act (an agent commits itself to do something or to have something to be done at a precise date); and
- in messages (sending and receiving dates) and information included in messages.

It enables one to define for example service expiry dates, service answer delays, service availability changes, service removal at precise dates, or all kinds of information changes.

Conditions under which capabilities are available, or commitments can be made, are precisely defined respectively in agent private-action descriptions and agent commitment rules. Those conditions can define limits of contracts between agents. For example, an agent can commit itself to do something only if it remains able to do it. If an unpredicted event occurs and disables an agent from doing something it was committed to, then the commitment made with a contract may be legally broken. Commitment rules are convenient for defining policies. Preferred or mandatory attributes or services offer choices or various decision rules dealing with conflicts between multiple agent activity and competition, and may be specified in the conditions of agent commitment rules.

Agent interfaces are defined by typed messages. Each type of message has a precise definition for each agent. These type definitions help interoperability between agents and also in understanding how each agent deals with message reception. For example, it can help answer questions like: what kind of message should be sent to an agent to obtain a specific service, what condition has to be fulfilled, what information has to be sent previously to have an effective understanding of a message, or why an agent does not react to a message as expected by the message sender. Observing the state transition of an agent following a message reception enables one to know the effect this message had and compare it with what was expected. For example, let us imagine a user agent that wants a commitment from a service provider agent to do a specific task at a precise time. After sending the appropriate message, the service provider agent can reply to the request with the effectively created commitment. The user agent can then compare it with the wanted commitment and, if it is not satisfactory, decide to cancel it or to start a negotiation process to improve it according to its own policy. To give another example, we can also imagine a provider agent of a weather forecast service informing a trader agent that its service is available for the France area. In reply, the trader agent sends the service provider agent some of its new beliefs on its weather services based on its service database updates. In these updates the service agent notices that the trader now believes that it provides weather forecast services for West Indies overseas French departments, which is wrong since its services are only available for metropolitan France. The service agent can then send a message to the trader agent to correct this information.

Agent behavior is controlled by a basic loopstep which consists in:

- reading incoming messages;
- updating state, i.e., beliefs on the truth value for pieces of information, private action capabilities, commitments towards itself or other agents according to these incoming messages, its current state, and its internal decision rules; and
- launching actions to achieve commitments in time.

This loop is time-bounded by the agent time grain.

This default behavior also forces an agent to adopt such basic policies as:

- **autonomy:** an agent launches actions for another agent only if it accepts the request and decides to do so;
- **veracity:** an agent always tells what it believes to be the truth; and

- **commitment:** an agent is compelled to perform a service it is committed to perform.

Finally, an agent-oriented programming approach provides powerful high-level abstractions to facilitate the description, and thus the understanding process, of the policy-oriented behavior of distributed system actors (piece of a system that plays a role). This approach also helps to model the dynamics of the states of these actors and the relationships between them. For example, by simulating the behavior of the agents of an enterprise viewpoint of an open distributed system, we see the state of a community as a network of temporal commitments.

13.6 Agent Communication Language for an Information Viewpoint

After various partnerships between agents have been defined according to their own policy, agent interoperability is needed to exploit them.

The main difficulty in software interoperability in an open distributed system comes with heterogeneity of information and computing entities.

Heterogeneous computing entities may consist of various conventional software items like mathematical Fortran programs, but also expert system applications, or databases. Each one of them is written in its own programming language, with different development teams, different development tools, and different computing environments.

Information heterogeneity may be found at a syntax level, like incompatibility between information formats, but it may also be found at a semantic level, like differences between the meaning of a concept used by different software, or at a pragmatic level, like inconsistencies in hypotheses made by interoperating agents.

Common standard information formats, such as GIF, JPEG for graphics, MPEG for animated pictures, and PostScript for complex images, mainly deal with the syntactical aspect of information heterogeneity. An agent base approach for interoperability also deals with all the other aspects

13.6.1 An Agent-Oriented Approach to Software Interoperability

One popular 'agentified' approach to the problem of software interoperability is promoted by people involved in ARPA Knowledge Sharing Effort (KSE) with their Agent Communication Language (ACL for short) (Genesereth, 1994).

With such a language, agents communicate in a common language whose semantics is agent-independent. This aspect has already been stressed in the previous section about agent-oriented programming regarding heterogeneity of computational entities, defining common descriptions of states and behavior. In this section we will focus on heterogeneous information communication problems.

To deal with this aspect of interoperability problems, three components of an ACL have been defined:

- KQML (Knowledge Query and Manipulation Language), a query language;
- KIF (Knowledge Interchange Format), a knowledge representation language; and
- Ontologies, which function as open-ended dictionaries to define the vocabulary used.

Messages sent using this ACL are KQML queries on KIF expressions using concepts defined in ontologies.

Let us now see how such an approach has already been followed in telecommunication domains such as distributed network management.

13.6.2 Network Management Agents

Like others, France Telecom is developing network management agent systems that provide their services to different kinds of users and for various needs. They are used internally by France Telecom to manage and control all its interconnected networks. Some network management services are also offered to customers to manage the France Telecom network resources they use for their own business. These network management services are important in offering customers complete network solutions to their telecommunication needs. Other services are also offered between telecommunication operators to manage and control international networks using multiple operator resources. Once again, these services are important in offering customers an integrated global international networking solution.

To offer the needed services, agents are able to send the appropriate command to each specific network equipment. They also embed all the strategic policies to allocate network resources according to their limitations, scheduled future requirements, quality of service stability, and profit optimization. Sometimes, they also have to be able to filter the information provided to various users or to propose actions, for example to optimize the network configuration or solve some detected problems. Expert system technology is used more and more often to implement this autonomous intelligent behavior.

Interconnection of multiple network resources implies interoperation of network management systems. To assure this, network management agents use standard communication protocols. Some protocols used in telecommunication network management have been defined according to standard recommendations established by the ISO (International Standardization Organization) OSI (Open System Interconnection) group.

A short presentation of these recommendations will now be given to point out their similarities with the idea of an Agent Communication Language. Further details on these recommendations can be found in ISO documents (ISO 10165-1, ISO 10165-2, ISO 10165-4).

13.6.3 Network Management Communication Protocols

To assure communication between two open systems, the ISO/OSI group defined a common information model specification language, a common query language associated with adapted communication protocols, and standard communication functions.

To define these distributed network management agents from an information viewpoint, a completely object-oriented information model specification language is used. It is defined as Guidelines for the Definition of Managed Objects (GDMO) (ISO 10165-4). Each piece of information exchanged or manipulated between two agents is encapsulated in an object, called a managed object. Such an object is defined according to a template which mainly specifies:

- its attributes with their properties such as default and permitted values, types, and allowed access;
- its actions;
- the notifications this object can send on occurrence of specific events; and
- an informal description of its behavior.

In order to ensure uniform access to a specific object, each object is associated with a single name, computed according to a naming tree. This naming tree is constructed by physical or conceptual containment relations between objects. Allowed containment relations are defined in the object template. An object name is constructed by the recursive concatenation of the object name that contains the named object and an identifier of the named object. Each object is contained in a system belonging to a company. Each company receives an internationally registered number to identify its systems. To guarantee unambigous object identification, each company has to manage its own local naming tree.

To interoperate, each agent has to specify in GDMO the information model associated with the services it offers.

To assume consistency and unambiguity between definitions in these models, each object defined in a model is defined with some inheritance relations with standard object templates that are internationally registered by international standards organizations like ISO, IUT-T or ETSI (European Telecommunication Standards Institute) or consortia like ATM-FORUM. This object template registration process provides commonly accepted concept definitions and unambiguous identification of these concepts.

Multiple standard information models have already been defined. Those standard models are defined for specific management services according to:

- the nature of the managed network, for example some models are specific to ATM networks;
- the abstraction level of these services, for example one model can define network-level management services on ATM networks, whereas another one defines equipment-level management services on ATM networks; and
- the nature of the user, for example one interface information model is designed for customer network management systems, whereas another one is designed for multiple telecom operator management systems.

These standard information models are assumed to be ontologies in the network management domain. Matching between each agent information model will be described below in the agent association establishment process.

The common query types that can be used are precisely defined as Common Management Information Service Elements (CMISE) (ISO 9595). Seven types of query are defined:

- M_CREATE: to create an object;
- M_DELETE: to delete an object;
- M_SET: to assign a value to an attribute of an object;
- M_GET: to know the value of an object attribute;
- M_CANCEL-GET: to cancel a previous get request;
- M_ACTION: to execute an object action; and
- M_EVENT-REPORT: to send a notification of the occurrence of a specific event.

More parameters can be added to identify the objects to which a query applies. For example, a scope parameter determines the depth of containment relationship to use for selecting all objects. A filter parameter to be applied on object attributes may be used to select only desired objects. A sub-naming-tree parameter determines the root of the global naming tree used to name the objects. Acknowledgement to confirm a query or a synchronization parameter can also be specified. Synchronization parameters are the atomic parameter, which ensures that all the queries will be executed on all requested objects or will be cancelled, and the best effort parameter, which will execute the query only on objects that will not raise errors. Query answers may also be time stamped and linked to a query identifier.

Queries allowed for each agent and the kind of interaction they can have depend on their communication role, which is defined when communication connection is established. When an agent wants to obtain some network management services from another agent, it has to define an association with it. Within this association, the asking agent will have a manager role and the other agent will have the agent role (it acts on the manager's behalf). In the following, the agent

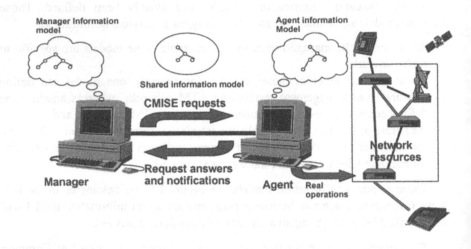

Figure 13.2. Agent communication within OSI protocols

with the manager role will be called the manager and the agent which has the agent role will be called the agent.

The types of interactions between a manager and an agent within an association are summarized in Figure 13.2. M_CREATE, M_DELETE, M_SET, M_GET, M_CANCEL-GET, M_ACTION, queries can only be sent by the manager. The agent can only reply to queries and send event reports. To assume a peer-to-peer communication relation between two agents, two symmetric associations can be established between these agents.

To understand each other, the manager and the agent must also negotiate a shared information model to which queries can be applied. This negotiation process consists in computing the intersection between the manager information model and the agent information model. Object definition using the standard information model guarantees some intersection. A more sophisticated matching process between objects has also been designed. Compatibility rules between objects have been specified to guarantee that objects are functionally equivalent to each other. This compatibility property is called allomorphism. For example, it allows a manager to send a query on an object which is not directly known by the agent, but can be replaced by another one known by the agent to serve the same purpose.

To improve interoperation between agents, common CMISE query types and Standard Information Model are standard communication functions, which, in the network management domains are named System Management Functions (SMF). These also include, for example, event report functions, event recording functions, a threshold computing function, an access control function, etc. Each of these functions is defined using a GDMO information model. For example, the event report function defines discriminator objects. To ask an agent to send to a manager only the notifications the manager is interested in, the manager asks the agent to create a discriminator on these notifications. This object has a filter attribute that allows conditions to be specified on notifications. If these conditions are satisfied, an event report containing the notification is sent to the appropriate agent. During the association establishment process, the SMFs applicable to each part of the agent information model are also negotiated. This negotiation mainly depends on the manager requirements and the functions implemented and available in the Agent. Shared Information Model and SMF negotiation largely increase open system interconnection flexibility.

13.6.4   Some Similarities with KSE/ACL

Although semantically less clear, GDMO assumes the same role as KIF in an ACL. Studies to formally define the semantics of GDMO are currently being undertaken (Keller, 1994).

CMISE and KQML purposes are nearly the same, even if CMISE defines fewer query types than KQML. But the large number of KQML 'performatives' was previously criticized as many were redundant (Cohen, 1994). Table 13.1 approximately shows how some KQML 'performatives' may be defined with CMISE queries.

Even if less sophisticated than the Mediator or Facilitator functions developed in the KSE using ACL language, the negotiation process between managers and agents improves agent interoperation efficiency. Trading, as defined by ISO/ODP recommendation functions, can also be integrated to help a manager to find the appropriate agent.

Table 13.1.

KQML	CMISE
tell	M_SET , or M_EVENT-REPORT
ask-one, ask-all	M_GET + scope + filter,
discard	M_CANCEL-GET
evaluate, achieve	M_ACTION
subscribe, monitor	M_CREATE Discriminator, M-SET filter attribute

13.6.5   What About Network Services Integration?

After the enterprise viewpoint of an Open Distributed System presented in the previous section, GDMO is presented as a language to specify an information viewpoint. CMISE and associated interconnection protocols define how to exchange and manipulate this information. GDMO and CMISE have been presented in a network management domain, but their use for other domains can be proposed. For example, GDMO was chosen by TINA-C (Telecommunications Information Networking Architecture Consortium) to specify an information model of intelligent network services (Dupuy, 1994).

In comparison with a more famous Interface Description Language (IDL) defined by OMG (Object Management Group), GDMO should be used to define an information model, whereas OMG/IDL should be used to define a computational model. In such a way, a GDMO information model describes the information accessible from an agent and an IDL computation model describes procedures to call in order to access or modify this information.

13.7   Mobile Agents: A Computational and Engineering Viewpoint Paradigm

After the enterprise and the information viewpoints of an open distributed processing system, we are now going to see how an agent-oriented approach can be useful for dealing with the computational and engineering viewpoints.

Current distributed computing technology may be categorized in two kinds of programming techniques: Remote Procedure Call (known as RPC) and Remote Programming enhanced by General Magic TeleScript[1] language.

Remote Procedure Call is becoming popular. In short, it consists in an agent (called a client) asking an accessible agent (called a server) to execute a procedure with the given parameters and to reply with the procedure results. The procedure request, the invoking parameters, and the final results are all transmitted through a communication network if these agents are physically distributed. To achieve this, a server agent often describes these procedures in an Interface Description Language (IDL) which is specified in CORBA OMG recommendations (OMG, 1991).

Remote programming, promoted by General Magic Inc., proposes another approach. To define this approach in a way that facilitates understanding, use, and control of the enabled processes, a metaphor based on mobile agents is used (White, 1994). Such agents are objects that act on behalf of an authority that may differ from the computer authority that executes their code. Mobility is used by an

---

[1] TeleScript is a trademark of General Magic Inc.

agent to go from one logical place to another in order to meet other agents to interoperate with them. 'Go' and 'meet' are thus the names of the most important methods of the agent class. Thus, location of the agent execution process can be dynamically modified at run-time according to service availability or various other circumstances.

France Telecom, as a member of the alliance with General Magic, like other telecommunication operators, has prototyped some services using this technology. One example is a service that integrates railway ticketing and car renting services and proposes the best solution according to price and time optimization. This service uses SNCF and ITI Minitel services (Léger, 1995).

Some attractive features of remote programming and more generally of the entire metaphor of mobile agents are presented below.

13.7.1 Local Communication

In comparison with RPC, the Remote Programming approach adds a new concept to access a service named a place. Places are logical locations where agents can be executed and can interact with each other. Communications between agents are thus local. One of the most important consequences is that once the agent has moved to the right place, the agent communication process does not generate network traffic. Thus, communication between agents can be more intensive without overloading the network, which increases the financial cost of communication or introduces performance degradation due to long communication delay.

With such intensive communication capabilities, the negotiation process between agents can be increased at low cost. Negotiation is an interesting and powerful feature. It can be used to solve conflicts found when defining service cost or quality of service, selecting the most interesting offer, or specifying the appropriate result expected from a service. Service personalization, online competition between services, flexibility between requirements, and available offers are enhanced by such a negotiation process.

Local communication between agents also solves the problem of communication delay. This can be important when a user wants his or her agent to react rapidly to some changes, for example, to buy or to sell stocks, to obtain concert or plane tickets becoming suddenly available. Delays introduced by network communication between the moment when an agent becomes aware of an opportunity and the effective execution of an appropriate action can make a user lose this opportunity. Thus, fast agent reaction is a quality of service that a user may require, and agree to pay for.

Local clock and agent synchronization is more easily achievable within a place than in remotely distributed computer systems. Agent synchronization may be useful, for example, to guarantee the transactional property of multiple actions of agents in the same place.

13.7.2 Asynchronous Computing

As they are in the same place, interacting agents must run on the same machine. Thus, no costly network connection between two remote computers has to be kept as in the RPC approach between a server and its clients. Once the user terminal has sent the user agent to the appropriate place, the user can also switch off his or her terminal and save his or her mobile computer battery, or simply close the related application in order to free some memory on his or her terminal. He or she does not have to wait for the agent's return. The agent's answers can be stored in the user mailbox located on a continuously available remote machine. The user will consult his or her mailbox later when he or she has time and is able to connect his or her terminal again.

In summary, firstly, instead of 'wasting' your precious time online in the network, navigating through multiple services, asynchronous computing lets an agent spend its time on your behalf. Secondly, instead of using your own computing resouces, asynchronous computing lets an agent consume service providers' resources.

13.7.3 Flexible Services Evolution and Customization

Agent capability to go in any authorized places for computing locally available information, and returning the result to its user, should improve service evolution and flexibility. For example, to obtain from multiple providers a new service better suiting his or her needs, a user will not have to wait for these providers to update their available services. A third party vendor should be able to propose a new agent that is programmed to offer this new service to all service provider places in order to be able to get this new service from all previously available services. The update of a service assumed by a newly available agent does not eliminate the previously available services. Multiple versions of a service can coexist, particularly earlier versions to keep existing users satisfied. Thus, users have more opportunities to find the exact service they want.

13.7.4 Natural Multiple Trading System

In short, to access a service, an agent must first go to a place, then if this place accepts it, ask the place for an available agent to offer a specific service interface. This service interface is defined by the class of the required agent. Thus, places have the responsibility of accepting or refusing an agent, and matching a user agent requirement with available offers. A service integration infrastructure organized in multiple places naturally introduces a multiple trading system. This is an important feature since a central trading system is often considered to be a distributed system bottleneck.

Some distributed computing technologies promote the idea of computing location transparency and could be seen as opposite to the TeleScript *go* instruction. This instruction allows one to distinguish physical and logical location transparency. When you want to book a flight ticket, for example, you do not want to cope with the physical address of the company agency that will provide you this service, you only care about the name of the company you want to fly with. It should be the same for an agent that books this ticket for you. It does not want to deal with any physical address but it needs a way to specify the logical name of the authority that will provide this service. It is one purpose of the *go* instruction to allow an agent to specify the logical name of a place where it wants to find a service that represents this authority.

13.7.5 Structured Service Offer

Places can also help to navigate through a huge service offer. Places can contain places. Those containment relationships may hierarchically structure all the available services. This structure can be defined so as to organize service access according to various topics' specialization.

13.7.6 Flexible Distributed Computing Execution

Distinguishing agents and places also isolates various decisions about the physical location for computing execution. More flexibility is thus introduced. Agents can decide to move themselves with regard to the place of the agents they want to work with, but places cannot decide to move themselves. Physical installation of places is a system management operation. In the ODP reference model, this process is defined in the engineering viewpoint. Machines that host places may also belong to companies that are different from those of the service providers. Thus, decisions on a place's physical location may be taken by another authority than the service provider. A place is a physical location of computing execution, thus these decisions are taken according to specific features such as multiple machine load balancing, information security requirements, system robustness, or communication cost induced by agent code transmission.

Conversely, an agent's logical location is decided according to the service provider authority, and according to the agent computation process. For example, to assume multiple partnerships between information providers, involved agents from each partnership can be grouped in the same place to provide more efficient and reliable services. This partnership has to be really flexible to take advantage of all possible offers available in the system. Thus, service agents can also decide to be mobile according to their evolving multiple partnerships. User agents also move from one place to another in order to navigate through all available services and select the more attractive ones. Thus, mobility decisions do not depend on engineering requirements but on the evolution of service availability.

13.7.7   Agents: A Useful and Attractive Metaphor

Finally, the use of the agent concept provides a useful and attractive metaphor for decision and execution processes undertaken in a system. Agents are presented to users as assistants that act on their behalf. This personification can also be useful for programming purposes.

This agent personification is brought by the various ascriptions that can be made on a TeleScript agent:

- He acts on behalf of his boss.
- He can communicate. To communicate, agents have to meet each other.
- He can move. To move, he needs some travelling tickets. Each ticket is available for a given destination.
- He has got hands to collect objects and can own them.
- He is limited by time and money and has to optimize these in order to satisfy his boss (its authority).

Let us now see how useful this metaphor is.

AI researchers give us some recommendations to evaluate this (Shoham, 1993; McCarthy, 1979). This personification of agents is useful when the ascriptions made help us to understand the structure of the system, its past or future behavior, or how to repair or improve it. It is most useful when applied to entities whose structure is not completely known.

From the end-user point of view, ascribing a task to a software assistant should faciltate the use of the computing resources available and provide the services he or she needs. Ease of use often comes from the right match between the end-user mental image of the system and the effective way the system evolves. Object-oriented graphical user interfaces, like those in drawing software or operating systems, engage users to manipulate objects. It seems that agent-based techniques for service architecture would engage end-users to ask agents to satisfy their service needs.

For programmers, an 'agentified' view of software should help them to be more efficient in developing code, debugging it, and improving it. As software developers are limited in the number of lines of code they can write, understand, and manage, development efficiency can be achieved by using more powerful abstractions. With such abstractions, each line of code can do more. In Section 13.2, we saw what kind of abstraction the agent concept provides. The multiple ascriptions made here on TeleScript agents correspond to previously defined behavior programmed in multiple object classes and public methods defined in TeleScript. This code is accessible and reusable for software developers to leverage service development. Such behavior seems really well suited to the development of sophisticated, multiple partnership, value-added services, and service personalization in distributed systems. In the previous paragraphs, we have seen some interesting aspects of agent mobility, and distinguishing agents from places. Thus, the metaphors used in these default behaviors should help developer to understand how to use them efficiently.

13.8 Conclusion

Telecom companies, and particularly France Telecom, are building infrastructures to allow software agents to provide more and more sophisticated services to multiple users.

We have seen that agent-oriented software techniques and know-how are becoming available to build such distributed systems. But links between techniques based on different viewpoints have to be defined. For example, TeleScript provides interesting technology to deal with the computational and engineering viewpoints of an agent system. However, links with the other ODP viewpoints of the reference model are also needed to efficiently manage large service integration architecture. For example, an information model of services should help for agent interoperability. Agents could then navigate in more knowledgeable places. From an enterprise viewpoint, contractual relationship definition between agents also seems to be an important topic to engage users to trust the system, and to provide support for flexible partnerships between competing service providers.

By providing a new way of thinking about distributed software, the agent-oriented approach fuels many attractive new ideas about new kinds of services or software features that end-users or programmers will find of interest. But many issues are still open, and France Telecom CNET is participating in this effort to meet these technical challenges.

Acknowledgements

I would like to thank Yoav Shoham from Stanford University for the discussions we had on Agent Oriented Programming and all my collegues from France Telecom CNET who helped improve this chapter.

References

Berndt, H., Minerva, R. (1994) Definition of service architecture, TINA-C Deliverable.

Cohen, P. R., Levesque, H. J. (1995) Communicative actions for artificial agents. In: *Proc. ICMAS'95*, 65–72.

Dupuy, F., Gunnar Nilsson, G., Inoue, Y. (1994) The TINA consortium: towards networking telecommunications information services. In: *Proc. ISS'95*, Vol 2, B5.2, April.

ITU-T X 901 Basic Reference Model for Open Distributed Processing, Part 1: Overview and Guide to Use.

ITU-T X 902 Basic Reference Model for Open Distributed Processing, Part 2: Descriptive Model.

ITU-T X 903 Basic Reference Model for Open Distributed Processing, Part 3: Prescriptive Model.

ISO 21-N-9122 Committee Draft ISO/IEC 13235, ISO/IEC JTC 1/SC 21 N 9122 Information Technology – Open Distributed Processing Trader.

ISO 10164-5 Distributed International Standard ISO/IEC 10164-5 Recommendation CCITT X 734 Information Technology – Open System Interconnection – Systems Management – Part 5: Event Report Function.

ISO-10165-1 Distributed International Standard ISO/IEC 10165-1 Recommendation CCITT X 720 Information Technology – Open System Interconnection – Structure of Management Information – Part 1: Management Information Model.

ISO-10165-2 Distributed International Standard ISO/IEC 10165-2 Recommendation CCITT X 721 Information Technology – Open System Interconnection – Structure of Management Information – Part 2: Definition of Management Information Model.

ISO-10165-4 Distributed International Standard ISO/IEC 10165-2 Recommendation CCITT X 722 Information Technology – Open System Interconnection – Structure of Management Information – Part 4: Guidelines for the Definition of Management Objects.

ISO-9595 Distributed International Standard ISO/IEC 9595 Recommendation CCITT X 710 Information Technology – Open System Interconnection – Common Management Service Definition (CMIS).

Genesereth (1994) Software agents. *Communications of the ACM*, 37(7), 48–54, July.

Keller, J., Dubuisson, O. (1994) Formal description technique for OSI management information structure. In: *Proceedings IS&N'94*.

Léger, A., White, J. E. (1995) Towards intelligent telematics. In: *Proceedings. of CNET 50th aniversary Multimedia forum*, 55–62

McCarthy (1979) Ascribing mental qualities to machines. Technical Report Memo 326, Stanford AI Lab.

OMG (1991) Object Management Group Inc., The Common Object Request Broker: Architecture and Specification, December.

Shoham, Y. (1993) Agent oriented programming. *Artificial Intelligence*, 60(1), 51–92.

Tokoro (1993) The society of objects. SONY Computer Science Laboratory Technical Report, SCSL-TR-93-018.

White, J. E. (1994) TeleScript technology: the foundation for the electronic marketplace, white paper, General Magic Inc.

14 Intelligent Agents in Portfolio Management

K. P. Sycara and D. Zeng
The Robotics Institue
Carnegie Mellon University

K. Decker
University of Delaware

14.1 Introduction

Due to advances in technology, diverse and voluminous information is becoming available to decision makers. This presents the potential for improved decision support, but poses challenges in terms of building tools to support users in accessing, filtering, evaluating, and fusing information from heterogeneous information sources. Most reported research on intelligent information agents to date has dealt with a user interacting with a single agent that has general knowledge and is capable of performing a variety of user delegated information finding tasks (e.g., Etzioni and Weld, 1994). For each information query, the agent is responsible for accessing different information sources and integrating the results. We believe that, given the current computational state of the art, a centralized agent approach has many limitations: (1) a single general agent would need an enormous amount of knowledge to be able to deal effectively with user information requests that cover a variety of tasks, (2) a centralized information agent constitutes a processing bottleneck and a 'single point of failure,' (3) unless the agent has beyond the state of the art learning capabilities, it would need considerable reprogramming to deal with the appearance of new agents and information sources in the environment, (4) because of the complexity of the information finding and filtering task, and the large amount of information, the required processing would overwhelm a single agent. For these reasons and because of the characteristics of the Internet environment, we employ a distributed collaborative collection of agents for information gathering.

We are currently working on a system where each user is associated with a set of agents which have access to the task and situation models and keep track of the current state of the task, situation, environment, and user information needs. Based on this knowledge, the agents decide what information is needed and initiate collaborative searches with other agents to get the information. During search, the agents communicate with each other to request or provide information, find information sources, filter or integrate information, and negotiate to resolve conflicts in information and task models. The returned information is communicated to display agents or agents that possibly combine it with information from other sources (e.g., the user) and/or filter it for appropriate display to the user.

This chapter focuses on the design of such a system of agents for the task environment of financial portfolio management, and on the key issues that we will be addressing. These issues include:

- **Gathering and integrating diverse information sources with collaborating software agents.** Because of the volume, complexity, and dynamic nature of the information available to support a user's goals, it is impossible for a single computational agent to find, access, and integrate all that information in a timely manner.
- **Case-based user, task, and situation models.** The utility of information depends on the user, task, and situational context. We propose to model user, task, and situations in cases. Cases organize information gathering plan fragments under currently valid user, task, and situation features; focus distributed agent information searches; and guide information filtering and integration. Case up-dates resulting from agent information gathering activities refine these models and reflect the current situation.
- **Adaptive integration of planning, co-ordination, scheduling, and execution.** We will explore the construction of individual agents that have the ability to be highly autonomous, quickly adapt to changes in the current environmental situation, and yet still be socially situated, balancing predictability and responsiveness.

In our system, case-based reasoning provides meta-level control and activation of agents. Depending on the task, user, and situation, case-based retrieval selects current planning goals, information needs, and information gathering goals. Based on the plans and information gathering goals, agent teams are activated 'on demand' to access, integrate, and filter information to fulfill these goals. New information can be incorporated in the case base and may give rise to new plans and information gathering goals (and as a result activation of potentially different agent teams). The system has two types of agents, task agents and information agents. Task agents have information about tasks and associated information gathering goals. Information agents have models of information sources, information access strategies, and associated task agents to whom the information should be returned. The reported work is a continuation of our previous work on multi-agent information access, filtering, and integration of everyday organizational tasks (Sycara and Zeng, 1995).

14.2 The Portfolio Management Domain

To evaluate our domain-independent agent control, organization, co-ordination, and architectural schemes, we have chosen financial portfolio management as a task domain. This is the task of providing an integrated financial picture for managing an investment portfolio over time, using the information resources already available over the Internet. This task environment has many interesting features, including:

- the enormous amount of continually changing, and generally unorganized, information available;
- the variety of kinds of information that can and should be brought to bear on the task (market data, financial report data, technical models, analysts' reports, breaking news, etc.);
- the many sources of uncertainty and dynamic change in the environment;
- information timeliness and criticality features that present the agents with hard and soft real-time deadlines for certain tasks;
- resource and cost constraints – not all data are available for free; and
- relatively well-structured evaluation criteria and experimentally verifiable testbed where decisions supported by the system can be evaluated using real-world data and feedback.

The overall task in the portfolio management domain, as stated by modern portfolio theory (Markowitz, 1991), is to provide the best possible rate of return for a specified level of risk, or conversely, to achieve a specified rate of return with the lowest possible risk.[1] Risk tolerance is one of the features that characterize the user of our system; other features include the user's investment goals (long-term retirement savings? saving for a house?) and the user's tax situation. In current practice, portfolio management is carried out by investment houses that employ teams of specialists for finding, filtering, and evaluating relevant information. Current practice as well as software engineering considerations motivate our multi-agent system architecture.

Previous work in the portfolio management domain (see Trippi and Turban (1990) for one collection) has focused on the portfolio selection process (i.e., 'stock picking') as opposed to portfolio monitoring – the ongoing, continuous, daily provision of an up-to-date financial picture of an existing portfolio. A multi-agent system approach is natural for portfolio monitoring because the multiple threads of control are a natural match for the distributed and ever-changing nature of the underlying sources of data and news that affect higher-level decision-making processes. A multi-agent system can more easily manage the detection and response to important time-critical information that could appear suddenly at any of a large number of different information sources. Finally, a multi-agent system provides a natural mapping of multiple types of expertise to be brought to bear during any portfolio management decision-making. Existing DAI techniques for resolving conflicting opinions, negotiation, and argumentation can be brought to bear on these problems (Sycara, 1989a; b).

---

[1] Risk can be specified via a statement such as 'I wish to be 95% certain that I endure no more than a 10% loss in value over any one year.'

The overall portfolio management task has several component tasks. These include eliciting (or learning) user profile information, collecting information on the user's initial portfolio position, and suggesting and monitoring a re-allocation to meet the user's current profile and goals. As time passes, assets in the portfolio will no longer meet the user's needs (and these needs may also be changing as well). Our initial system focuses on this ongoing portfolio monitoring process.

The task of monitoring individual portfolio assets gives rise to a variety of concurrent goals, such as monitoring an asset currently being held (should we continue to hold it? sell some or all of it?), or monitoring the buying or selling of an asset. Buying and selling at this high level are not instantaneous transactions, but also require careful planning and monitoring of plan execution. For example, let us assume that in the process of monitoring the system comes to recommend that an asset be sold. The way in which it is sold will be determined in part by the reason for the sale – perhaps the asset is no longer performing as required for its role in the portfolios asset allocation mix. Perhaps it is performing *too* well, and there is a growing possibility that the asset has reached a peak. In this second case, it is often prudent not to sell one's entire holdings all at once, but to sell in phases and place the appropriate standing orders to protect the user from a sudden downturn (while avoiding worry over simple daily price fluctuations).[2] Thus the goal of selling an asset is not one that requires only a simple short sequence of actions, but one that requires careful planning and monitoring of that plan as it is executed, over an extended period of time.

14.3 Case-Based Situation and Task Models

A real-world information gathering and decision making/aiding system, such as a portfolio management system, typically operates in a dynamically evolving environment, where information gathering can be user, task, and situation dependent. Good models of the user, task, and situation help focus information gathering and filtering activities so that relevant information can be efficiently found. On the other hand, due to the unpredictability of the information and decision-making environment, new goals come into the system in the midst of execution, actions may fail due to exogenous events and need to be replanned, and there is incomplete information about the world.

We are proposing to model the information gathering task as a planning task where planning and execution are interleaved and search is guided by user, task, and situation models. We believe that cases that incorporate user, task, and situation models can effectively provide instantiations of the situation-dependent task structure and the associated team of information gathering agents. The case base contains cases of successful and unsuccessful information gathering episodes

---

[2] There are of course tax considerations on sales as well.

and information evaluation. After each information gathering cycle the case base is updated. Thus, learning is integrated with problem solving and is achieved automatically. This feature makes case-based reasoning very preferable in application domains with an open and dynamically changing world model (Sycara et al., 1995). Case-based reasoning offers three general advantages. First, since it relies on reusing specific experiences rather than reasoning from a general world model, it provides for more efficient planning. Second, since it can start with few cases in memory and incrementally acquire new cases based on a reasoner's interactions with the world, it makes few assumptions about the completeness and correctness of world knowledge. Third, previous past failures warn the planner about the possibility of failure in current circumstances and, hence, help avoid future failures.

Each case will be automatically labeled with identifying information such as user's name (a user could be a software agent), time of creation, time of modification, etc. So, a case will carry a complete audit trail of its origin and modifications. This information is essential for careful analysis of all the planning knowledge that is exchanged during system operation, and we will rely heavily on it during the initial stages of knowledge acquisition and development. In addition, this information can be used to evaluate the performance of the system under different planning scenarios, since each item will be clearly identified.

The library of cases we propose can be viewed as a case-based scheme for meta-control that offers agents access to task and situation specific information. The agents use this information to focus search and filtering. The asynchronous information gathering activity of the agents results in new information about the world (new cases) that gets incorporated into the case base. Case base updates result in formation of new memory indices. These new indices, along with any new user inputs (e.g., information gathering requests, change in context) activate a new set of cases that reflect possibly new information seeking goals, and new sets of agents. In this sense, the case base can be viewed as (1) tracking the user's intentions and his/her evolving information needs, (2) reflecting changing situations, (3) recognizing new events, and (4) learning information retrieval tactics/heuristics.

Figure 14.1 shows an active case base which receives as input notification of events, either directly from the user or from new information that becomes available (e.g., from other software agents). Updates of the case base with the addition of new information finding episodes and new indices are also considered an event that results in the activation of a new round of reasoning. In the following, we use an example to illustrate the general case-based agent invocation process. Given a situation, the case base calls a certain task assistant, say Analyst Tracking Agent, which the reasoning process determines is relevant to meeting the information gathering goals (which in turn might be information requests from Portfolio Manager Agent). Portfolio Manager Agent calls upon Earnings Analysis Agent, News Classifier, etc., to locate information from the infosphere directly (in

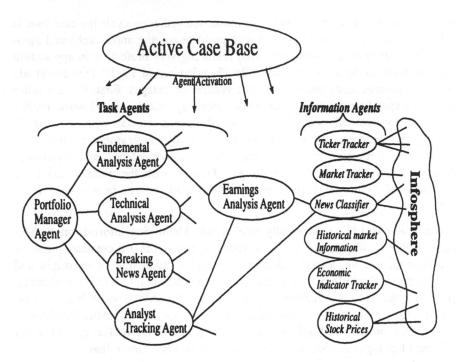

Figure 14.1. A 'direct invocation' agent organization for a portfolio mamagement system

the case of News Classifier) or indirectly (in the case of Earning Analysis Agent). Note that there is no hierarchy of agents here: in a different situation Earning Analysis Agent might have been called directly by the case-base reasoning process. After collaborating to find and filter information, Analyst Tracking Agent updates the case base with new information finding episodes that include a timestamp and the results of the search. If unexpected news (unexpected in terms of the current situation) has been found during information retrieval (such as major corporate merge news), the case-based process will interrupt the regular plan execution and take other emergency actions. For example, the case-base process might invoke the interface agent to notify the user right away.

From the perspectives of case-based reasoning, there are a number of important research questions that we need to address. The most fundamental question is *what constitutes a case?* A case in case memory describes a specific information scenario including: (1) information needs and goals which might come directly from the user or from other software agents, (2) global features which give an abstract characterization of the situation in which this information gathering operation takes place, (3) features of local nature which describe in detail the information about information sources, inter-agent interactions, etc., (4) information retrieval plan skeleton, (5) feedbacks/evaluations with respect to acquired information and information retrieval effectiveness/efficiency, and (6) potential failures and re-trial, plan modification information.

At the most abstract level, we might index an asset monitoring task plan fragment using several broad situation characteristics. These characteristics are represented in the case base and used as indices for the retrieval of plan fragments, associated information gathering goals and associated lists of agents to be activated. Depending on the situation, at different times, different task and information plans could be active, thus activating different agent teams.

- **Goal-to-plan-for:** We described some abstract monitoring goals above, such as monitoring a held position, monitoring an acquisition, or monitoring the sale of all or part of a position. This is a main index for plan fragment retrieval.
- **Asset type:** US stocks, US government bonds, mutual funds, gold, etc. The high-level, abstract plans used for monitoring these different types of investments are themselves quite different.
- **Sector:** With stocks, for example, this is the industry sector such as electronics or health care. (Actually, there are several well-defined hierarchical classification systems used in the industry.) While this will only have a minimal effect on the high-level abstract plan an agent uses, it will have a larger effect at more detailed levels. For example, the types of information (and the evaluation processes) that are needed to evaluate an investment in a financial institution such as a bank are very different from those need to evaluate the stock of a manufacturing company. It also offers an index for learning sector-wide information such as economic forecasts and cross company earnings reports effects (see Section 14.4.2).
- **Name:** Again, the particular stock being monitored is an important index at the more detailed levels of plan retrieval, and will be used for indexing task execution times, storing historical data, and so on.
- **Ownership records:** Information about how much was purchased, when, and at what price. This information interacts with the user's investment goals and tax situation to produce situation-specific buy/sell plans.
- **Tax status:** Assets held in non-taxable trusts like an IRA require different treatment than those that are subject to taxes on realized capital gains.
- **Portfolio status:** What else is in the portfolio? What is the current asset allocation, and what role does this asset play?
- **User profile:** What are the user's investment goals for this portfolio? Expectations on return? Risk tolerance?
- **Other:** Other information, such as brokerage commissions.

We are currently investigating other important issues such as efficient case indexing mechanisms, case retrieval/matching approaches, and initial case collection. To address the initial case collection issues, we envision that a limited number of standard finance information gathering and decision making procedures (default cases) can serve well for the initial case base. This is due to another nice property of case-based reasoning: a partial case base can be a starting point of a case-based system that will gather cases through user interaction and problem solving incrementally.

14.4 Organizational Structure

We propose a general system organization in which agents are directly activated based on the top-down elaboration of the current situation (as opposed to indirect activation via manager or matchmaker agents, or self-directed activation). These agent activations, guided by case-based retrieval according to the current situation, dynamically form an organizational structure that fits in with the user's current profile, tasks, and other situational features. This organization will change over time, but will also remain relatively static for extended periods (for example, while monitoring currently held investments during stable market periods). Information that is important for decision-making (and thus might cause an eventual change in organizational structuring) is monitored at the lowest levels of the organization and passed upward when necessary.

In this type of organization (see Figure 14.1), 'task agents' or 'task assistants' (Sycara and Zeng, 1995) continually interleave planning, scheduling, coordination, and the execution of domain-level problem-solving actions. Task agents interact with one another and with 'information agents' or 'information assistants' that encapsulate network information sources. Task agents retrieve, coordinate, and schedule plans based on local knowledge modulated by situational context. A task assistant decomposes an information request into information seeking goals and subgoals and interacts with the information assistants to gather the information. In this architecture, a task assistant does the final filtering and fusing of information before passing it on to agents above it in the organizational structure (requesting agents). This incremental information fusion and conflict resolution increases efficiency and potential scalability (e.g., inconsistencies detected at the infor-mation-assistant level may be resolved at that level and not propagated to the task-assistant level) and robustness (e.g., whatever inconsistencies were not detected during information assistant interaction can be detected at the task-assistant level). In addition, a task assistant composes a new case that incorporates its findings to be stored in the case memory.

In this architecture, information assistants would have models of their associated information sources, learn the reliability of those sources, as well as strategies for low-level information fusion and multiple methods for responding to information requests. As an example of the latter, a stock ticker monitoring agent might have several methods available to it that trade off time, cost, and quality:

- one or more sources of 15-minute delayed values (with varying reliabilities and average response delays);
- one or more sources of real-time quotations that charge a fee (more reliable response but still not guaranteed); and

- the ability to guess a quote based on recent data and simple models (very fast but of low quality).

On the other hand, task-specific assistants have a model of the task domain, executable methods for performing the task, knowledge of an initial set of information assistants relevant to their task and strategies for learning models of pertinent information assistants.

Figure 14.1 shows a top-level portfolio manager agent which receives as input notification of events, either directly from the user or from the case base, or from information that becomes available (e.g., from task and information agents). Given the current situation, the portfolio manager agent:

- instantiates task plans and associated information gathering goals according to the current situation;
- coordinates those plans with other agents (this includes task assignment actions that activate task assistants); and
- schedules and monitors the execution of its local actions.

In Figure 14.1, the fundamental, technical, news, and outside-analyst task agents have been activated in this manner. These agents are task assistants that can either locate information via information assistants, or by calling upon other task agents. There is not a strict hierarchy of agents – the same task and information agents may be called upon by different parts of the portfolio management organization. After collaborating to find and filter information, task agents update the case base with new information finding episodes that include a time stamp and the results of the search.

This architecture has potential advantages and drawbacks. The advantages include:

- There is a finite number of task assistants that each agent communicates with.
- Because information processing is done by all the task agents at every level (rather than by having one task agent receive all data from every information agent) we avoid having a single computational bottleneck point.
- The task assistants are responsible for checking information quality, filtering irrelevant information, recognizing important information, and integrating information from heterogeneous information sources for their respective tasks.
- The task assistants are responsible for activating relevant information assistants and coordinating the information finding and filtering activity for their task.

All the above characteristics, by imposing some structure through definition of task assistants, contribute to overall system responsiveness. On the other hand, there are potential drawbacks:

- The portfolio manager is a single point of failure. Such failures can be mitigated by expending the resources to have, for example, a redundant portfolio manager that takes over in case of failure.

- Each task assistant also constitutes a single point of failure for that task. This can be mitigated by having more than one task assistant (either clones of each other or not). In the case where two different assistants exist for the same task, the task assistants must negotiate to resolve inconsistencies. We propose to explore the use of negotiation strategies for resolving inconsistencies.

In the stock portfolio example, task assistants for areas such as earnings analysis might be replicated and allowed to specialize on various industry groups (one agent to handle banking industry earnings, one for manufacturing, etc.). Such agents might begin as clones, but learn specialized case information. In the event of a failure, a non-specialist would still be able to retrieve useful plans for a task inside its area of expertise, but outside of its specialty.

14.4.1 The Portfolio Monitoring Task

We can represent the plans that are retrieved using TAEMS task structures (Decker, 1995; Decker and Lesser, 1993). TAEMS task structures are based on abstraction hierarchies, where task plans are elaborated via a 'subtask' relationship into acyclic directed graphs that have actions, called executable methods, at their leaves. Such structures are compatible with most planning representations, and provide the necessary information both for scheduling activities that arise from multiple plans (Garvey et al., 1993), and for coordinating the activities of multiple agents (Decker and Lesser, 1995). As shown in Figure 14.2, a top-level portfolio management agent interacts graphically and textually with the user to acquire information about the user's profile and goals; as mentioned earlier, we will assume in this chapter that the system has gone through an initial usage period and has reached a 'steady state' of monitoring the current portfolio.

Such a monitoring task includes gathering opinions from various task experts, integrating this information, and then making or updating the recommendation (such as buy, sell, or hold) for the asset under consideration. These tasks are persistent, in that they are continuously present. An agent will be dealing with many such tasks simultaneously. Gathering opinions from the area experts (fundamental analysis, technical analysis, news, and the opinions of other analysts – the published output of similar human organizations) requires registering with them and then either waiting for new opinions to be received or asking for them directly. An opinion consists of not just a buy/sell/hold recommendation but a short list of positive and negative reasons for holding that opinion, and potentially both symbolic and numeric measures of uncertainty. Information integration involves removing redundant information, resolving conflicts (or declaring them unresolvable), and forming a coherent group opinion, that can then be used for decision-making (in the light of the user's risk tolerance, investment goals, asset allocation, tax status, and so on). The conflict resolution process may involve negotiation between the agents involved.

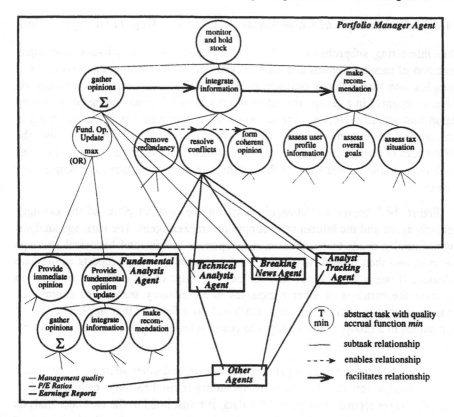

Figure 14.2. A task structure representing high-level portions of the monitor-stock-and-hold task

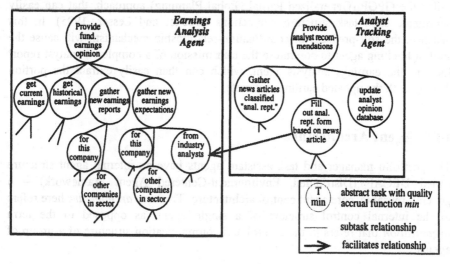

Figure 14.3. A task structure showing one co-ordination relationship between tasks in the domain of the earnings report agent and the human analyst tracking agent

14.4.2   An Example of Co-ordination: Earnings Report Interpretation

One interesting subproblem in portfolio management is acquisition and inter-pretation of earnings reports and earnings estimates. The earnings analysis task is a complex one that includes estimating the impact of one company's earnings on other companies in a sector, the information contained in one company's earning report that actually releases information about all companies in a sector, timing in the release of earnings reports (especially for smaller companies), and the differences in actual earnings versus expectations. It is important to track revisions in earning estimates over time, as they often give important clues as to future price moves.

Figure 14.3 shows a relationship between the abstract plans of the earnings analysis agent and the human analyst opinion tracker agent. The earnings analysis agent initially needs to get data on a company's current and historical earnings patterns, and then it needs to keep up to date on new earnings reports as they are released. It needs to track not only the new earnings of the company in question but also the earnings of other companies in an industry sector. For example, a change in the portion of earnings attributed to sales is often applicable to all companies in a group, unlike changes to costs (sales minus earnings) (Joh and Lee, 1992).

The analyst tracking agent gathers, from news and other sources, existing and updated analyst reports on a company, including revised earnings estimates (often part of a larger report). This part of the data, if transmitted to the earnings analysis agent, can somewhat speed up (i.e., facilitate) the process of gathering earnings expectations. We have demonstrated the use of general coordination mechanisms, called the GPGP (Generalized Partial Global Planning) approach, that can easily coordinate such task structure interactions (Decker and Lesser, 1995). In this instance, the soft-predecessor-coordination-relationship mechanism will cause the analyst tracking agent to commit to the transmission of a completed analyst report form to the earnings analysis agent, which can then easily extract the portion dealing with the updated earnings estimate.

14.5   Agent Architecture

The portfolio manager and task assistant agents have an internal agent structure called DECAF (Distributed, Environment-Centered Agent Framework) – a general, reusable, core agent control architecture. The term *architecture* here refers to the internal control structure of a single agent, as opposed to the term *organization* that refers to the control and communication structure of a group of agents.

The important features of the DECAF architecture are:

- A set of clearly defined control modules (planning, coordination, scheduling, decision-making, and monitoring) that work together to control an agent. The implementations of these modules are not fixed, only their interfaces are. It is often helpful to imagine these modules as acting asynchronously (or multi-threaded) even if they are not implemented in this manner. Each module has an essentially null implementation, so agents do not have to be any bigger than they need to be. The idea is that properly developed modules can be re-used and traded.
- A core task structure representation that is shared by all of these control modules. This core structure can be annotated and expanded with all manner of details that might be 'understood' only by one or a few control modules, but there is a core, shared representation.

Briefly, the main control functions consist of a *planner* that creates or extends the agent's view of the problem(s) it is trying to solve, called the *task structure*. The *coordinator* notices certain features of that structure, and may annotate it, expand it, communicate parts to other agents, or add scheduling constraints to it. The *local scheduler* takes the rough plan and creates a low-level schedule or schedules that fix the timing and ordering of actions. The *decision-maker* chooses a schedule – if there is more than one – that best meets the agent's current needs or performance goals. The *execution monitor* takes care of actually executing the next desired action (perhaps including pre-emption of the action in true real-time execution).

Previous work has focused on the design of the coordinator (Decker and Lesser, 1995), the local scheduler (Garvey et al., 1993), and how they interact with the decision maker (Garvey et al., 1994). Details of the implementation of these components can be found in the cited papers. We intend to extend this work to include more sophisticated execution monitoring, using such techniques as the TCA (Task Control Architecture) approach (Simmons, 1994).

14.6 Conclusions

We have presented the overall framework and design decisions made in our multi-agent system for the management of financial portfolios through information access, filtering, and integration. Within this framework we will explore research issues of agent coordination and negotiation and case-base structuring for user, task, and situation modeling. In addition, there are a number of learning-related research issues we want to explore. How do we formulate the learning task in the context of multi-agent interactions where procedural and control knowledge must be learned? Concept learning has been the focus of most machine learning research (e.g., (Michalski and Tecuci, 1994). Learning of control knowledge has been explored using case-based reasoning (e.g., Kambhampati and Hendler, 1992;

Veloso, 1992; Miyashita and Sycara, 1995), and reinforcement-type learning techniques (e.g., Sutton, 1988; Moore, 1993). This research has been conducted almost exclusively in a single-agent setting. We want to explore strategies for multiple-agent learning of control knowledge during agent interactions. Within each formulation of the learning task (e.g., as a case-based learning, or reinforcement learning), there are additional more specific issues to be explored. For example, for multiple-agent case-based learning, new case indexing and retrieval algorithms might be necessary. In addition, the number of training cases that must be incrementally acquired through agent interactions for reliable learning is an open issue.

References

Decker, K. S. (1995) *Environment Centered Analysis and Design of Co-ordination Mechanisms*. PhD thesis, University of Massachusetts.

Decker, K. S., Lesser, V. R. (1993) Quantitative modeling of complex computational task environments. In: *Proceedings of the Eleventh National Conference on Artificial Intelligence*, 217–224, Washington, July.

Decker, K. S., Lesser, V. R. (1995) Designing a family of coordination algorithms. In: *Proceedings of the First International Conference on Multi-Agent Systems*, 73–80, San Francisco, June, AAAI Press. Longer version available as UMass CS-TR 94-14.

Etzioni, O., Weld, D. (1994) A softbot-based interface to the Internet. *Communications of the ACM*, 37(7), July.

Garvey, A., Decker, K. S., Lesser, V. R. (1994) A negotiation-based interface between a real-time scheduler and a decision-maker. In: *AAAI Workshop on Models of Conflict Management*, Seattle. Also UMASS CS TR-94-08.

Garvey, A., Humphrey, M., Lesser, V. R. (1993) Task interdependencies in design-to-time real-time scheduling. In: *Proceedings of the Eleventh National Conference on Artificial Intelligence*, 580–585, Washington, July.

Joh, G., Lee, C. (1992) Stock price response to accounting information in oligopoly. *Journal of Business*, 65(3), 451–472, July.

Kambhampati, S., Hendler, J. A. (1992) A validation-structure-based theory of plan modification and reuse. *Artificial Intelligence*, 55(2-3), 193–258.

Markowitz, H. (1991) *Portfolio Selection: Efficient Diversification of Investments*. B. Blackwell, Cambridge, MA, Second Edition.

Michalski, R., Tecuci, G. (1994) *Machine Learning: A multistrategy Approach*, Vol IV. Morgan Kaufmann Publishers, San Mateo, CA.

Miyashita, K., Sycara, K. (1995) Cabins: a framework of knowledge acquisition and iterative revision for schedule improvement and reactive repair. *Artificial Intelligence*, 76(1-2).

Moore, A. W. (1993) Prioritized sweeping: reinforcement learning with less data and less real time. *Machine Learning*, October.

Simmons, R. (1994) Structured control for autonomous robots. *IEEE Trans. on Robotics and Automation*, 10(1), February.

Sutton, R. S. (1988) Learning to predict by the methods of temporal differences. *Machine Learning*, 3, 9–44.

Sycara, K. (1989a) Argumentation: planning other agents' plans. In: *Proceedings of the Eleventh International Joint Conference on Artificial Intelligence (IJCAI-89)*, Detroit, Mich.

Sycara, K. (1989b) Multi-agent compromise via negotiation. In: M. Huhns, L. Gasser (Eds.) *Distributed Artificial Intelligence*, Vol 2. Pitman.

Sycara, K., Zeng, D. (1995) Task-based multi-agent coordination for information gathering, in: C. Knoblock, A. Levy (Eds.) *Working Notes of the AAAI Spring Symposium Series on Information Gathering from Distributed, Heterogeneous Environments*, Stanford, CA, March. AAAI.

Sycara, K., Zeng, D., Miyashita, K. (1995) Using case-based reasoning to acquire user scheduling preferences that change over time. In: *Proceedings of the Eleventh IEEE Conference on Artificial Intelligence Applications (CAIA '95)*, Los Angeles, February, IEEE.

Trippi, R., Turban, E. (Eds.) (1990) *Investment Management: Decision Support and Expert Systems*. Van Nostrand Reinhold, New York.

Veloso, M. M. (1992) *Learning by Analogical Reasoning in General Problem Solving*. PhD thesis, Carnegie Mellon University.

15 The FinCEN AI System: Finding Financial Crimes in a Large Database of Cash Transactions[1]

H. G. Goldberg
US Department of the Treasury

T. E. Senator
National Association of Securities Dealers

15.1 Introduction

This chapter discusses the FinCEN Artificial Intelligence System (FAIS) and its continued development as a case-study of AI analysis of a financial database. We first present a brief description of the system, along with an update of what has been accomplished since the system was reported in (Senator, 1995). The version of FAIS reported there is V2.0, which has been in operation since December 1994. We next discuss some generally applicable conclusions regarding knowledge discovery in databases (KDD), in particular, the essential role of data preparation and database transformation steps in knowledge discovery systems. Finally, we discuss our plans for system improvements and future development in the context of an expanded agency mission, including not only incremental changes but also a major redesign, referred to as V3.0 of FAIS.

15.2 FAIS: Case Study and Progress Report

The Financial Crimes Enforcement Network (FinCEN) is an agency of the US Treasury Department whose mission is to establish, oversee, and implement policies to prevent and detect money laundering, in support of federal, international, state, and local law enforcement. A key data source available to FinCEN is reports of large cash transactions made to Treasury according to terms of the Bank Secrecy Act (BSA) and other, related legislation.[2] FAIS links and evaluates

---

[1]The authors of this chapter are employees of the Financial Crimes Enforcement Network of the US Department of the Treasury, but this chapter in no way represents an official policy statement of the US Treasury Department or the US Government. The views expressed herein are solely those of the authors. This chapter implies no general endorsement of any of the particular products mentioned in the text.

[2]12 U.S.C. sections 1730d, 1829b, 1951-1959, and 31 U.S.C. sections 5311-5326.

all reported transactions for indications of suspicious activity characteristic of money laundering, with the objective of identifying previously unknown, potential high value leads for follow-up investigation and, if warranted, prosecution.

FAIS integrates intelligent software and human agents in a co-operative discovery task on a very large data space. It is a complex system incorporating several aspects of AI technology, including rule-based reasoning and a blackboard. FAIS consists of an underlying database, a graphical user interface (GUI), and several pre-processing and analysis modules. The database functions as a blackboard and is implemented in Sybase. The GUI is implemented in Neuron Data's Open Interface. The suspiciousness evaluation module is a rule-based reasoner implemented in Neuron Data's Nexpert Object (now called Smart Elements). Alta Analytics' NetMap provides a link analysis module. Other FAIS programs, which asynchronously load and pre-process the data, are written in SQL and C. FAIS runs on a network of Sun servers and workstations under the UNIX operating system.

FAIS has been in operational use at FinCEN since March 1993 by a small group of analysts, processing approximately 200 000 transactions per week. FAIS operates in two modes: data-driven and user-directed. Over 500 investigative support reports, referring to over 1500 individual subjects, have resulted from using the system. These reports reflect transactions on the order of $1.5 billion in potential laundered funds. FAIS's development is continuing, to remain current with changes in money laundering techniques and statutes, to increase its effectiveness, to add additional features, and to support FinCEN's policy and regulatory responsibilities in addition to detection and investigative support.

FAIS's unique analytical power arises primarily from a transformation of view of the underlying data from a transaction oriented perspective to a subject (i.e., person or organization) or account oriented perspective. FAIS enables a process that was not feasible without automation, both because of the data volume and the need to link together related transactions prior to evaluation. FAIS permits analysts to focus on significant items of interest in the database, enabling more detailed and complex analyses on these items. FAIS allows law enforcement to derive increased value from the reported data, to ensure that all reported transactions are evaluated at least once, and to reduce the likelihood of missing any significant reported illicit financial activity.

In this section, a summary of the system as previously reported is followed by an update of subsequent, recent efforts.

15.2.1   FAIS V2.0 Summary

This section describes FAIS V2.0 – its task, architecture, and use.

15.2.1.1 Task Description

Money laundering is a complex process of placing the profit, usually cash, from illicit activity into the legitimate financial system, with the intent of obscuring the source, ownership, or use of the funds. Money laundering typically involves a multitude of transactions, perhaps by distinct individuals, into multiple accounts with different owners at different banks and other financial institutions.

To combat money laundering, the BSA requires reporting of cash transactions in excess of $10 000 (see Figure 15.1). This record keeping preserves a financial trail for investigators to follow and allows the Government to systematically scrutinize large cash transactions. Approximately 10 million transactions are reported each year[3] (see Figure 15.2). The data reported on the forms are subject to errors, uncertainties, and inconsistencies that affect both identification and transaction information.

Because of the volume of forms received, the number and variety of fields on the forms, and the quality of the entries on the forms, it is not feasible for human analysts to review all forms even on an individual unlinked basis. Additionally, the detection of money laundering is a complex task requiring years of experience and judgement by well-trained analysts, due in large part to the lack of both formal domain models and normative data regarding the cash economy. These factors all contributed to the belief that AI was a necessary component of FAIS. The original task of FAIS is the automated review of *all* BSA filings to generate potential leads. The expertise required for the FAIS task is the ability to detect potential indications of money laundering *in the BSA database*, as distinct from the (at least as important) ability to detect money laundering based on other clues.

15.2.1.2 Application Description

This section briefly describes FAIS V2.0 – how it operates and its system architecture. Figure 15.3 depicts the FAIS architecture and its two modes of operation, data-driven and user-directed. The key functional modules of FAIS are:

- the underlying database,
- the data load programs,
- the database extension updating programs,
- the suspiciousness evaluation programs,
- the link analysis tool, and
- the interactive query interface (IQI).

---

[3]A recent Congressional mandate to reduce the filing burden on financial institutions has produced regulatory changes that are expected to reduce filings by 30%.

Form **4789**
(Rev. October 1995)
Department of the Treasury
Internal Revenue Service

Currency Transaction Report
▶ Use this 1995 revision effective October 1, 1995.
▶ For Paperwork Reduction Act Notice, see page 3.   ▶ Please type or print.
(Complete all applicable parts—See instructions)

OMB No. 1545-0183

1   Check appropriate box(es) if:
a ☐ Amends prior report   b ☐ Multiple persons   c ☐ Multiple transactions

Part I   Person(s) Involved in Transaction(s)

Section A—Person(s) on Whose Behalf Transaction(s) Was Conducted

2 Individual's last name or Organization's name	3 First name	4 M.I.

5 Doing business as (DBA)	6 SSN or EIN

7 Address (number, street, and apt. or suite no.)	8 Date of birth M M D D Y Y

9 City	10 State	11 ZIP code	12 Country (if not U.S.)	13 Occupation, profession, or business

14   Describe method used to verify identity:
a ☐ Driver's license/State I.D.   b ☐ Passport   c ☐ Alien registration   d ☐ Other ....
e Issued by: _____   f Number: _____

Section B—Individual(s) Conducting Transaction(s) (if other than above).
If Section B is left blank or incomplete, check appropriate box(es) below to indicate the reason(s):
☐ Armored Car Service   ☐ Conducted On Own Behalf   ☐ Mail Deposit or Shipment
☐ Night Deposit or Automated Teller Machine (ATM)   ☐ Multiple Transactions

15 Individual's last name	16 First name	17 M.I.

18 Address (number, street, and apt. or suite no.)	19 SSN

20 City	21 State	22 ZIP code	23 Country (if not U.S.)	24 Date of birth M M D D Y Y

25   Describe method used to verify identity:
a ☐ Driver's license/State I.D.   b ☐ Passport   c ☐ Alien registration   d ☐ Other ....
e Issued by: _____   f Number: _____

Part II   Amount and Type of Transaction(s). Check applicable boxes to describe transaction.

26 Cash in $ _____ .00   27 Cash out $ _____ .00   28 Date of Transaction M M D D Y Y

29 ☐ Foreign currency _____ (Country)   30 ☐ Wire transfer(s)   31 ☐ Negotiable Instrument(s) Purchased

32 ☐ Negotiable Instrument(s) Cashed   33 ☐ Currency exchange(s)   34 ☐ Deposit(s)/Withdrawal(s)

35 ☐ Account number(s) affected (if any):   36 ☐ Other (specify)

Part III   Financial Institution Where Transaction(s) Took Place

37 Name of financial institution	Enter Regulator or BSA Examiner code number from the instructions here. ▶ [ ]

38 Address (number, street, and apt. or suite no.)	39 SSN or EIN

40 City	41 State	42 ZIP code	43 MICR No.

Sign Here ▶

44 Title of approving official	45 Signature of approving official	46 Date of signature M M D D Y Y
47 Type or print preparer's name	48 Type or print name of person to contact	49 Telephone number ( )

Cat. No. 42004W

Form **4789** (Rev. 10-95)

Figure 15.1. The CTR

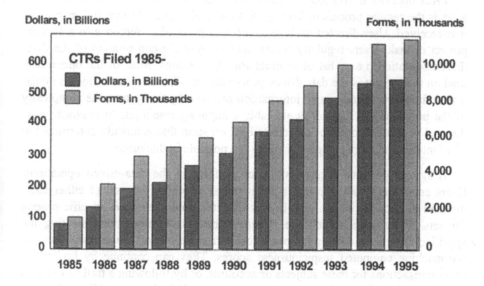

Figure 15.2. CTR filling

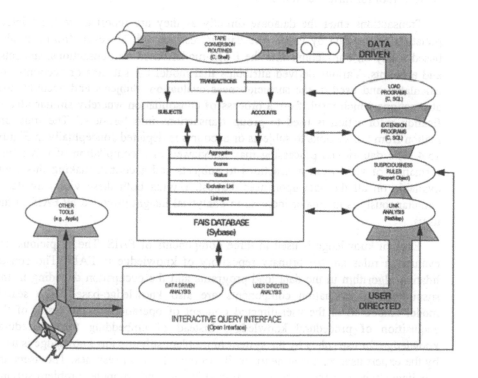

Figure 15.3. System architecture

FAIS operates in two modes: data-driven and user-directed. Data-driven operation is the regular process of loading, linking, and evaluating new information as it is received. User-directed analysis is *ad hoc*, initiated in response to a specific project or task. Users regularly review and analyze the end product of the data-driven operation, i.e., a list of subjects sorted by scores. Most of the operational load on the system is the data-driven processing of all transactions. Because data-driven functions operate on all information received by the system, the complexity of the processing is limited by available computing resources. In contrast, user-directed processing operates on selected information that is already determined to be of interest, so more complex analyses are possible in this mode.

A system operator is responsible for performing the data-driven operations. Users enter the system through a main menu in which they select either user-directed or data-driven analysis. In user-directed mode, users set specific criteria for sets of transactions and the system retrieves all transactions meeting the specified criteria. In data-driven mode, users retrieve sets of transactions based on the machine computed suspiciousness scores. They can continue by finding all other transactions for these subjects or accounts, or by following a trail of linkages by looking for other subjects and accounts that are linked to a specified subject or account. At any stage, a user can load sets of transactions into the NetMap link analysis tool for further analysis.

Transactions enter the database directly as they are reported, with no interpretation of the data by FAIS. The data is restructured, however, from a model based solely on transactions into the FAIS model based on transactions, subjects, and accounts. Various derived attributes that model the subjects or accounts are calculated and used in the suspiciousness evaluation. Subjects and accounts are abstractions which result from a process of consolidation whereby similar identification information is used to group transactions into 'clusters.' The transformation from transactions to subjects or accounts is depicted conceptually in Figure 15.4. The data-driven processing may be viewed as a compilation of this transformation of view from transactions to subjects and accounts, making this view available on all the data upon user request. Having both these views available simultaneously is the major increase in analytical insight provided by FAIS to the users.

Explicit knowledge is used in three components of FAIS. The suspiciousness evaluation rules are the primary repository of knowledge in FAIS. The consolidation algorithm in the data load programs and the occupation decoding in the suspiciousness evaluation components are also knowledge-based. The search model embodied in the user-directed concept of operations is the result of the acquisition of procedural knowledge. Instead of embedding this procedural knowledge for use solely by the system in problem solving, this knowledge is used by the expert user to reason heuristically through his own searches. The users are intelligent agents in the context of a mixed human and computer problem solving

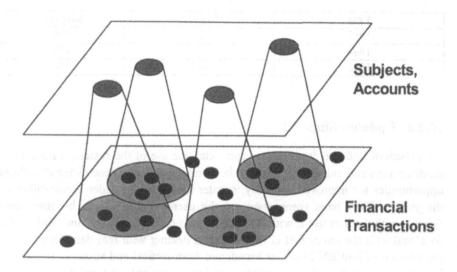

Figure 15.4. Transformation of perspective

system. The human and software agents co-operate via the database. The FAIS database serves as a blackboard, and the FAIS programs as automated agents.

15.2.1.3 Application Use and Payoff

FAIS has been used operationally since March 1993. As of April 1996, 30 million transactions have been entered and linked together, resulting in four million consolidated subjects and three million accounts. A group of intelligence analysts is engaged full time in reviewing, validating, and pursuing potential leads generated by the system. These analysts have as their primary responsibility the process of BSA suspiciousness analysis. An additional responsibility is to serve as the primary sources of knowledge for system development.

As the analysts have gained experience with the system, it has become more productive. Table 15.1 summarizes reports by year in terms of number of reports produced and number of subjects identified. These reports correspond to well over $1.5 billion in potential laundered funds.

A key benefit of FAIS is that it has allowed analysts to see the BSA data as it has not been seen before. Queries against the FAIS database have yielded insights useful for BSA policy decisions, form redesigns, and identification of required compliance actions.

Table 15.1. Leads resulting from FAIS

Year	Reports	Subjects
1993	27	276
1994	75	403
1995	448	>1500

15.2.2   Update – Since V2.0

As a result of both the development and extensive use of the system, a number of modifications and enhancements have been implemented. These changes address opportunities for improved accuracy, greater utility, and broader applicability of the system. They have come about as the users of FAIS have become more familiar with the data itself, with the best ways to explore, display, and analyze the data, and with the errors that always occur in dealing with real data. In addition, the mission of FinCEN itself has broadened from tactical and strategic support of law enforcement to include regulatory policy, oversight, and enforcement. The agency also has a role in guiding and assisting the financial community in self-policing efforts. Analyses of the BSA data are important in all these efforts.

15.2.2.1 System Development Efforts

The dual approaches to search in FAIS (i.e., data-driven and user-directed) are merged in the user interface in response to the need for users to manually refine the scope of a search by selecting broad categories of transactions, and then request system-provided evaluations of subjects or accounts linked to those transactions. This was done by combining the two modes of search in the one query interface.

Additional improvements to the query interface have yielded greater throughput in the case analysis process by allowing the users to spend less time in routine tasks such as producing output for investigators, plotting aggregate monetary values, or exporting them to a spreadsheet.

A geographical information system (MapInfo) was purchased and integrated into the system. Geographical displays both of filing institutions and of finished and pending cases have been produced. We expect even further use of this tool as the complexity of the cases increases.

The link analysis and visualization tool (NetMap) was upgraded and enhanced to include additional data from the BSA database. While this tool is essentially a separate program, processing a file of data that has been output from FAIS, we prototyped a call-back feature where the user of NetMap can reach back into the database to perform additional analyses. We expect this feature to be used extensively as we integrate these tools more closely into the system.

Upgraded versions of the system software have provided improvements in both speed and capabilities. New hardware was purchased to increase the performance of the queries which form the basis of the system's analyses. All together, a speed-up of 5–10 times has allowed us to keep up with the increasing database size and complexity of the cases.

15.2.2.2 System Use – Results from a Year in the BSA Database

The past year of case analysis has seen a huge increase in the number and complexity of cases that the users of FAIS were able to produce. Although we are unable to discuss specific details of these cases, a few illustrative examples may be described in a general fashion.

A bank account with an inordinately large number of transactors was discovered and a case was opened (see Figure 15.5). This led to the uncovering of a ring of small businesses, owned or operated by members of the same ethnic group, which were exchanging cash in a suspicious fashion. This organization was uncovered without any prior leads from law enforcement. While some of the businesses and individuals involved were known to investigators, the full extent of the network was not. FAIS, through its automated consolidation and linkage, was able to perform the search and present the results in a meaningful way to its users and to investigators in the field.

A federal law enforcement agency involved in a large-scale multi-agency investigation requested authorization to use BSA data provided by FAIS in an affidavit pursuant to a search warrant. The agency had contacted FinCEN earlier in the investigation for development of leads and to get a better feel for the scope and extent of the criminal organization under investigation. Specific BSA information uncovered with the help of FAIS proved vital to identifying in advance documents able to be seized under the terms of the warrant.

In addition to investigative case analyses, the system was used in support of FinCEN's role in regulatory policy making. Statistical analyses of the BSA data supported a study of ways to reduce the filing burden on banks without loss of value to law enforcement. While the system's AI capabilities were not employed in this study, the experience led us directly to the development of a separate extraction of profiles of financial activity for filers of BSA reports. This filer profile database is a part of the design for V3.0, and will provide a continuous monitoring capability for the units at FinCEN which deal with financial institutions policy and compliance.

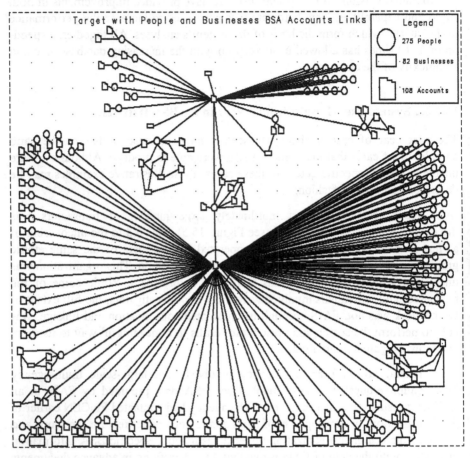

Figure 15.5. A complex case

15.3 Knowledge Discovery and Analysis in Real Databases

The FinCEN AI System is an example of an operational knowledge discovery system which integrates intelligent software and human agents in a co-operative discovery task on a very large database. KDD has recently been recognized as an application area of AI involved in the analysis of real databases with the goal of finding useful, unknown knowledge about the things they represent. AI techniques of machine learning and knowledge representation, as well as non-AI techniques such as database management, statistical analysis, and visualization of data are all of interest. In (Fayyad, 1996), the process of knowledge discovery in databases is broken into five stages: selection, preprocessing, transformation, data mining, and interpretation. While some of these stages may be performed by humans, there is a clear recognition that all are critical to the ultimate goal of discovering knowledge in databases. We use this model to describe what happens in FAIS.

15.3.1 Preprocessing

Real databases are very unfriendly places for AI algorithms. They are filled with errors as well as being incomplete and not truly representative of the real world. They often contain incomplete, inconsistent, or multiple identifications of entities of interest. To perform the task of finding complex patterns, anomalies, trends, and ultimately knowledge about the real world in a database such as the BSA trans-actions it is essential that the data be significantly improved.

In the financial database with which FAIS deals, the major concern is with errors in identification data fields. This is because so much subsequent analysis depends upon decisions which are based on these data. A number of tools have been developed for cleaning them up. The Soundex algorithm built into most commercial DBMSs is the oldest of these (and fairly inaccurate due to its reliance on English phonology). However, there are a number of refinements to data cleanup for matching, including models of keyboard errors, use of non-English language phonology, and attempts to place names and addresses into canonical form.

FAIS was implemented with a fairly rudimentary set of data-cleanup algorithms. It was believed that, as long as data was not lost and ID matches were generous, comprehensive search would compensate for inaccuracy in initial identification of people and businesses. This has generally been the case, although we have identified a number of problems, from general sources of error, such as confusion over non-English language names or mis-keyed data, to specific ones such as the incorrect use of ledger accounts on the forms and the use of identi-fication phrases like 'known customer' in place of actual ID numbers. Future improvements to the system will attempt to clean up and normalize some of these data.

15.3.2 Transforming the Database

The key problem in dealing with the BSA transactions is to group them together into related sets for more detailed analysis. Since money laundering is often only recognizable as a pattern of activity over a number of transactions, it is essential that the correct transactions be grouped together before an assessment can be made of the potential criminality of a subject's activities. These ideas are discussed in detail in (Goldberg, 1995).

A shift of viewpoint is often essential to successful application of many algorithms for machine learning, as well as more traditional knowledge-based methods of analysis. FAIS accomplishes this shift through processes we call consolidation and linkage. *Consolidation* is the process of matching the various errorful and incomplete identifier fields on individual transactions in an attempt to identify all transactions involving individual, real entities (people, businesses, and accounts). *Linkage* is the identification of pairs of subjects and/or accounts which share a common transaction. A more comprehensive notion of linkage would also link entities which share common attributes, e.g., people with a common address. For the initial accumulation of data in FAIS, this type of linkage is not considered important enough to warrant the cost of cross comparison of data. Furthermore, some of these links are subsumed in the process of consolidation. After an interesting data set is identified, further analysis can yield such linkages. This is, admittedly, a compromise for performance which we may re-assess.

When these links are followed, a user can find a full set of all related transactions and the real entities they involve. The user interface is designed to present the data so one can easily follow these linkages and build up such a set. The set can then be analyzed with NetMap, MapInfo, or a spreadsheet, and can be managed automatically as a single unit.

Both consolidation and link formation – the essential components of FAIS database transformation – may be interpreted as changes of representation from the identifications originally present in a database to the real-world entities of interest. Practical implementations of these transformations in commonly available commercial relational database management systems are possible using indexing. Where these methods involve large numbers of comparisons, they can be sped up at a slight cost in accuracy by techniques like the band join (Hernandez, 1995).

15.3.3 Selection

Disparate financial activities produce a mixture of data that superficially looks the same because they arrive via the same data collection instrument. Thus the input stream of transactions must be categorized and perhaps physically separated – if that is required for performance. This mixture of transactions causes the system problems of two kinds.

Performance both of consolidation and linkage, and of *ad hoc* user queries is affected by the size of the databases because these queries have to look at the whole data set. While this problem can often be addressed by purchase of larger, faster hardware, or a query accelerator (using special indexing), within the budgetary context of any particular project, performance may always be a critical issue.

The second type of problem is interference. Some consolidations will be incorrect no matter how much effort is spent developing the match algorithms, causing incorrect higher-level entities to be abstracted. Categorization decisions can help to focus the matching activity over a smaller, more relevant database. In addition, rules or cases used in inference will interact if they must be applied to too wide a variety of activities. It is better to refine the domain of the intelligent agents in the system to focus on a single population of data. If one also needs to correct the partitioning decisions, that is a good function to separate out into additional agents.

Although Fayyad et al. (1996) place the selection stage ahead of data preparation and transformation, we have found that we need the results of the data cleanup and the consolidation and linkage stages to properly segment the entire data stream. The users of FAIS have identified a number of relevant categories of these data which depend upon grouping new transactions with previously input ones according to matches of participating subjects and accounts. Thus the success of the data categorization depends upon the accuracy and precision of the previous stages.

Other sources of knowledge to be used in this stage are data from a variety of outside databases, each relevant to particular categories. These include, for example, identifiers of known subjects of past investigations, subjects reported by banks via the new Suspicious Activity Report,[4] and accounts identified as having high activity in postal money orders. Matches against these databases will provide additional evidence for the categorization. For example, matches against a database of known subjects of prior investigations will be used to segregate data that is useful for training from data useful for identification of potential leads.

15.3.4 Data Mining and Interpretation

Data mining involves the application of any of a variety of automated learning algorithms such as clustering, data summarization, learning classification rules, finding data dependency networks, analyzing changes, and detecting anomalies (Piatetsky-Shapiro, 1994). There are also a number of statistical methods for refining measures of a population of data values, identifying correlations, and testing hypotheses. The goal of all these approaches is to derive unknown, not easily observed, information from data. This information may be very specific facts, or more global patterns and trends. The key concept is that the information is not accessible to straightforward query, but requires the use of the more complex methods mentioned above to discover.

To a large extent, data mining in FAIS has been done by the human agents using the system. Early attempts to apply machine learning were unsatisfactory due to data errors and inaccurate consolidations. Most of the information presently mined is specific facts, i.e., potential leads, rather than broad trends or generally applicable patterns. However, the thrust of future efforts will be in the latter direction, and it is expected that improved data preparation, categories, and an

---

[4]Treasury form TD F 90-22.47, which combines information previously reported on the Criminal Referral Form and on CTR forms marked suspicious.

accumulated base of past cases will provide the necessary support for these efforts. In addition, data mining activities can be automated to a greater degree. Different categories can be mined for different things. For example, we can mine for target patterns of behavior by clustering in the known cases of financial crimes. We can develop regulatory categories by correlating data values to exemptable businesses and thus derive meaningful policies for filing exemptions.

In FAIS the interpretation stage is also performed by the users. The critical technology to allow this is visualization of complex relationships in the data. Entities (subjects and account) abstracted from the transactions form the basic units of the displays. The users see derived attributes and summaries of financial activity as easily as they once saw individual data fields in older database query interfaces. A major component of the system is the link analysis and visualization tool, NetMap.

15.4 Future Directions – Towards an Agent Paradigm

The idea of introducing information analysis, retrieval, and manipulation agents into a discovery system such as FAIS is particularly attractive. Tasks for which agents are well suited have been characterized as: tasks which are boring or repetitive, involve search through a lot of data, or involve memory – keeping track of more than the human short-term memory can accommodate. We find a number of these types of tasks in the knowledge discovery problem which FAIS addresses, and we believe that there are a number of opportunities for adding automated, intelligent agents to the system.

We have characterized FAIS as a discovery system comprising co-operative components for both computer and human analysis. Much of the initial power of the system stems from the abilities of the various 'components' to co-operate in an effective and meaningful fashion. FAIS is also evolving towards greater complexity of its automated components, as well as greater variety of its tasks. The agent paradigm, in which components exchange information consistently and usefully, and in which new components can be added with relative ease, is thus motivated by this increased complexity and variety.

The preceding sections have given a broad picture of the problem addressed by FAIS and the system architecture with which it has been implemented. As with many fielded systems, FAIS is undergoing significant modification both to improve its performance and to address new and expanded tasks. This section will address some of the details planned for this phase of the project with an eye towards the ways in which agents can contribute. Our goals are to improve performance, accuracy, and user productivity, as well as to provide new capabilities for analysis of the BSA data. We are aiming towards an architecture in which a number of intelligent agents can effectively co-operate in classifying, transforming, evaluating, linking, and monitoring tasks. Specialized agents, whether human or automated, will operate on particular subsets of the data, allowing a match of particular techniques and knowledge to the appropriate task.

15.4.1   Database Re-organization for Improved Performance and Accuracy

Although in concept the FAIS system still operates on one nationwide database, we are introducing the notion of a preliminary categorization and data-sorting step in order to divide the data into a number of smaller categories in which different investigations can be pursued. The separation by category is based on real, observed differences in the data and in how to deal with it. For example, the data associated with high-volume businesses, or casinos, may be of interest to regulatory analysts interested in formulating policy, while the BSA filings keyed to subjects identified in a postal money order database will be of interest to investigators looking for money laundering involving those.

The evolution of this idea shows the value of having a real, operational system with committed users in the development of the system architecture. From its inception, FAIS was viewed as a simple classification system, identifying all transactions as either suspicious or not. We recognized immediately the need for a separate, user-driven mode for user exploration of the data in order to develop expertise in a new domain. We also recognized, very early on, the need to transform the database of transactions into one of subjects and accounts and of networks of these linked together – and that the task was to classify these higher-level abstractions. However, we designed the suspiciousness classifier to operate uniformly over the entire database. This monolithic approach to data analysis is a common shortcoming in database systems which has led to the proposed data selection step in the KDD process. Unless this step can be performed accurately, it is difficult to develop and capture specialized expertise relevant to sub-populations of the database.

As a result of operational use, analysts identified a number of categories into which transactions should be placed. One example is transactions by banks, casinos, credit unions, etc., at other financial institutions, another is high-volume transactors, and a third is transactions of large retail businesses. In addition to the transactions which trigger categorization, any transactions which are associated via consolidation are also included in the category. This operationally motivated classification allows specialized analyses to be performed on appropriate subsets of the database, allowing more detailed analyses with the computing resources available. It should be apparent that agents, specialized to work in the different sub-populations of data, might be an effective means of segmenting the analysis along with the data. The fact that the selection is never completely accurate means that these agents will need to co-operate with one another, passing new information, and even correcting the data categories as they go.

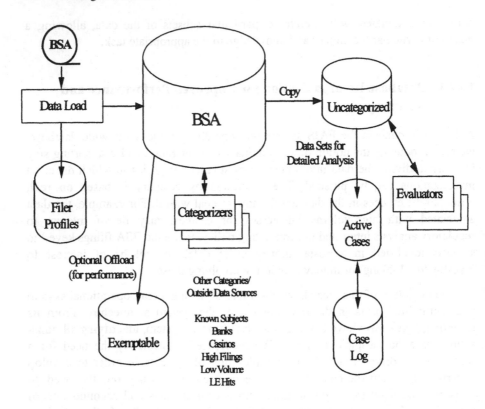

Figure 15.6. Planned categorization of data in FAIS V3.0

An additional benefit of the categorization step is that these groupings of the data can support a variety of new analyses required by FinCEN's expanded mission. A study of the bank and casino transactions can support compliance studies, or broad studies of retail business activities can be made using the appropriate category of transactions. Categories that are derived from matches against known or suspected financial crimes activities can be used in automated learning methods to train even better classifiers and suspiciousness evaluators.

We are implementing the categorization of the data in a single database with transactions flagged by separate categorizer agents (see Figure 15.6). This design is robust to changes as new categories of BSA filings are identified, or old ones cease to be of value. The database will become very large and overall queries will be slow. However, most user-interactive querying will be done within the smaller, case analysis database. We have chosen the single database option, primarily because of its robustness. FAIS must be able to operate in an environment of constantly and rapidly changing requirements, whereas raw database performance is something that the commercial sector can and will surely provide steadily through time.

15.4.2 Usability and User Productivity

Modifications to FAIS, whether cosmetic or functional, which increase user productivity are essential in a human-machine co-operative process such as BSA analysis. We are developing a case log, tracking, and reporting module that will be integrated with the proactive case analysis database. These sorts of tools can become increasingly intelligent, perhaps by learning the appropriate data transformations and reporting formats which the users select. These case management and reporting agents will take over more and more of the routine, tedious tasks of preparing output products.

Although routine, this is a critical part of the system. The entire process of finding and reporting suspicious patterns in the data is not completed until feedback from the field is received and tallied. Then the most effective analyses can be reinforced, and the less effective ones eliminated. Human agents must have the tools to rapidly find and evaluate new patterns in the data, produce reports for the field, and track the results. The most effective strategies will be re-applied by automated agents in an evolving community of specialized analyses.

15.4.3 Improved Intelligence

Improvements to FAIS's knowledge-based components are being made in both the consolidation and linking and in the rules which govern suspiciousness evaluation and the new data categorization.

15.4.3.1 Consolidation and Linking

Grouping BSA transactions in FAIS is accomplished by consolidation and linkage. Consolidation accuracy is critical. Under-consolidation produces too many, small clusters, while over-consolidation groups together data from different real-world entities. In the current system, the evaluation rules are applied to these consolidated sets to evaluate individual subjects and accounts. If the sets do not reflect reality, the evaluations do not. Similarly, overly generous linkage, such as joining two businesses because they share a common currency exchange service, will create spuriously large sets. However, missing links can cause critical associations to be lost.

When consolidation and linkage are accurate enough that we are confident of most of the sets that are formed, we can automate much of this set management. Sets can be classified, evaluated, or archived automatically. Manual operations will be more efficient, since users will not have to spend as much time following links and building the sets by hand.

Significant improvements can be made in this area through the use of specialized, knowledge-based agents such as language-specific name matchers or agents which understand how to verify bank ID numbers or addresses. A learning agent, which observes a user correcting a group of bad consolidations would then be able to apply that learned knowledge in similar situations. A link traversing agent, which can group subjects and accounts together into a meaningful network, might request guidance from a user (e.g., in determining the validity of linking via an account used by a bank to record all foreign currency exchanges). Or it might pass the user a hint about the presence of a single business as the hub of a number of otherwise unconnected networks. By reinforcing the most beneficial hints, the users can 'tune' this agent to their liking.

15.4.3.2 Evaluation and Dissemination

Knowledge about money laundering and financial crime is FinCEN's stock-in-trade, and analysis of the BSA data is an important source of such knowledge. It is important that the results of knowledge development be made available to the rest of FinCEN, and that the expertise of all of FinCEN be able to be incorporated into FAIS. We will institute an agency-wide effort to capture the expertise of FinCEN's diverse staff for specialized rule development. Indeed, a number of efforts have already begun at FinCEN, such as threat assessment in specific financial arenas and simulation of new financial crimes and countermeasures.

The various rules which are discovered or invented will be codified, tested, and compared in a consistent and thorough manner. As new rules are discovered by the users, (or discovery programs), agents can be launched to do the repetitive evaluations, eventually resulting in a graded set of proposed new rules. Dissemination of rules might eventually take the form of 'knowledge publishing' where rules, in computer processable form are sent out to participating financial institutions. In this case, the agent paradigm of separable knowledge 'units' is of particular value, since outsiders are more likely to accept simpler, more modular evaluations. This feature of the agent approach is particularly important for communicating our findings. Agents act 'for' the user, in understandable ways, over limited domains, thus enhancing their acceptance and the acceptance of their discoveries.

15.4.4   New Capabilities

The categories into which we will sort the BSA transactions can support FinCEN in a variety of studies, from gaining a better understanding of non-bank financial institutions to assessing the threats posed, for example, by postal money orders or franchised retail businesses.

We are already planning to integrate identification information from a variety of law enforcement databases. As new sources for useful 'outside' information are identified, they will be incorporated. A classic application for agent technology is the information retrieval task. Rather than requiring global matches of all data, against these new sources, agents can respond to requests for this outside information as it is needed.

Finally, because of its ability to present volumes of BSA data in meaningful ways to the users, the FAIS system has become a very useful resource for investigating new trends and patterns of financial crime, for experimenting with new technologies for data analysis and visualization, and for training FinCEN and outside analysts. We have no idea yet where these investigations may lead. The system architecture must be able to accommodate a variety of new analyses with a minimum of effort. We believe the agent approach holds great promise for accomplishing this goal.

15.5 Conclusion

The changing and more complex uses for FAIS have led to a number of modifications. Regulatory oversight and compliance monitoring and enforcement must be supported by 'strategic' analyses of the data. New data sources have become available and are deemed critical to the success of the system. There have been changes to the rules governing the collection of the basic data, to reduce the burden on filers, by making the forms simpler and exempting a number of routine businesses. Finally, working with the data has taught valuable lessons about how to partition data into meaningful populations prior to analysis, how to transform the data for more meaningful analysis and discovery, and how to present data at various levels of abstraction to humans working in close co-operation with the system. As a result of paying close attention to the data and following where it has led us, we are moving towards an agent paradigm of co-operating human and machine intelligence. Specialized agents for data analysis, retrieval, and manipulation are attractive because they are simpler to build and understand, can be adapted to new tasks more readily, and can learn many tasks from the system's users, thus allowing a gradual evolution towards a more highly automated system.

Acknowledgements

The authors would like to acknowledge the contributions of their colleagues at FinCEN who shared in the development of FAIS: Christina Klinger, Winston Llamas, Mike Marrone, and Rey Wong. We would also like to thank the analyst-users of FAIS: Matt Cottini, Steve Navicky, and Jerry Wooton, for their hard work and dedication.

References

Fayyad, U. M., Piatetsky-Shapiro, G., Smyth, P. (1996) From data mining to knowledge discovery – an overview. In: U. M. Fayyad, G. Piatetsky-Shapiro, P. Smyth, R. Uthurusamy (Eds.) *Advances in Knowledge Discovery and Data Mining*, 1–34. AAAI Press/MIT Press, Menlo Park, CA.

Goldberg, H. G., Senator, T. E. (1995) Restructuring databases for knowledge discovery by consolidation and link analysis. *Proceedings of the First International Conference on Knowledge Discovery & Data Mining* (KDD-95), 136–141. AAAI, Menlo Park, CA.

Hernandez, M. A., Stolfo, S. J. (1995) *A Generalization of Band Joins and The Merge/ Purge Problem*. Department of Computer Science, Columbia University, New York, NY.

Piatetsky-Shapiro, G., Matheus, C., Smyth, P., Uthurusamy, R. (1994) KDD-93: Progress and challenges in knowledge discovery in databases. *AI Magazine*, 15(3), 77–81, AAAI, Menlo Park, CA.

Senator, T. E., Goldberg, H. G., Wooton, J., Cottini, M. A., Khan, A. F. U., Klinger, C. D., Llamas, W. M., Marrone, M. P., Wong, R. W. H. (1995) The FinCEN artificial intelligence system: identifying potential money laundering from reports of large cash transactions. *AI Magazine*, 16(4), 21–39, AAAI, Menlo Park, CA.

16 Adding Value with Intelligent Agents in Financial Services

D. Wenger
Swiss Bank Corporation

A. R. Probst
University of Lausanne (HEC)

16.1 Introduction

Companies working in the financial service industry are almost pure information factories. The information produced is their product. Thus, we can say that adding value to the business means adding information.

The metaphor we use for applications in the financial service industry is the concept of the *intelligent agent* (Guilfoyle, 1994; Shoham, 1993; Unland, 1995; Woolridge, 1995). Instead of using the term 'intelligent agent,' we prefer the term 'artificial information agent' because it suggests an analogy with a human information agent. In the financial service sector, human beings are human information workers since they produce information (commodities). This contrasts with human workers in manufacturing who produce goods instead of information. Just as the production of goods has largely been automated by artificial agents (robots, machines), so it is the objective of financial information engineering to increase the level of automation in financial services. We can say that artificial information agents are the 'information machines' of the information factory. One of their primary characteristics is to be active; they are not just passive tools. From a production point of view, they behave in a well-defined context like human information agents – only more efficiently. Hereinafter, we shall refer to artificial information agents simply as agents.

One of the main issues involved is how to develop agents. Systems engineering, as it has been understood over the last twenty years, does not provide a solution as it was intended to produce database-oriented systems, now known as legacy systems. Boosting these methodologies with object-oriented technologies has only increased their ability to support the same wrong products in an even more complex way. A fundamentally different approach is needed. Techniques from artificial intelligence (Breuker, 1987; Bylander, 1987; Chandrasekaran, 1986; Gaines, 1990; Spirgi, 1990; Spirgi, 1992; Wielinga, 1992) look promising.

But the scope of intelligent agents is much broader. The objective of this chapter is to show the importance of the agent concept for the corporate information system of financial service companies and to outline the vision of a business-driven and business requirement-driven information technology.

The first part of this chapter describes the characteristics of agent-based applications and illustrates them with some examples. The second part outlines the 'added value' concept – which drives the structure – and related concepts, such as information and knowledge. Next, the corporate dimension of intelligent agents is elaborated. Since the significance of the intelligent agent paradigm limited to the application dimension would not be sufficient, the corporate dimension will also be stressed. The final section emphasizes how intelligent agents can meet future requirements in financial services, such as direct banking and cross-selling. The paper concludes with the fundamental concept, i.e., that structural conflicts between business and information technology are eliminated – or at least sharply reduced – by the agent paradigm. Reducing these structural conflicts makes financial service companies much more flexible and easier to manage and control.

16.2 Agent-Based Systems

16.2.1 Characteristics

Agent-based systems by their nature are active, autonomous, and modularized.

Active – in the context of financial services – means producing information, i.e., adding value.

Autonomous and modularized mean having a human-like behavior. Figure 16.1 illustrates our metaphor for how agents collaborate. Like human beings and together with human beings, artificial agents collaborate in work groups in order to produce services. An agent is an expert in a clearly defined domain contributing to the work group. A primary characteristic of agent-based systems is that the collaboration among human and artificial agents is natural and seamless.

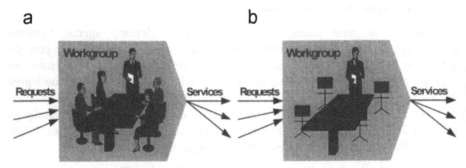

Figure 16.1. Metaphor for the collaboration of agents

The agent approach causes a fundamental paradigm shift as control of the system moves from the system to its components, the agents.

16.2.2 Examples

16.2.2.1 Sales of Mortgages

Figure 16.2 shows a work group of agents that, as a work group, sells mortgages. Each agent is an autonomous unit of the work group providing services. Autonomous means the agents themselves know when they have to become active. Agents may have a user interface for interacting with users. The work group is started by the agent 'Process initial order data,' which provides the initial data about the customers and their real estate. Based on these data, the agent 'Analyze

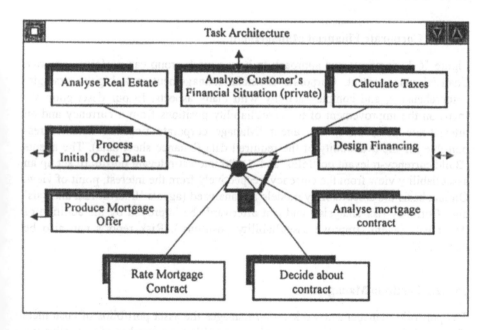

Figure 16.2. Work group selling mortgages

customer's financial situation' and the agent 'Analyze real estate' become active. In addition, the agent 'Calculate taxes' provides tax information about the customer. In a first stage, all this information is imprecise since the data from which the information is derived is very incomplete. The agent 'Design financing,' taking the information about the customer and the real estate into account, proposes the financing part of the mortgage. Then, the proposed contract is analyzed (agent 'Analyze mortgage contract') and rated, and an attempt is made to reach a decision. It may happen that the agent 'Decide about contract' asks the other agent for more precise information. This in turn causes other agents (e.g., the agent 'Analyze real estate') to ask themselves for more data in order to generate more precise information (in this case about real estate). This way the mortgage sales work group with artificial agents acts like human bankers by asking for further details if the situation is not clear. Thus, the more complex the situation is, the more information is requested and the more the customer is consulted. In this way we achieve an optimal process in terms of efficiency, covering the range from simple to complex cases.

16.2.2.2 Corporate Financial Management

Figure 16.3 represents one approach to how a work group can perform corporate financial management. Corporate financial management is a highly strategic, comprehensive, and complex activity with many aspects. In our description we focus on the improvement of the asset/liability positions from a currency and an interest-rate perspective. The agent 'Manage corporate financial data' is responsible for the availability of the required data (balance sheet data). The agents 'Build currency-relevant portfolio' and 'Build interest-relevant portfolio' set up an asset/liability view from the currency, respectively from the interest, point of view. On that basis the asset/liability models are analyzed (agents 'Interest risk analysis' and 'Currency risk analysis') and can afterwards be improved by the addition of derivatives (agent 'Improve asset/liability positions'). Risk reports can also be generated.

16.2.2.3 Portfolio Management

The portfolio management work group manages the asset portfolios of customers (Figure 16.4). One portfolio manager is responsible for a number of portfolios (up to several hundred). A set of artificial agents is available for this purpose. A first agent loads the set of the portfolio manager's portfolios (agent 'Load set of asset portfolios'). This enables the portfolio managers to manage the portfolios as a whole. They can view, analyze, rate, and improve the portfolio(s). They can generate bulk trades, define constraints and strategies, etc.

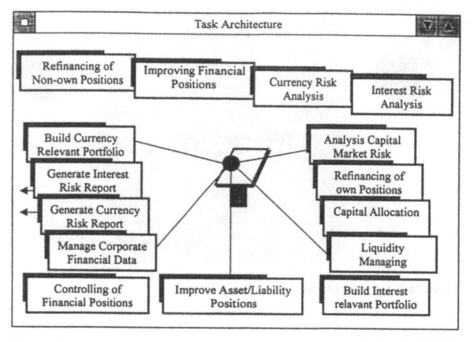

Figure 16.3. Work group performing corporate financial management

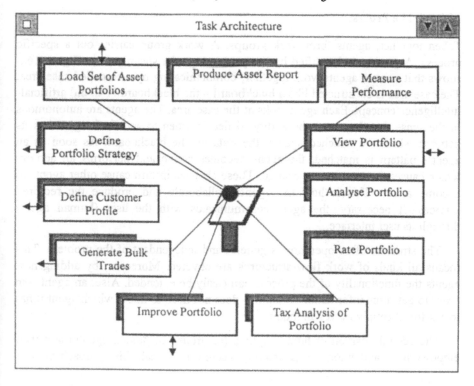

Figure 16.4. Work group for performing portfolio management

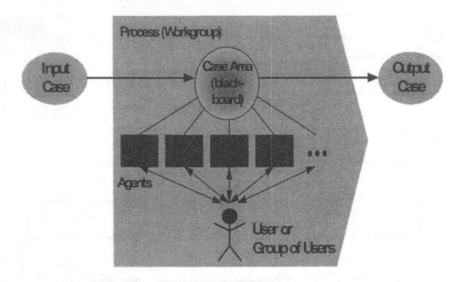

Figure 16.5. Architecture for the collaboration of agents

16.2.3 Architecture

16.2.3.1 The Process

Taken together, agents form work groups. A work group carries out a specific process. A process is identified by the processing of a specific case. Figure 16.5 shows that a set of agents work together, communicating by a so-called case area. The case area is constructed like a blackboard – the blackboard is an old artificial-intelligence concept. Each agent looks at the case area. The agents are autonomous in the sense that they have the ability to decide when to act. Each agent has its patterns which are matched against the data on the blackboard. As soon as an agent's pattern is matched, the agent becomes active and performs an activity which causes the case area to change. These changes in turn cause other agents to become active. This is how the agents collaborate and produce the required services. If necessary, the agent communicates with the user (human agent) through its user interface.

The structure of co-operation is general and independent of the problem. This means all kinds of work flow structures are covered. Moreover, by adding new agents the functionality of the process can easily be extended. Also, an agent – in order to get some information as input – does not need to know which agent it has to ask for. It simply makes an inquiry.

The central position of human agents (or groups of human agents) and their empowerment and autonomy is striking. Therefore, we call this approach human-

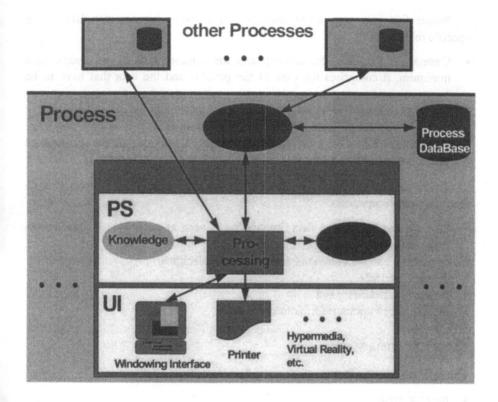

Figure 16.6. Internal structure of an agent

centered and human-empowered. We can say that agent orientation implies human-centered distributed computing.

16.2.3.2 The Agent

After having described the agents working collaboratively as a group, let us now look at the internal view of an agent (Figure 16.6). Here, too, we need to be aware of the arbitrariness of the definition. However, this definition is extremely useful for a systematic, methodical development process. It first divides the agent into the problem-solving component (PS) and the user interface (UI). The processing area is central. It is responsible for all data traffic within the agent. Processing takes data from the case area and the diverse user-interface areas, stores these data in the agent-case area, requests information from other processes, and delivers the results produced back to the case area. Processing acts as the engine, and is backed up by knowledge, acting as the brain. The knowledge area drives and controls processing. It contains the theory used to construct the information produced.

Notice that case area, agent-case area, and knowledge are just data but in specific roles:

- **Case area:** The case area encompasses the common data of the agents. At a minimum, it comprises the case of the process and the data that have to be communicated among the agents.
- **Agent-case area:** The agent-case area holds additional case-specific data that the agent uses for producing the required information.
- **Knowledge:** Knowledge drives the processing. It contains all the information that is not specific to the case.

To develop an agent, we have to develop the internal models. We can identify the following components:

- the case and knowledge data (knowledge is seen as encompassing the knowledge data and processing);
- the interface to the common case area on the blackboard;
- the user interface;
- the process database; and
- the interface to other information processes.

16.2.3.3 The Data Model

The data model describes

- the case area;
- the agent-case area; and
- knowledge (see Figure 16.6).

The modeling concepts (or building blocks) of the data model are those of the object-oriented approach such as class, instance, attribute, and generalization.

16.2.3.4 The Processing Model

The processing model describes:

- the processing component of an agent (see Figure 16.6).

Analogous to the data modeling concepts, we need processing modeling concepts. Whereas it is relatively easy to define the data modeling concepts, as the concepts of the object-oriented approach are used by general agreement, the definition of the processing concepts is much more problematical. We also should be aware that the definition of abstract concepts is, to a certain extent, always arbitrary. Therefore, to arrive at our process modeling concepts, we apply two criteria which are:

- adequacy for modeling processing, and
- usefulness for development.

Adequacy for modeling processing requires that technical issues, such as the fact that most computer languages are sequential, do not dominate the definition of the process-modeling concepts. The natural, adequate representation of the product to be developed – which is an agent – is the key issue.

Usefulness for development for process-modeling concepts calls for different granularities and different purposes. The different grain size is important for a step-by-step, methodical development; e.g., stepping directly down to a single command of a computer language is certainly too far.

The proposed process-modeling concepts are *activity agent, sub-activity agent, activity method, processing block, access method, service function* and *effect method* (Figure 16.7). Processing consists of activity agents. An activity agent has a pattern and an activity method. The pattern makes the activity agent autonomous and pro-active in that it checks and matches the environment against its pattern. As soon as its pattern can be matched, the activity agent becomes active. An activity agent can be broken down into sub-activity agents which are similar to the activity agents. The reason for doing so is to eliminate redundancy. Then, the activity method and sub-activity methods are further refined into what we call processing

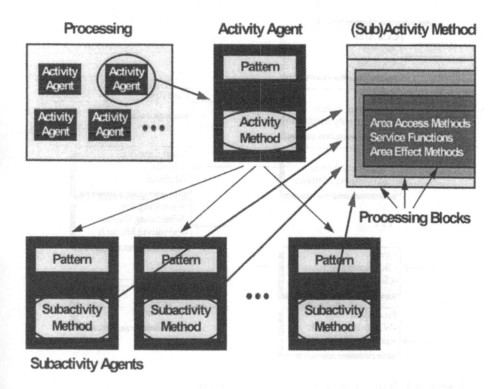

Figure 16.7. Process-modeling concepts

blocks. Processing blocks carry out iterations or selections. They contain area-access methods, service functions, and area-effect methods. Finally, the area-access and area-effect methods consist of primitive access and effect methods.

16.2.3.5 Fractal Architecture

As mentioned above, the processing elements, such as process or agent, are similar, so why not simply reduce the processing elements to only one concept, agent, and allow an agent to consist of agents? This would enable us to achieve a fractal processing structure for an application. Our model would certainly become much more flexible and homogeneous.

We should in fact be moving in this direction, but we are not yet ready to do so. Currently, it is easier to work out the required development knowledge with explicit levels of processing elements.

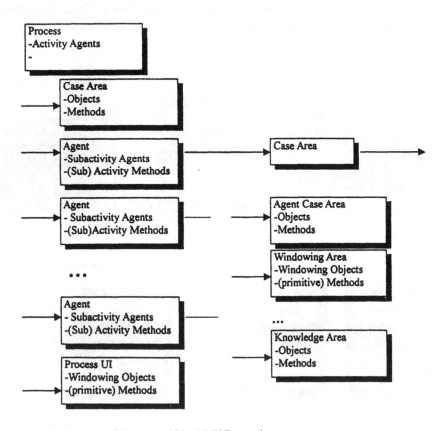

Figure 16.8. System architecture within ART*Enterprise

16.2.4 System Structure

Figure 16.8 represents the system architecture of the process of how they are developed at Swiss Bank Corporation. Systems at the right are subsystems; e.g., the 'Case area,' the various agents and the 'Process UI' system are subsystems of the system 'Process.'

This architecture allows:

- a highly modularized development;
- a highly standardized development (a developer knows how to find what he or she is looking for without knowing the application); and
- a highly parallel development (each developer works on one agent, the case area serves as common communication).

16.3 Principles of Intelligent Agents for Adding Value

16.3.1 The Manufacturing Metaphor

The manufacturing metaphor is perhaps the most powerful rationale for the new direction of IT. By setting the two concepts information and goods (commodities) equivalent and by looking back over the last two hundred years at the history of manufacturing, we can discover many important ideas and insights. This metaphor also touches on the relationship between data and information. It is similar to the relationship between goods (commodities) and material: Information is made up of data just as goods (commodities) are made up of material. Please refer to our definition of information in Section 16.3.2.

In the information area, as in the goods area, we can distinguish among the three activities transportation, storage, and production. In manufacturing, goods are stored and transported to or from machines, and new goods are produced by machines from input goods. Manufacturing technology is comprised of transportation, storage, and production, with production by machines being the most prominent part.

However, in the early years of manufacturing, transportation and storage were more predominant because production was done manually by workers. At that time, only a few central machines which were driven by mills and later by steam engines existed. The automated production of goods was limited by the central engines.

A first parallel can be seen in the form of central computers. Computers are the engines, applications the machines. In the age of central computers, storage and transportation of information dominated. Information production could only be carried out centrally. This was a very limiting factor as it meant only central activities, such as accounting, could be automated. All other activities, i.e., the majority, were out of range. As in the early years of manufacturing, the central engine was the limiting factor.

The essential, big step in the evolution of manufacturing came along with electricity, which enabled decentralized production of goods. Production was no longer bound to a central location. The engines became more and more powerful, as did the machines, and production became more flexible and dispersed.

In the last few years the parallel with the information sector has become increasingly obvious. Computing power is available where information is produced. Applications can be developed to support the production of information.

We can learn from the manufacturing metaphor that information production, like goods production, will become the primary activity in the future, and the storage and transportation activities will take on the role of auxiliary activities, enabling the production of information. This becomes clearer if we compare the information production process and the goods production process.

The process of producing goods is analogous to the information producing process. Business process re-engineering can learn an awful lot from process engineering in manufacturing, e.g., from computer-integrated manufacturing (CIM). There, the interaction between automation and the structure of the process was worked out as a main emphasis – the impact of the machines on the overall process design. The impact of information-producing applications on the business process will become a key issue in the design of business processes or information processes. Note that information process and business process are used here interchangeably. The term information process is preferred because it is more general – not every information process has to be a business process.

The primary character of production and the auxiliary character of transportation and storage is enforced by the fact that the production of goods is the value-adding component. For IT and especially for business process reengineering, this means that automation only adds value to the business process if the information production is automated by applications.

Another important parallel is the distinction between tool and machine. A tool is passive and transfers the energy of a human being to a certain effect. For example, a hammer transfers the energy of the hand to a nail. The tool itself is passive. A tool in IT, e.g., an editor or word processor (at least an older one), is passive, too. Like tools in manufacturing which were gradually extended with active parts, tools in IT have recently started to become more active. An example is newer word processors which help structure the layout and help to find errors.

The next parallel envisions the improvement of machines and applications. In order to obtain machines that exploit the technological possibilities, we must constantly improve them and develop them further – a machine, such as a loom, has achieved a high level of quality because it has a long history of predecessors.

16.3.2   Service, Added Value, and Information

Service, added value, and information are closely related in the financial service industry. A service consists of information which is provided to the customer and in that way generates added value.

Information is an essential concept in our context, but it is also an extremely general one. It needs to be explained and defined in more detail here. Our definition of the concept of information is based on our manufacturing metaphor.

The world can be seen from an information perspective and from a physical one. The basic concept in the physical (or commodity) world is material. The physical object that can be used and is produced from material is called a commodity. In the information world the basic concept is data. An information object that can be used and is produced from data is called information. Thus, by analogy with material and commodity we arrive at our definition of data and information.

16.3.3   Kinds of Added Value

A financial service company, as the name indicates, offers services. Producing services means adding value. Another service is helping customers use the services. We can differentiate between a primary and a secondary service. The secondary service generates two kinds of value: first, by selling this service to the customer; second, by utilizing primary services.

An example is custody account management and portfolio management. Custody account management is a primary service, offered by a bank. Portfolio management is a secondary service, utilizing the service of custody account management.

Agents are employed to produce primary and secondary services and can be classified according to these two kinds of services.

16.3.4   Knowledge/Competence

In order to produce a commodity or information you need knowledge. Knowledge is the theory under which the agents work. Developing knowledge is the essential step in developing agents.

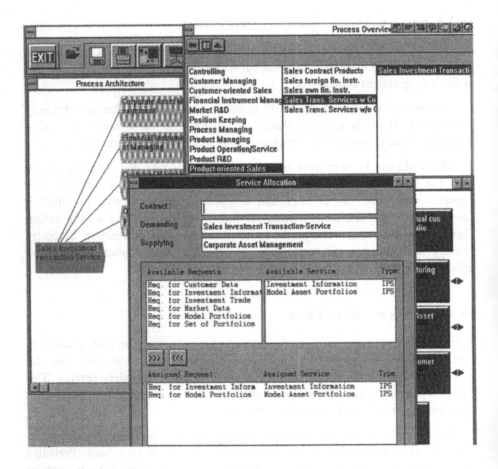

Figure 16.9. Interaction among processes

16.4 Agent-Based Corporate Banking: The Bank as a Set of Intelligent Agents

16.4.1 The Fractal Business Service Modeling Environment (FBSM-E)

A company can only be structured down to the agent level with the help of a tool. Companies encompass – depending on their size – a few hundred processes resulting in more than a thousand agents. A tool provides the necessary facilities for handling such a huge model; e.g., it provides the required consistency checks. Figure 16.9 shows some of the windows of the tool that has been developed. This tool maintains the various processes and their interactions which consist of the services the processes provide to each other. Each process is supported by a set of agents, acting as a work group. The tool demonstrates the interaction among the agents through animation.

The abstract structure of the process, allowing inheritance and an easier and more compact handling of the entire model, is essential.

The tool produces all the necessary reports, such as the input/output specification of an agent. An agent is then developed on the basis of this specification.

16.4.2 Example

As an example, let us look at the process 'Sales of investment transaction service.' This process is aimed at advising investors and selling them optimal investment transactions (e.g., equities).

This example is illustrated by screens of the fractal business service modeling environment (FBSM environment).

The upper right window 'Process overview' of Figure 16.9 provides a hierarchical overview of a part of the process structure (from left to right). The upper left window 'Process architecture' represents the interaction among the processes. It indicates the processes that deliver services to our current process. An example of an interaction is defined by the window 'Service allocation.' It shows all the requests of our current process (upper left) and the available services of the supplier process 'Corporate asset management.' The actual interactions are combinations of a request and a service, and are listed at the bottom.

Figure 16.10 shows the agents, their interactions, and the services they consume or provide. The interaction among the agents is represented as a work group metaphor in which the agents communicate with each other by the internal services they provide to a common area. For example, the window 'Agent description' encompasses the interaction of the agent 'Analyze actual customer portfolio.' We see that this agent produces an internal service 'Customer portfolio analysis,' requests model portfolios and consumes the service 'Model asset portfolio' as input. This consumed service comes from the supplier process 'Corporate asset management.'

Figure 16.11 illustrates this supplier process and how the services are produced. Here, we see that our previous consumed service 'Model asset portfolio' is produced by the agent 'Set up model asset portfolios.'

As already mentioned, the agents interact in the services they provide and consume. This interaction implicitly defines working scenarios (Use case) which are shown as animation in the FBSM environment.

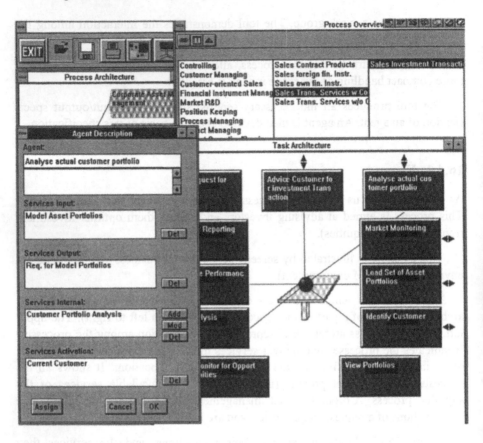

Figure 16.10. Agents of the process 'Sales investment transaction service'

All these processes, agents, and services are specified in more detail on a specification level; e.g., the specifications for the services are carried out at the data element level.

16.4.3 Granularity Levels

The FBSM environment offers the user three levels of granularity: the process, the task, and the specification level (Figure 16.12).

The process level provides the 'big picture,' showing the processes and their interactions by their services.

The task level presents the task of a process, the interactions by their internal services and their connection to the services to or from other processes.

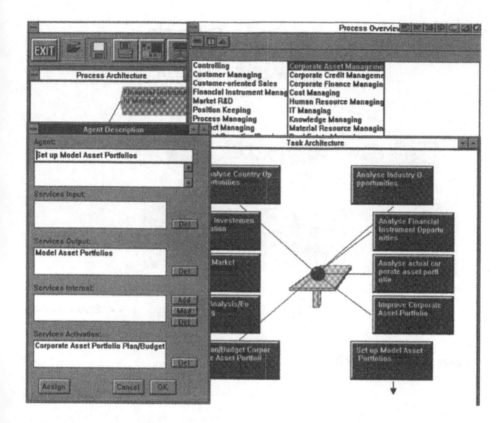

Figure 16.11. Showing the supplier process 'corporate asset management'

The specification level encompasses the detailed specification by process, service, and task.

16.4.4 The Various Architectures

The driving architecture is that of the processes. However there are other architectures such as the organization structure, the data architecture, the technical architecture, security architecture, communication architecture, and application-systems architecture. All these architectures are matched against the process architecture.

As an example, Figure 16.13 illustrates the match with the data architecture. The process database, as a logical database, may consist of the enterprise server database (part of it), components of server databases and perhaps of client databases. This structural conflict represents the current situation and not the targeted one.

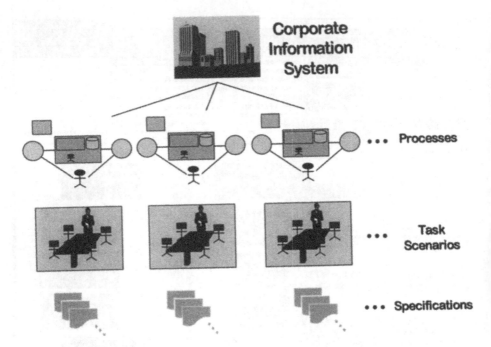

Figure 16.12. Granularity levels

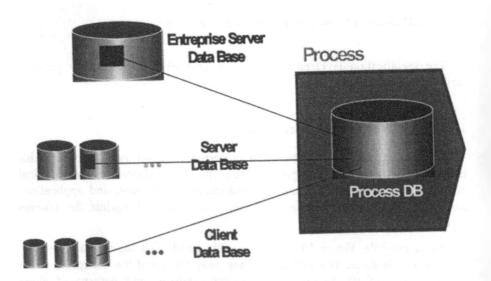

Figure 16.13. Data versus process architecture

The ultimate goal is that all other architectures are driven by and congruent to process architecture.

16.4.5 Corporate Processing Versus Corporate Data Model

As a consequence of our approach, the corporate data model will change fundamentally. In the last ten years, corporate data modeling and data warehousing have been extensively discussed. We should be aware that these terms were strongly influenced by central host computing and therefore are inherently centralist.

The issues in this chapter related to that context are:

- The primary model is not the corporate data model, but the corporate processing model which consists of the processes.
- The corporate data model can be derived from the corporate processing model and consists of the models of the process databases. It is therefore inherently decentral and conceptually dispersed.

Figure 16.14 attempts to depict a model of a corporate information system consisting of processes.

Once again, we note that the data architecture is driven by the process architecture.

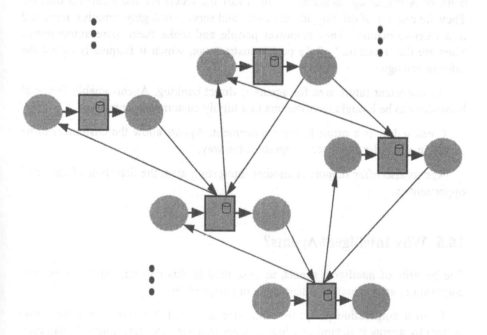

Figure 16.4. Representation of a corporate-wide system consisting of processes

16.5 Meeting Future Banking Requirements With Intelligent Agents

Some of the trends in financial services are:

- Financial services are becoming cheaper.
- Financial services will become more complex.
- Customers want a more tailored and specific service.
- Customers want to use an increasing number of financial products themselves.
- Customers want to use financial services whenever and wherever they desire.
- Financial services and advice must consider the entire financial context of a customer.

All these trends will dramatically change the relationship between the bank and the customer. The following aspects of banking requirements can be identified:

- The automation even of complex financial services has to be stepped up.
- Bankers need a better, highly active, and automated support in their customer relationships (advice, sales, and service).
- Customers require a better, highly active, and automated assistance in advice, sales, and service.

In general, these are the requirements for an agent-based information factory which is characterized by a seamless collaboration between human and artificial bankers. Artificial agents are active and available whenever and wherever desired. They are capable of offering advice, sales, and service in highly complex areas and in a flexible manner. They empower people and make them more autonomous. They are the 'machines' of the post-industrial age, which is frequently called the information age.

An important future area for agents is direct banking. Agents enable financial know-how to be brought to customers in a highly customer-oriented way.

Cross selling is a major future requirement. Agents allow the customers to be served in a broader and more comprehensive way.

Agents also offer support in another interesting area: the detection of risks and opportunities.

16.6 Why Intelligent Agents?

The benefits of intelligent agents, as described in this chapter, can be seen from corporation, application, and development perspectives.

From a corporation perspective the structuring of the corporate information system by agents is natural and business-appropriate. The fundamental character-istic of our agents is to produce information in an active and autonomous way. In the financial service sector, producing information is the addition of value. Since adding value is the primary objective of a corporation, it makes sense and is necessary to structure the corporate information system according to the element which is adding the value. Clustering agents into a process means bringing them together in a group (work group). Thus, a process can be seen as a group of agents producing certain services. Since a service is the added value, structuring the corporate information system into processes results in a value-added-oriented corporate information system. Automating a corporation by artificial agents is the most natural way of eliminating structural conflicts between business and technology and thus making the corporate information system efficient and flexible (entrepreneurial flexibility) with minimal costs. Moreover, these artificial agents provide an evolutionary and smooth means of transforming a company to a higher level of automation, since corporations are structured according to their human agents (individual human agent, groups of human agents, groups of groups, etc.) and thus the artificial agents fit into this structure. Also note that what makes managing and controlling a company so difficult lies in the structural conflicts – the more structural conflicts the more difficult it is to manage and control a company. Companies normally have a serious structural conflict with their information technology, which the agent approach can reduce or even eliminate. Based on the agent approach, managers can employ management methodologies and tools which enable them to directly control and manage their companies since their corporate information systems are directly driven by the business. To summarize, the agent-oriented model of a corporation is extremely expressive and powerful.

From an application perspective, artificial agents are the information machines of a company. Instead of producing goods, artificial agents produce information. Both the production of goods and the production of information add value. Thus, the most efficient way of pushing ahead automation within a financial service company is to implement artificial agents. The interaction among human agents and artificial information agents will be similar to that of human agents and machines in the manufacturing sector.

From a development perspective, the agent approach is a development metaphor and a new paradigm, replacing and extending the functional and object-oriented paradigm. The 'right' metaphors allow the development of the right product in the right way, i.e., in a systematic and methodical way. On the one hand, the agent approach is the answer to clumsy, out-dated legacy systems – which hinder corporations in their development because of the structural conflict they produce – while on the other, it is the answer to the unstructured, unsystematic, and inefficient development of client/server applications. The agent approach is a paradigm shift, as control of the system is moved from the system to its components which are the agents.

16.7 Conclusion

Companies working in the financial service industry are almost pure information factories. As in manufacturing, production becomes increasingly significant since producing information means adding value. The approach presented here structures a company's IT model according to the information produced. The information produced becomes the key element which requires the next key element: the intelligent agent. The intelligent agent is *the* element responsible for the production of information.

This approach is used within Swiss Bank Corporation for migrating its old corporate information system into its new one.

References

Breuker, J. (Ed.), Wielinga, B., Schreiber, G., de Greef, P., de Hoog, R., van Someren, M., Wielemaker, J., Billault, J. P., Davoodi, M., Hayward, S. (1987) Model Driven Knowledge Acquisition: Interpretation Models, Del A1, Esprit p1098, University of Amsterdam.

Bylander, T., Chandrasekaran, B. (1987) Generic tasks for knowledge-based reasoning: the 'right' level of abstraction for knowledge acquisition. *Int. J. Man-Machine Studies*, 26, 231–243.

Chandrasekaran, B. (1986) Generic tasks in knowledge-based reasoning: high-level building blocks for expert system design. *IEEE Expert*, 23–30.

Gaines, B. R. (1990). Knowledge representation servers: a generic technology for knowledge acquisition and knowledge-based systems. *Proceedings of the First Japanese Knowledge Acquisition for Knowledge-Based Systems Workshop, JKAW'90*, 413–430.

Guilfoyle, C., Warner, E. (1994) *Intelligent Agents: the New Revolution in Software*. Ovum Limited, London.

Shoham, Y. (1993) Agent-oriented programming. *Artificial Intelligence*, 60, 51–92.

Spirgi, S., Probst, A., Wenger, D. (1990) Knowledge acquisition in a methodology for knowledge-based applications. *Proceedings of the First Japanese Knowledge Acquisition for Knowledge-Based Systems Workshop, JKAW'90*, 382–397.

Spirgi, S., Wenger, D. (1992) Modeling in EMA. *Proceedings of the 7th AAAI Knowledge Acquisition for Knowledge-Based Systems Workshop, KAW'92*, Banff.

Spirgi, S., Wenger D. (1992) The knowledge-based methodology-application EMA. *Proceedings of the 7th AAAI Knowledge Acquisition for Knowledge-Based Systems Workshop, KAW'92*, Banff.

Unland, R., Kirn, S., Wanka, U., O'Hare, G., Abbas, S. (1995) AEGIS: Agent Oriented Organizations. Arbeitsbericht des Instituts für Wirtschaftsinformatik der Westfälischen Wilhelms-Universität.

Wielinga, B. J., Schreiber, A. Th., Breuker, J. A. (1992) KADS: a modeling approach to knowledge engineering, *Knowledge Acquisition*, 4(1), 5–53.

Wenger, D. (1996) Financial Information Engineering: The Development of Artificial Information Agents; Cooperative, Declarative Methodologies based on Agents and Objects, PhD, University of Lausanne.

Woolridge, M., Jennings, N. (1995) Intelligent agents: theory and practice, *The Knowledge Engineering Review*, 10(2).